# The Gospel according to
# MOSES

# The Gospel according to
# MOSES

## What My Jewish Friends
## Taught Me about Jesus

By
## Athol Dickson

**Brazos Press**
A Division of Baker Book House Co
Grand Rapids, Michigan 49516

© 2003 by Athol Dickson

Published by Brazos Press
a division of Baker Publishing Group
P.O. Box 6287, Grand Rapids, MI 49516-6287
www.brazospress.com

Printed in the United States of America

Library of Congress Cataloging-in-Publication Data
Dickson, Athol, 1955-
   The Gospel according to Moses : what my Jewish friends taught me about Jesus / by Athol Dickson.
   p. cm.
   Includes bibliographical references.
   ISBN 1-58743-048-7
   1. Theology, Doctrinal. 2. Bible. O.T. Pentateuch—Criticism, interpretation, etc. 3. Christian life. 4. Bible. N.T.—Relation to the Old Testament. 5. Judaism—Relations—Christianity I. Title.
   BT78 .D53 2003
   22'.106—dc12                                            2002152790

Unless otherwise marked, Scripture is taken from the HOLY BIBLE, NEW INTERNA-TIONAL VERSION®. NIV®. Copyright © 1973, 1978, 1984 by International Bible Society. Used by permission of Zondervan. All rights reserved.

Scripture marked JPS is taken from Tanakh, The Holy Scriptures, The New JPS Translation according to the Traditional Hebrew Text, (Philadelphia: The Jewish Publication Society, 1985).

Scripture marked KJV is taken from the King James Version of the Bible.

Scripture marked NRSV is taken from the New Revised Standard Version of the Bible, copyright 1989 by the Division of Christian Education of the National Council of the Churches of Christ in the USA. Used by permission.

Published in association with the literary agency of Alive Communications, Inc., 7680 Goddard Street, Suite 200, Colorado Springs, Colorado 80920.

For my mother,
Mary Katherine Garrett Dickson.
She considered it all joy.

# Contents

# Introduction

*A Stranger among You*

The Torah was given in the desert, given with all publicity in a place to which no one had any claim, lest, if it were given in the land of Israel, the Jews might deny to the Gentiles any part in it.

—Mekilta on Exodus 19:2[1]

Life's most important moments are often disguised as the commonplace. Take this moment for example. As Philip and I make small talk about business and family, we say the things one says when catching up with a casual aquaintance. Then the conversation shifts to religion. He says his Reform Jewish temple has interfaith gatherings every year to reach out to members of other religions. Since I am a Christian, he wants me to come to a thing called *"Chever Torah,"* in honor of something else he calls an "interfaith *Shabbat.*" My ignorance of Judaism is prodigious, so I ask Philip the meaning of *Shabbat* (it means "Sabbath") and of course those mysterious words, *Chever Torah* (the "Torah Society," or "Torah Group"). Chever Torah, says Philip, is basically a Bible study. Will I come?

1. *The Talmudic Anthology*, ed. Louis I. Newman and Samuel Spitz (West Orange, N.J.: Behrman House, 1945). Note: All references from the Talmud at chapter headings and elsewhere throughout this book are from *The Talmudic Anthology* unless noted otherwise.

9

Unaware that Philip's simple invitation will change my life as a Christian forever, I accept.

Two weeks later, filled with trepidation at the thought of studying the Scriptures with people who don't believe in Jesus, I knot my tie and head to temple. There I enter a hall filled with about one hundred and fifty people, half of whom are members of a local church invited for the occasion. Chever Torah meets in a lofty room clad in brick. To my surprise, the place reeks of modernity. I am disappointed, having hoped to experience something more along the lines of dark wood paneling and rough-cut ashlars, preferably lit by candles and partially obscured by wavering tendrils of incense. But the crowd sits at rows of ordinary folding tables draped with white paper. There are no dated black hats, no unkempt beards, no parchment scrolls. These people are as hopelessly modern as the architecture. Many have large books open on the tables before them. Bibles, I suppose. Peering surreptitiously at a woman's copy across the way, I observe the controlled chaos of Hebrew text on the pages, row after row of dots and squiggles. My disappointment fades slightly. At least this is something Jewish.

A man in a dark suit rises to speak. For the benefit of the Christians present, he introduces himself as Rabbi Sheldon Zimmerman. Although he wears no yarmulke or prayer shawl, his full gray beard and proper bald spot lend the bookish air one expects of a rabbi. He speaks of his pleasure at seeing so many new faces this morning, his large brown eyes sparkling as he surveys the crowd. Rabbi Zimmerman is good with words, and I begin to hope something unusual might yet be salvaged from the otherwise mundane morning. Then the rabbi identifies a man sitting to his left as Dr. George Mason, pastor of Wilshire Baptist Church. His complimentary remarks about Dr. Mason sound ominously like the introduction of a featured speaker. This suspicion is bitterly confirmed when the rabbi steps back and the pastor approaches the podium.

My mood turns sour. Have I been lured away from my comfortable Saturday morning routine with false expectations of the exotic, only to be subjected to a Bible study led by a fellow Christian? I sigh and settle in, feeling the inevitable sermon-inspired drowsiness rise behind my eyelids.

After five minutes, it is clear that Dr. Mason is every bit as fine a public speaker as the rabbi, but this does little to improve my frame of mind. Then a hand is raised, an elderly gentleman near the front asks the pastor a question, and my grouchy train of thought is stopped dead in its tracks.

This is not a Christian kind of question.

It is more aggressive somehow, less deferential to the subject at hand. It may not be asked in the exotic, incense-tinted atmosphere I had hoped for, but it is different nonetheless . . . definitely different. I sit a bit straighter. Perhaps I will get some sense of the Jewish world after all.

As it happens, I get much more than that. The instant Dr. Mason finishes answering the old man's question, hands shoot up everywhere. Penetrating comments fly across the room with astonishing candor as these Jews become determined miners sifting a rich stream of biblical material with questions unbounded by fear of heresy and unlimited by preconceived notions. I crane my neck to see what kind of people would ask such remarkable things, but these Chever Torah Jews still look like my father, or my wife, or my friend—the usual faces one sees in a crowd. Who could have known?

All too soon it is over. Outside on the sidewalk, Philip asks for my reaction. Basking in the afterglow of this Chever Torah experience, I gush, "I loved it! I wish I could come every week!" After a moment's pause, Philip says, "Well, I don't see why you couldn't."

And so began the five-year odyssey that led me to write this book.

I am ill prepared to teach a Jew about his or her own religion, and fortunately not foolish enough to try. Where important differences between Judaism and Christianity arise within these pages, I will do my best to explain both perspectives fairly, but Reform Jews will undoubtedly have some objections to my presentation of their perspective. For this I apologize in advance. Jewish friends have read rough drafts of this work and attempted to correct my errors, but any remaining mistakes are mine alone and not the responsibility of those who tried to help.

Among those who read early drafts of this book is Philip, the casual aquaintance who first invited me to Chever Torah. Philip has become my dearest friend over the years and is a very devout Jew. He expressed concern that Jews who do not know me may mistake my purpose, believing this is just one more thinly veiled attempt to convert them to Christianity.

It is not.

But after five years at Chever Torah, I know why Philip is worried, so let me be clear about my intentions. In *The Gospel according to Moses*, I will show that Christianity is a reasonable response to the books of Moses, the writings, and the prophets. For Christian readers, I hope this will be a welcome confirmation that the most basic tenets of our faith are rooted in the earliest moments of creation, in the Garden, in the cool of the day. Ours is a Torah-based faith. For Jewish readers, I hope this will demonstrate that our religious differences flow from a genuine divergence of informed opinion on the meaning of the Hebrew Scriptures, not from scriptural ignorance.

Some of my friend Philip's concern about Jewish suspicion of my motives may also be relieved if I promise not to disguise my beliefs only to unveil them when the reader's back is turned. Within these pages I will describe how my faith has been informed and enriched by contact with Jews and Judaism, but make no mistake: this book is about *Christian* faith. And just as honesty forbids the disguise of my bias within these pages, it also means I must not compromise basic tenets of the Christian faith, not even to build bridges. I agree wholeheartedly with these words by a famous atheist:

> The other day at the Sorbonne, speaking to a Marxist lecturer, a Catholic priest said in public that he too was anticlerical. Well, I don't like priests who are anticlerical any more than philosophers who are ashamed of themselves.
>
> —Albert Camus[2]

2. *Resistance, Rebellion and Death*, trans. Justin O'Brien (New York: Knopf, 1960), p. 71.

Like Camus, I am not much for the easy religious pluralism one often hears espoused today. The differences between Christianity and Judaism are too important to ignore or minimize.

That does not mean there is little value in learning from each other. When I first wrote this book, the newspaper headlines were already filled with churches burning, synagogues defaced, and hate-filled men attacking Christian and Jew alike. While this book was being considered for publication, Muslim terrorists inflicted history's most deadly attack on the United States in the name of their religion. In this time of increasing violence against persons of faith by those who hate us for our specific beliefs, or simply because we do believe, all "people of the book" should stand together. But we are often divided by misunderstandings, which have grown through centuries of isolation between the Christian and Jewish communities. If ever there was a time to learn the truth about our differences *from each other* rather than reinforce false assumptions among ourselves, it is now. And we must respect those differences, even as we search for genuine common ground and cultivate it side by side. As the novelist Tom Clancy once wrote: "One hallmark of intellectual honesty is the solicitation of opposing points of view."

So while I do intend to avoid proselytization, I have no intention of leaving the reader untouched. This applies to Christians and Jews alike. Unless we are gagged and blindfolded by preconceived ideas, all worthwhile encounters change us in some important way. Heaven knows the Jews of Chever Torah have changed me. Being a conservative Christian at a liberal Jewish temple has never been easy or painless, but I have accepted the cost because my religion teaches that constructive growth is worth a little pain.[3] Key positions of Christianity have been strongly disputed almost every week at Chever Torah by highly intelligent people who know the Scriptures well and find very different truths there. At first I responded to the challenges with dogmatic inflexibility, experiencing a range of unpleasant emotions from anger to anxiety. Only God's subtle prodding can explain why I kept returning. Then somehow—again, I believe this can only be explained as an act of God—I found the ability to set aside my preconceived notions and truly *hear* the new ideas

3. James 1:2.

these Jews tossed back and forth. From that moment on, the people of Chever Torah began to coach me in that decidedly Jewish pastime: wrestling with God. Now, after years of Bible study among them, I have learned to think about important things like faith and obedience, justice and mercy, and rebellion and redemption in Jewish ways, and in so doing have found deeper meanings within every word uttered by Jesus and his apostles. Strange as it may seem, the Jewish perspective of Chever Torah has given me a richer, more solid foundation for my own faith. It has become a cliché in Christian circles to say, "Judaism is the root of Christianity," but Chever Torah has breathed real life into those words for me. I have uncovered my Jewish roots, examined them, and fed upon the nourishment that flows up into the sheltering branches of my own belief.

Years ago I exposed myself to the possibility that Judaism might have great truths to offer, and Chever Torah rewarded my open mind with radical improvements in the way I live and view my Christian faith. In the same way, with openness and proper respect for the importance of ideas, it is my earnest hope that something within the covers of this book will challenge the preconceived notions of every reader and result in a deeper relationship with the One who made us all.

# one

# God on the Spot

Frequently questions or objections, which men might raise to
something in God's conduct of affairs in the world, are put into
the mouth of the angels, to give God, so to speak, occasion to explain or justify his ways.

—Bereshit Rabbah, 8, 3

"What was the difficulty for Rashi?"

Rabbi Peter Berg, the newest addition to the staff at temple
has just posed a question that is centuries old. The tall and slender rabbi searches our faces for an answer. It is a question rabbis
love to ask, a question I too will learn to cherish. The medieval
French rabbi and Bible scholar known as Rashi (an acronym for
his full name, Rabbi Shlomo ben Isaac) found many difficulties
in the Bible. These included apparent contradictions, apparent
flaws in logic, enigmatic stories that occupy pride of place within
the text yet have no apparent rhyme or reason, verses that seem
out of context, and words, phrases, or entire stories that are repeated for no clear purpose. In Rabbinic Judaism, such difficul-

15

ties are called *koshim*. They can be volatile, dangerous stuff. Once they drove me far from God.

My foundation in Bible study was laid in my parents' devout Christian home, where I began memorizing simple Bible verses almost before I could read. I remember "Bible drills" when I was seven or eight years old. My Sunday school class was given a verse to look up as quickly as possible. The first to find it won something, usually a little sticker to affix inside the cover of his or her Bible. By the time I was eight or nine I had already been taught much of the doctrine that the church has long associated with each of these verses: the nature of sin, faith, and redemption, and the attributes of God and humanity. But by the age of sixteen, I had more questions than answers. For example, there are two accounts of the gathering of the animals into Noah's ark, the famous one when they come in pairs, and another, rarely mentioned in churches, in which they come in sevens. Why two accounts? Why pairs in one and groups of seven in the other? Such difficulties in a document I had been taught to view as the flawless word of God were disturbing, but they were merely the tip of the iceberg. More far-reaching issues surfaced as my mind matured. How can God promise Abraham that his descendants will be a blessing to all nations, knowing full well that he will send those same descendants into Canaan with a command to slaughter every man, woman, and child? And how can God be so holy that he will not allow sin into his presence, yet also exist everywhere simultaneously in a universe filled with sin?

I became convinced that the Bible was filled with mistakes and half-baked truisms. I reacted to these difficulties by abandoning the faith of my childhood for a time, descending to a life of hedonism and destructive behavior. But although Rashi also found these kinds of difficulties, his response and mine could not have been more different. Rashi confronted his koshim squarely, with an open and inquiring mind. The result was one of the most widely respected commentaries on the Hebrew Scriptures in existence, a body of work on the order of Augustine's *City of God* or Calvin's *Institutes of the Christian Religion*.

Why did Rashi and I respond to the difficulties in such radically different ways?

On one level, it is an impossible question to answer. Our times and civilizations surely played a role in causing these dissimilar reactions, but with nine centuries dividing us there is no way to accurately access the psychological and cultural disparity between Rashi and me. On another level, our diverse responses can easily be explained by an all-important difference in religious backgrounds. Rashi was trained to wrestle with God like Jacob at Bethel, to bargain with him like Abraham at the trees of Mamre, to argue with him like Moses at Mt. Sinai. Rashi's people have an ancient tradition of questioning God "face-to-face, as a man speaks with his friend."[1] Conversely, I abandoned my faith because it seemed I had no right to question the difficulties, much less expect answers. I had been taught to accept ready-made dogma rather than to personally take my doubts to God.

Make no mistake; I do not blame the church for my lost time. I might well have fallen away no matter what. But it is just possible that several years of painful isolation from the Lord might have been avoided had I learned at an early age this simple truth that most Reform Jews know:

God loves an honest question.

Before I learn Rashi's secret, many of the questions asked by the Jews of Chever Torah appall me. Nothing seems to be out of bounds, no subject too sacred for doubt and challenge. I squirm in my seat as they dare to ask if God might be limited, or "in a learning process," or fickle, or mean spirited. One Chever Torah woman even suggests that Adam might have been a homosexual!

I stare at the ceiling, watching for lightning bolts.

More than once I think of leaving, but I stay, irresistibly drawn to Chever Torah in spite of my discomfort with these outlandish questions. And now, long after the novelty of studying with people of another religion has disappeared, I remain enthralled, thinking back to last week's lesson or looking forward to the one to come. Yet those questions, those heretical, sometimes even blasphemous, questions often fill me with fear and indignation.

1. Exodus 33:11.

I am attracted and repelled simultaneously. It is such a strange sensation. What does it mean? Why does questioning God make me so nervous? Why does it attract me anyway? Who am I to search for *more?*

Abraham stands on a high place speaking with the Creator, and Abraham is worried. God has said he may destroy Sodom and Gomorrah because of their wickedness. But Abraham's nephew, Lot, and Lot's wife and daughters live down below, and for all Abraham knows, there are others in the cities who are innocent of those crimes.

What to do?

Abraham, the original Jew, does what the people of Chever Torah do. He takes a deep breath and questions God. Listen to the nerve of the man:

> Far be it from you to do such a thing—to kill the righteous with the wicked, treating the righteous and the wicked alike. Far be it from you! Will not the Judge of all the earth do right?
>
> —Genesis 18:25

When we read that question at Chever Torah, the rabbi laughs and says, "You've got to admire the *chutzpah* of this guy." Suddenly, I look at the story with brand new eyes. It is true: not only did Abraham ask God a question; he questioned God's very motives! Then, far from punishing Abraham, far from cursing him or withdrawing from him, God responded by making him an offer:

> If I find fifty righteous people in the city of Sodom, I will spare the whole place for their sake.
>
> —Genesis 18:26

Later that day, while walking with my mother and my wife at an arboretum near my home, I am troubled. I linger behind, shuffling along in the shade, pondering the meaning of this enormous story. How is it possible that a man could question the motives of God Almighty, yet be drawn closer as a result? Surely no one could get away with asking, "Will not the Judge of all the earth do right?"

And yet . . . and yet. . . .

God actually bargained with Abraham, from fifty righteous people, down to forty-five, to thirty, to only ten, giving him the answer he wanted each time he asked. Somehow, Abraham's impudent questions seemed to deepen his relationship with God.

Alone beneath the pecans and oaks, I feel as if the Lord has driven me like Abraham to a high place and left me standing there, aching to ask a question of my own. It goes against everything I have ever believed about approaching God. "Will not the Judge of all the earth do right. . . ." Such a question! How dare he doubt the Lord that way?

Dare I?

The story is there in the Bible. It must be true. And if it worked for Abraham at the oaks of Mamre, maybe it could work for me at the oaks of the arboretum. So, in a moment of utter recklessness, I accept the challenge. I ask God my own first truly honest question in many years.

I ask if I may ask.

The answer comes instantaneously, as if God has been waiting on the edge of his throne. It is simple, profound, and so undeniably clear it might have been spoken aloud:

"Asking is not doubting. It is trusting."

In that instant, I understand that it takes more faith to ask than it takes to fear the asking. It takes faith to be ready for whatever answer comes, and faith to persevere with more questions if the answer is not understood. Asking an honest question means being ready to change in response to the answer, and short of martyrdom, change may be the ultimate act of faith.

How wonderful now to know I can question the Lord without fear of faithlessness! How wonderful to be unafraid to ask God, knowing he will answer. Every time that happens, my faith in him grows stronger.

Genesis teaches that I am made in God's image. Granted, the Lord is the essential reality and I the mere reflection, but if I reflect him, then surely some of my most basic instincts began in him. I think one of those instincts is a desire to be the focus of attention. I experience a small thrill when someone says, "May I ask you a personal question?" They have just revealed a wish to know me more deeply. It could be that God feels that thrill as well.

Consider the most basic question in any new relationship: "What's your name?" No matter how separated by language and culture, two people invariably make that question part of their meeting ritual, a way to demonstrate interest in each other and show good intent. Even the most primitive of responses—"Me Tarzan, you Jane"—is a sign of respect between persons, an acknowledgment of another's existence as an individual.

But the response cannot come until someone asks a question.

When God appears to Moses as a voice within a burning bush, he tells Moses to go to Egypt to bring the Hebrews to the Promised Land. Then Moses, feeling the need to understand who is sending him, demonstrates his desire to know more about God by asking a question:

Suppose I go to the Israelites and say to them, "The God of your fathers has sent me to you," and they ask me, "What is his name?" Then what shall I tell them?

—Exodus 3:13

Because of Moses' question, humanity draws a step closer to God at this pivotal moment when the Creator answers:

I am who I am. This is what you are to say to the Israelites: "I Am has sent me to you."

—Exodus 3:14

This is more than an answer. It is an overture to increased intimacy. The Lord answers with his most intimate personal name. "I Am" is not just some variation on a Cananite word for God, like "Elohim" or "El Shaddai." It speaks directly to God's fundamental essence. It is as if the Lord has said, "You don't have to call me 'Mister Jones' anymore. You can call me Bill." God reveals his desire to be on a first-name basis with humanity, and that remarkable breakthrough comes about because one man dares to ask the Lord a question.

Dare I?

At the church of my youth, I somehow got the idea that only a prideful person would dare to question the Lord. At Chever Torah I have learned that sometimes asking questions is a way to demonstrate humility, because inherent in the question is the assumption that I do not have the answer; God does. Sincere questions give God respect. They acknowledge his power. They honor him.

Moses learns this as he leads the Israelites out of Egypt. With the famous ten plagues of Egypt and the divided sea behind him, it seems Moses may be getting a bit smug. This is only natural. After all, Moses' outstretched hand parted the waters, Moses prophesied the ten miraculous plagues that convinced Pharaoh to let the people go, and Moses alone had been chosen by the Creator of the universe for the job of leading his people. Small wonder this man begins to believe his own wisdom is up to the task of answering every single question in Israel. So Moses sets himself up as Israel's only judge, the final authority for all disputes. Only pride run amuck can explain such foolish behavior from an otherwise intelligent fellow. In the ordinary course of things God might let the natural result run its course, teaching Moses as most of us are taught, through the school of hard knocks. But in this case there is no time. The next event on God's to-do list is the revelation of the Torah at Mt. Sinai. God wants Moses to come to the mountaintop *now*, and in order to survive such close encounters with the Master of the universe, all self-centered pride must be checked at the door. So the Lord sends Moses a message through his father-in-law, a Midianite priest named Jethro:

> Listen now to me and I will give you some advice, and may God be with you. You must be the people's representative before God and bring their disputes to him.
>
> —Exodus 18:19

To his credit, Moses follows his wise father-in-law's advice and by so doing humbly admits that he is not up to answering all of the people's questions after all. I too would be wise to follow Jethro's advice, taking my questions to the Lord, along with the humble acknowledgment that I am not up to answering them myself.

Of course, there is true humility, and there is false humility. The two are easily confused. Is it humility or is it a warped kind of pride to assume the Lord cannot stoop low enough to hear my little questions? The Hebrew Scriptures are clear: God is not above a little stooping now and then:

> You give me your shield of victory; you stoop down to make me great.
>
> —2 Samuel 22:36

I must never think, "I've sunk too far. Even God cannot help me now." Believing I am beneath the Lord's reach is the same as believing I am above it. Above or beneath—either way I pretend I am beyond God's power, and that is something he will not tolerate.

This does not mean there are questions I must not ask. It simply means I must be careful of my attitude when I do the asking. For example, again and again as the Hebrews move through the wilderness of the Sinai Peninsula, they complain to Moses. Many of their complaints are framed as questions. As they stand trapped at the edge of the Red Sea with the Egyptian army intent on their destruction and approaching fast, they ask Moses, "Was it because there were no graves in Egypt that you brought us to the desert to die? What have you done to us by bringing us out of Egypt?"[2] Wandering thirsty in the wilderness, they grumble again, asking, "What are we to drink?" and "Why did you bring us up out of Egypt to make us and our children and livestock die of thirst?"[3]

Even Moses sometimes joins in this spirit of discontent. He questions God's motive in burdening him with the responsibility

2. Exodus 14:11.
3. Exodus 15:24; 17:3. See also Exodus 14:11; 16:3; and Numbers 14:2–3 for additional examples of questions the Israelites asked Moses.

of the Israelites, complaining that he "cannot carry these people," saying he would rather die than continue in the role God chose for him. At one point, he actually questions the Lord's ability to provide enough food for the people. And before all of this, when God first appeared to him at the burning bush, Moses questioned the wisdom of his entire plan, asking, "Who am I, that I should go to Pharaoh and bring the Israelites out of Egypt?" and, "What if they do not believe me or listen to me and say, 'The Lord did not appear to you'?"[4]

When the Israelites ask their questions, bad things often happen. During the Korah rebellion the ground opens and swallows those who question the exclusivity of Moses' relationship with God. An entire generation is condemned to die in the wilderness when they question the wisdom of entering the Promised Land.[5] Childhood feelings of fear and revulsion inspired by these stories are probably one reason I was hesitant to question God before I went to Chever Torah. Such wrathful responses to the Israelites' questions led me to view the God of the Hebrew Scriptures as a stern and isolated entity, one I dared not approach merely to satisfy my curiosity. I was not worthy. I was beneath even God's ability to enlighten.

But now I notice that Moses' questions bring very different results. They are no less brazenly doubtful than those of the other Israelites, yet Moses' questions are always answered and invariably lead to an enriched relationship with the Lord. Why this radical difference in God's responses? The answer becomes clear when I look at the questions again.

Israel questions Moses.

Moses questions God.

The difference has nothing to do with the audacity of the questions. Moses doubts from the very beginning. Some of Moses' questions are indeed an affront to the Lord. Some even make him angry.[6] But Moses takes his questions and doubts to God openly and honestly. Moses doubts God's plan, he doubts God's abilities, he even questions God's motives, but he never

---

4. Numbers 11:11–15, 21–22; Exodus 3:11; Exodus 4:1.
5. Numbers 16:32; 14:27–30.
6. See Exodus 4:14.

doubts God's desire or ability to give answers, and that makes all the difference.

For religious reasons, certain primitive peoples are deathly afraid of cameras. They believe photographs capture the soul. This fear is not entirely based on ignorance. These people know one points the little black box in a person's direction and pushes a button and gets a nearly perfect image on paper. They could even use a camera themselves. But their knowledge stops at the outside of the box. Their fear prevents them from searching for a deeper understanding of the how and the why of the thing. Their fear is both the cause of the problem and the barrier to the solution.

In my own life, fear of questioning God accomplished the reverse of Peter's admonition to "always be prepared to give an answer to everyone who asks you to give the reason for the hope that you have."[7] Until I began to question God at Chever Torah, I knew *what* I believed, but I had only a superficial idea *why* I believed. Paranoia masquerading as awe kept me ignorant of the deeper truths God has commanded me to explain.

If I seem to be vacillating between boldly questioning God and approaching him with awe, it is because these concepts must be so carefully balanced. At the oaks of Mamre looking down on Sodom, Abraham boldly bargains with God but offers nothing in return for the Lord's concessions. The patriarch of Israel knows he is merely a begger. I too must never fear to ask, but like Abraham, I must also remember that every time I approach the Lord I come with empty hands. God owes no answers and does not respond to ultimatums. Indeed, one sure way to receive the haunting answer of silence is to frame my questions as demands.

At Chever Torah I have learned several other reasons why I might seem to receive no answer from God. For example, all too often I accuse him of speaking gibberish, when it is really my own limited mentality that makes God's elegant explanation sound like nonsense.

7. 1 Peter 3:15.

Imagine a little girl who questions Albert Einstein about physics and receives this answer: "Let us begin with the theory of general relativity. Now then, this is essentially a theory of gravity I discovered that supersedes Newton's theory of gravitation, which is reproduced as a weak-gravity, low-velocity special case, and replaces the Newtonian notion of. . . ." Dr. Einstein could go on like this for hours, but the child is already frowning, convinced he is making fun of her. Stomping her pretty little foot, she says, "I'm serious, Uncle Al. Tell me about *physics!*"

And so it goes. No matter how many questions the little girl asks or how sincerely the youngster wants to know, she will not understand the answers. Of course, she should not blame Dr. Einstein. Their failure to communicate is due to a vast gap between his knowledge and the girl's limited experience. He can no more help being one of the world's great scientific geniuses than she can help being a little girl. For the child to complain about this state of affairs would be the height of . . . well . . . childishness.

Of course, the comparison of my intellect and God's is poorly illustrated by this example. If Dr. Einstein tried to explain the theory of relativity to a one-celled organism it would be closer to the true relationship between God and me. Small wonder then that I sense a haunting silence when I ask foolish questions such as this: "What was it like before creation?"

Even the words I use to frame such a question reveal my ignorance. By definition, before creation there was no "it" because nothing had been created. Yet I cannot visualize the concept of an "it" as anything other than a "thing." For that matter, there was no "was" since the concept of a past tense verb is tied to time, which almost certainly did not exist before creation's "first day." Yet I cannot even say "there was no 'was'" without making an inherent reference to time.

Obviously, only God can understand some questions, much less grasp the answers.

So one reason I might feel God has not answered is because I rudely demand an answer, and another is my own inability to understand. Here is a third explanation for divine silence: I am probably unable to safely handle some of the answers out there.

Just as Dr. Einstein would not dream of giving our little girl access to highly radioactive material, God may withhold some answers for my very survival. At Chever Torah, I find biblical illustrations of this all the time. For example, on Mt. Sinai Moses dares to ask to see God's "glory" or *kevod*, a word that literally means "weight." But Moses is shown only God's "back" and told, "No one may see me and live."[8] It is as if the Lord's weight would crush this man. Much of the text of Exodus and Leviticus is concerned with highly detailed rituals intended to prepare Israel's priests to survive a close encounter with the Lord. For example, the rising smoke of incense in the tabernacle is there so the priests will not see God and die.[9] The deadly seriousness of drawing near to the Creator of the universe is also seen in the story of Aaron's sons, Nadab and Abihu, who violate a small portion of the ritual. Brief as it is, their story teaches one of the most important lessons of the Bible. Aaron's sons approach the Lord's tabernacle with incense as God had commanded, but their censors contain something the Torah calls "alien fire." (The rabbis explain that the coals Nadab and Abihu used are probably from a source other than the fire on the tabernacle's sanctified altar.) Because of their mistake—or their cavalier disregard for the glory of God—Aaron's sons are burned alive by something the Torah calls "fire from the Lord."[10] Some at Chever Torah believe this is a hard-hearted response on God's part. They say he should have given Aaron's sons another warning, or punished them less severely. But I wonder if such thinking misses the point entirely. If our little girl ignored Dr. Einstein's warnings and played with the reactor core, would we blame the reactor, or the girl's foolishness?

I have seen that answers may be withheld because I am disrespectful, unable to understand, or unable to cope, but there is at least one more reason why God is sometimes silent: God may answer my question with silence because the answer *is* silence. In

8. Exodus 33:18–20.
9. Leviticus 16:13.
10. Leviticus 10:1–2.

other words, sometimes my questions themselves are answer enough.

> Good questions have a legitimacy of their own. They add to our understanding even before we can come up with an answer—and sometimes we glean insights precisely because we can't supply an answer. In such cases the significance of the knotty question derives not from cutting the knot, but instead from the annoying fact that no analytic knife seems adequate to the task.
>
> —Avigdor Bonchek[11]

When the Lord offers no clear answer to my questions, it may mean I will learn greater truths by continuing to ask the question. Sometimes questions have many possible answers, so God declines to point to a "correct" one. The most common examples of this phenomenon are bound up in the many paradoxes of the Scriptures, which I will explore more fully in another chapter. Here the point is this: if I feel a need to ask a question because of a loving desire to draw closer to God, I should ask in as many ways as possible, even if the only answer is repeated silence. So long as I do not attribute that silence to a deficiency on God's part, merely asking can be a learning experience.

The answer of silence should not stop me from asking God questions. I may receive a pat on the head and those all too familiar words, "I'll explain it when you're older," but if I want to know what I *can* know, I must ask anyway, accepting the fact that the boundaries of God's answers are established by my shortcomings, not by his.

As a Christian, one of my reasons for belief in Jesus flows from the things I have learned at Chever Torah about questioning God. I already mentioned that Genesis says humanity was created in God's "image" and "likeness." I also explained why I believe this leads to the conclusion that God enjoys being asked a question for the same reasons I do: it makes both of us feel loved

---

11. *Studying the Torah, A Guide to In-Depth Interpretation* (Northvale, N.J.: Jason Aronson, 1996), p. 170.

and honored. The Lord wants to communicate with me as badly as I want to communicate with him. After all, it was he who provided the Scriptures, which are filled with answers. God also caused my curiosity about him, which is proof that answers are out there, just as my thirst is evidence of crystal clear water and my longing for love testifies to the splendid miracle that another heart can touch me deep inside. The very intensity of my desire to ask God questions is evidence that he wants to provide the answers. I must not be ashamed or afraid to ask, because for each honest question, no matter how brazenly doubtful, God has prepared a special answer, just behind the *koshim,* or "difficulties," in the Bible.

Long before the time of Rashi, another rabbi said it very well indeed:

> Ask and it will be given to you; seek and you will find; knock and the door will be opened to you. For everyone who asks receives; he who seeks finds; and to him who knocks, the door will be opened.
>
> —Matthew 7:7–8

If it is true that the Lord wants to communicate with me, it follows that he would try to answer my questions in the most complete and comprehensible way possible. Yet how can this be done when God and I are mentally farther apart than Einstein and amoebas? It seems to make sense that the Lord would do what Einstein might do when faced with an inquisitive little girl: he would stoop down to my level.

God loves an honest question.

And to me, Jesus is the Creator of the universe on hands and knees, a proud Daddy talking baby talk to all humanity, a God who has become man so that I can better understand his answers.

two

# Our Mutual God

God's voice at Sinai was heard in all languages.
—Shabbat, 88b

I settle in on this rainy March Chever Torah morning, glad
that the temple's heating system is fully functional and grateful
for a little foam cup of warm coffee. Soon after I have arranged
my Bible and my copy of the Torah commentary before me on
the table, Rabbi Zimmerman arrives, well dressed as usual in a
dark suit, eyes warm and merry behind his wire-rimmed glasses.
He invites announcements and leads us in the opening prayer for
Torah study. Then he begins the class with this statement:
  "Today we read the most important words a Jew can know."
  This instantly captures my attention. I wonder . . . if Christianity had such words, what would they be?
  The rabbi continues:
  "They should be the first words of Torah that our children
learn, the first words that we speak when we rise every morning,
the last that we speak before we go to sleep at night, our comfort
in life's most trying times, and the final words upon our lips at
death. Please repeat the *Shema* with me now."

All around me everyone speaks the Hebrew words in unison. I lower my eyes, embarrassed that I alone am silent, embarrassed because I do not know the meaning.

"Shema Yisrael Adonai Elohim Adonai echad."

As with every Hebrew prayer, Rabbi Zimmerman repeats the words in English. "Hear, O Israel, the Lord our God, the Lord is one."[1]

I am surprised. Why are these Judaism's most important words when the Bible contains so many others more profound? Why not: "In the beginning God created the heavens and the earth?" or: "I will make you into a great nation"?[2] Now that I think about it, there seems to be no end of more suitable creeds the Jews could pick. The twenty-third Psalm or the Ten Commandments, for example. Why select these simple words instead?

The general characteristics of a religion can often be determined by examining the wise sayings or particular portions of Scripture it chooses to accentuate. In Christianity, this is probably the most widely memorized verse of all:

> For God so loved the world that he gave his one and only Son, that whoever believes in him shall not perish but have eternal life.
>
> —John 3:16

Those simple words speak of the depth of God's love for us, of the universality of his love, of the Trinity (two of three are mentioned), of a reconciliation process composed of faith on my part and grace on God's, of the inevitability of death without him, and of the gift of life with him. Thousands of books have been written on each of the ideas within this single verse. By contrast, when I first encounter it, the Shema seems very one-dimensional.

Such was my ignorance then.

The first clue that I have missed something important appears a few weeks later as I read a New Testament story in which Jesus is asked by a Jewish scholar to name the most im-

1. Deuteronomy 6:4.
2. Genesis 1:1; 12:2.

portant commandment. Somehow it had always escaped my notice before, but with all the Torah to choose from Jesus begins his answer with the very words I have so confidently dismissed as insignificant:

> "The most important one," answered Jesus, "is this: 'Hear, O Israel, the Lord, God, the Lord is one. Love the Lord your God with all your heart and with all your soul and with all your mind and with all your strength.'"
>
> —Mark 12:29–30 (quoting Deuteronomy 6:4–5)

Most Christians probably know that Jesus said loving God wholeheartedly is the most important commandment, and loving our neighbor as we love ourselves is second. But how many of us realize Jesus prefaced both of these with the Shema?

It is the first of many examples of Jesus' fundamental Jewishness that I will discover at Chever Torah. And if, like the rabbis of the Talmud, Jesus places the Shema at the head of the most important commandments, clearly there is something important to be learned from these words.

What could it be?

Jews throughout the centuries have spent a lot of time pondering the implications of a God who is one. This is only natural, since they are the people who first received that revelation from the Lord. But I cannot recall listening to a single sermon on the subject in church. Christians tend to take the oneness of God for granted, and focus instead on the Trinity. Again, this is only natural since that is the revelation we received. But in my case at least, overlooking the Shema led to a complete lack of appreciation for its importance in understanding God. Then at Chever Torah I began to understand that the statement "God is one" is the foundation for virtually everything I can know about the Lord.

The light began to dawn when I discovered the work of Rabbi Moses ben Maimon, better known as Maimonides.[3] It seems that one of Maimonides's important contributions to Judaism

---

3. The twelfth-century author of two of Judaism's most famous books, the *Mishnah Torah*, which is a codification of the entire Talmud, and *The Guide of the Perplexed*, possibly the Jewish world's first attempt to reconcile the teachings of the Bible with Western philosophy.

is his Thirteen Principals, which define the essential beliefs of his religion. The Shema is central to Maimonides's second fundamental principle of Judaism, which states that the oneness of God means there is no subdivision or composite aspect to his nature. God is whatever he is in the most complete and pure way possible, meaning no characteristic can apply to him in a partial or limited way. In other words, the Lord is like a flawless diamond. When people say a gem is without flaws, they mean it contains no cracks, no grain of a different mineral, no combination of colors—it is one thing only. God is what he is, absolutely.

That idea leads to a series of important conclusions about God.

For example, it seems almost unnecessary to point out that the Shema's assertion of divine oneness means there is no pantheon of other gods. But that idea inspires another, which is less obvious. If the Shema is correct, and there are no other gods capable of adding something to or taking something away from the Lord, then God is beyond the power of any other force in the universe. Simply put, the Shema leads to the conclusion that God is omnipotent, or all-powerful.

That idea in combination with Maimonides's assertion that God is pure, or "one" in his essence, leads to the conclusion that God is also unchanging. After all, change requires a combination of at least two things: a cause and an effect. But I have already seen that the Shema leaves no room for a cause or force powerful enough to change God from without, and if Maimonides's understanding of God's perfectly pure oneness is correct, there is no combination of things within God that could cause a change.

Thinking further, I soon find that the Shema reveals other important aspects of God's nature. For example, the Lord's changelessness means he does not grow or learn, unlike the theories in vogue among some modern theologians. Growth and learning would require the addition of new information to God's "mind," or essence. Such an addition would represent a change in God; yet as I have seen, the Shema and the logic of cause and effect make that impossible. So the oneness of God stated by the

Shema also leads to the conclusion that God is already all-knowing, or omniscient.

A similar argument can be made from the Shema to show that God exists throughout the universe simultaneously. The only alternative is the idea that God is present in some places, yet not present in others. But if that were true, God would be here and then be there, and his state of being would be different in each place. In other words, he would change when moving in relationship to space, as I do. But since the Shema does not allow the possibility of a change in God, he must be everywhere all the time.

Pure, all-powerful, unchanging, all-knowing, and ever-present —it seems Jesus' choice of the Shema to preface his definition of the most important commandment speaks volumes about the God who makes commands. But the Shema teaches one other lesson about God, and as an imperfect human being striving vainly to understand the world around me, that last bit of information may be the most important of all.

I already learned that Maimonides's second fundamental principle of Judaism interprets the Shema to mean that God is flawless. That leads directly to the idea that God is the ultimate example of those characteristics that reveal his nature. If the Lord is good, he is perfectly good; if he is just, he is perfectly just; and so forth. Otherwise, God would be a composite creature as I am, part good and part bad, sometimes fair and sometimes unfair. But the Shema oneness of God means he is not a consolidation of things, and must therefore be fully and completely whatever he is. In short, the Shema means God is perfect.

Why does this matter? As I mentioned a moment ago, God's pure oneness means I do not suffer from the eccentricity of a cadre of gods as did the Mesopotamians, Babylonians, Egyptians, Greeks, and Romans. Their shallow divinities shared the human foibles of inconsistency, lust, groundless rage, and petty jealousy—traits that left human beings languishing in an arbitrary and chaotic world where one's spiritual fortunes depended not upon established standards but on the gods' whims. Homer's *Iliad* describes such a world, with the course of the war between the Achaians and Trojans molded this way and that by the gods' fickle alliances and divine impulsiveness. Consider these mournful words of Agamemnon:

> First he bowed his head and promised that I should sack the walled castle of Ilion and return safe; but as it seems now his will was to ruin and deceive. . . . Such I suppose is the pleasure of Zeus. . . .
>
> —Homer[4]

In contrast, if the God of the Torah is "one" in the sense of flawlessness in both essence and deed as Maimonides said, then the Lord will not engage in any halfway measures. He will not be fair today but unfair tomorrow or good now and evil later. In a world of confusion and frightening change where I sometimes feel like a shipwrecked sailor clutching at waves, it is a great comfort to believe I can count on God to be completely and consistently what he is, forevermore.

This is a vital message with important implications for my daily life. Consider this question of a polytheist adrift in a tossing sea of divine caprice.

> "What is truth?" Pilate asked.
>
> —John 18:38

Without the Shema, this is a question without an answer. It is also the question of a thoroughly modern man, indeed, a postmodern man, convinced he can redefine truth to provide the excuse he needs to avoid a messy political situation by sentencing an innocent Jew to death. In contrast, since the giving of the Torah, people of the book have believed that certain truths are self-evident. They faced those truths as something independent of their own convenience. They arranged their lives to accommodate that truth rather than the other way around, and they did that regardless of the personal cost.

Were they right?

4. *The Iliad*, trans. W. H. D. Rouse (New York: Mentor, 1950), p. 25.

Assuming that God does not change and God is good, it follows that "truth" and "good" do not change either.[5] So long as the sun continues to shine, sunlight remains warm and bright even if I stand shivering in the shade, because sunlight depends upon the sun, not on me. Similarly, if God is one, his goodness must remain a constant even if it burns me now and then, because God's one-ness—his Shema perfection—sets the standard when it comes to moral reality. Although I enjoy thinking of myself as the center of the universe, that is a foolish fantasy. If the Shema is true, then truth and justice do not depend on me. Like sunlight from the sun, they emanate as fixed realities from a flawless God who is one.

Does this theological idea have any parallels in observable fact?

I believe it does. I believe it expresses itself throughout the physical universe. Consider time, for example. If I am late for an appointment, it is no good trying to escape the consequences by saying that time is different for me. Time is measured by things far beyond my control, such as the Earth's orbit around the Sun and rotation on its axis. It is not only illogical to assert that time is different for me, it is undesirable. For example, without one single, unchanging system for tracking time, ten minutes worth of air to a scuba diver might be sixty minutes worth to the man who filled his tanks—a disconcerting prospect to a diver eighty feet below. Or consider gravity. A person falling from a great height knows all too well that the truth about gravity is not rela-tive to humanity. Most things are beyond our control precisely because there is a reality connected with those things—a truth—that is also beyond our control, whether we believe in it or not. So any monotheist who claims that truth is relative to the human condition is trying to have it both ways. The Shema leads inexo-rably to the conclusion that truth does not change, because God does not change. I can no more adjust the truth to suit my per-sonal circumstances than I can turn back time, reverse gravity, or change God Almighty.

Just as there are those who believe truth and justice can be ad-justed to fit the circumstances, there are also those who question whether morality exists at all except as a human invention. Be-

5. In the next chapter I will explore the logical basis for the assumption that God is good.

cause many ethical and moral dilemmas seem unsolvable, it becomes tempting to say the rules of the puzzle do not matter. But
if the Shema is true, that is taking the dishonest way out, because
in the most fundamental sense there are no human inventions;
there are just human rearrangements of God's handiwork. In
every culture, on every continent, a similar set of basic rules for
human behavior has existed for at least as long as history has been
recorded. Morality is not made by us; it is made a part of us. So
although it is often hard to know what is right and wrong, true and
false, as Rabbi David Stern recently said to me, "We must be careful not to blur the distinction between the indiscernible and the
nonexistent." Things are true or false, right or wrong, whether I
can see the difference or not, because truth and righteousness ul-
timately emanate from a single, unchanging source.

Thus, the Shema lays the foundation for the Judeo-Christian
concept of morality.

Hear, O Israel, the Lord, God, the Lord is one.

I will not underestimate these Jews again. Because of their unrelenting focus on God's oneness, I now have logical proof in my
own mind that God is all-powerful and all-knowing. Most important, the Shema means God is pure and unchanging; therefore
he is the standard for all truth and morality, and a solid foundation I can build upon when the evil of the world seems overwhelming. It is the second important lesson I have learned at
Chever Torah, after the fact that God loves an honest question.
But now many new Chever Torah kinds of questions come to
mind: If the Shema means the Master of the universe is pure in
every way, then why is evil allowed to exist in the first place?
Why do I need a foundation of truth and morality at all? Why not
create a world where everything is just as pure as God?

Although I have a better understanding of the Lord thanks to
Judaism's Shema, I do not know the answer to these troubling
questions. Fortunately, there are many Chever Torahs in my future—and many more chances to learn.

three

# God in Chains

All expressions concerning the description of God must never be taken literally; they are simply due to the inadequacy of human language "to make the ear listen to what it can hear."
—Abot de-Rabbi Nathan, 2

On this Shabbat we have reached the passage in Deuteronomy that states, "Out of all the peoples on the face of the earth, the Lord has chosen you to be his treasured possession."[1] Filled with the boundless enthusiasm for Torah that seems to pervade all the rabbis at temple, Rabbi Deborah Robbins discusses this idea with a man at the back of the room. She stands an inch or two over five feet tall, and rises on her toes from time to time to peer over those seated up front. The rabbi smiles slightly as she listens, then suddenly she takes us in an unexpected new direction.

"The Torah says we are God's 'treasured possession,'" she says, "his chosen people. This has been central to our faith throughout

1. Deuteronomy 14:2.

the centuries." She pauses dramatically, suddenly very serious. "But is it time to abandon this idea?"

For me, it is a confusing question. This "idea," as she calls it, is the heart of the promise that binds Jews together. They *are* God's chosen people, according to the Torah, and even if they wanted to refuse such an honor, is it not God who does the deciding on such a cosmic level? Does anyone have the right or the power to "abandon the notion" of a covenant with God?

Oh . . . wait a minute.

It occurs to me that this is just what Rabbi Robbins wants. She has deliberately asked an outrageous question to make us think about the meaning of this covenant. I relax and glance around, certain someone will rise to the bait. Surely no Jewish congregation would seriously consider abandoning their covenant with God. But to my surprise, the first comment she receives is in favor of doing just that.

Across the room a man says, "I think it's a curse to be chosen. I wish God would change his mind."

Hands shoot up all around as I search this fellow's face for signs of levity. He is deadly serious. Next the rabbi calls on Margie, the woman who reads us a prayer or a poem at the beginning of every Chever Torah session. Margie speaks eloquently about the Lord's great love for his Jews; she speaks of God's provision for Israel's every need as they cross the wilderness, of his patient endurance of their complaints and his repeated offerings of forgiveness. God, she says, has not cursed his chosen people. There must be another explanation for the tragedies Jews have endured throughout the centuries.

In response, an elderly woman sitting near to me lifts her voice. She has a Dutch accent. My friend Philip leans close to my ear and whispers that this lady narrowly escaped the Nazis and lost many members of her family to their insanity. Her words are simple, yet devastating to Margie's position.

"If God is so loving" (she pronounces it "lovink"), "please explain the Holocaust."

And so a classic debate is joined, with the Jews of Chever Torah quickly dividing into two camps: those who side with Margie, viewing God as benevolent, and those of the Holocaust survivor's persuasion, who view God as ambivalent toward humanity at best and sometimes downright hostile. Because of the horrors suffered by these people it should come as no surprise that a Jew, Rabbi Harold Kushner, has found a way to frame the debate in its simplest terms:

Why do bad things happen to good people?[2]

This is a question I often hear at temple, but Rabbi Kushner and my friends at Chever Torah are hardly the first Jews to ask. It is an ancient dilemma, the question of the prophet Habakkuk:

Your eyes are too pure to look on evil; you cannot tolerate wrong. Why then do you tolerate the treacherous? Why are you silent while the wicked swallow up those more righteous than themselves?

—Habakkuk 1:13

Obviously, since Habakkuk's question is in the Bible, it is acceptable to God. I am relieved to find this verse, because for me, this is no shallow point of theology to occupy dry old men in the ivory towers of academia. As I listen to this Chever Torah debate, I think about my mother who has recently been diagnosed with inoperable cancer. For me, this is a time of deep and unceasing grief, and I join the Jews at Chever Torah in asking for an explanation. If God is so loving, why must a fine woman like my mother, a kind person who has served the Lord with deep humility all of her life, die such a torturous death? Many explanations are offered in the ensuing Chever Torah conversation, some of which seem to flirt with blasphemy. One is so shocking it demands my undivided attention.

As Rabbi Robbins rises to her toes to watch and listen, a young woman near the door asks, "Is God limited in some way, unable to restrain evil or protect us?"

Outrageous as this question seems to a conservative Christian like me, I understand why such a possibility might find voice here in temple. A limitation of divine power is one way to reconcile rampant evil like holocausts and cancer with the idea of a loving God, but understanding why the question was asked does not mean that I condone it. These people are descended from

---

2. Harold S. Kushner, *When Bad Things Happen to Good People* (New York: Avon, 1997).

those who first realized that "the Lord is God; besides him there is no other."[3] I am dismayed that Jews in particular can seriously think of God as limited in any way. So I fidget and check my watch and try not to roll my eyes while waiting impatiently for this Chever Torah session to end. Finally, it is over. Still distressed at what I witnessed here today, I head for my car without lingering as usual to talk to Philip. A limited God indeed! What about the Shema and the idea that God's oneness means he alone controls the universe? Such intellectual dishonesty is difficult to excuse. How I wish that I had said, "Our God is in heaven; he does whatever pleases him."[4] But I have yet to summon the courage to speak at Chever Torah. Perhaps I never will, because as I drive away I seriously consider never going back. But then, turning into my driveway, I remember my very first Chever Torah lesson.

God loves an honest question.

Who am I to say that even the idea of a limited God is beyond the pale? Perhaps I am the one abandoning his intellectual convictions. Instead of denying the hypothesis out of hand, I should take up the challenge and see where this outrageous Chever Torah question leads. So I shut off the car's engine and sit still for a moment, asking God right out loud, "*Are* you limited? Is there anything you cannot do?"

At first, I hear nothing but the ticking of my automobile's cooling engine. Then with unusual clarity I remember something I learned in Chever Torah a month or two ago. At the time I chalked it up as irrelevant trivia. Suddenly I'm not so sure.

Grabbing my copy of the Torah, I charge from the car into the house and up the stairs without bothering to greet my wife. In the study, I begin searching through my slowly growing file of Chever Torah notes.

Ah. Here it is. . . .

In a collection of mystical rabbinic teachings called the Kabbalah, the idea of God's interaction with his creation through

3. Deuteronomy 4:35.
4. Psalms 115:3.

"separation" came to be known as *tsimtsum*, or "withdrawing." The kabbalistic rabbis believed God's act of creation involved *tsimtsum*. They saw this withdrawing as a voluntary limitation that was necessary because God had to "make space for the creation."[5]

Reading in Genesis about the creation of the universe with the idea of *tsimtsum* in mind, a pattern that I have never noticed emerges. I find that God "separated the light from the darkness." Next, he "separated the water under the expanse from the water above it," then the water was "gathered to one place," separating it from the land, and after that, God established "lights" in the sky to "separate the day from the night."[6]

It seems that creation itself is somehow tied to the concept of separation. But does the idea of separating to "make space for the universe" mean that God "withdrew" as the Kabbalists said? Is this separation/withdrawal a kind of limitation of God?

Back to the Torah!

In the very first verse of the Bible I find that "the heavens and the earth" are established. So before this event, there was no world and no outer space. But take away the earth and the heavens and what is left?

The Bible's underlying assumption is that "God was first." This is seen in the Hebrew Scriptures' opening words: "In the beginning, God. . . ." If this most basic of all Biblical messages is false, then nothing else in the Bible can be trusted. But if it is true, then God must have existed completely alone at some point. Before there was matter, energy, space, or time, the Lord completely filled everything that was, because God *was* all that was.[7] From this, it also follows that God had to withdraw, or engage in *tsimtsum*, in order to allow space, time, energy, and matter to exist somewhere outside himself. Here I am, filling this space, and since I am not God, God is not here—at least not in the way that I am here. He has withdrawn. He has limited himself.

5. Lavinia and Dan Cohn-Sherbok, *A Popular Dictionary of Judaism* (Richmond, Surrey [U.K.]: Curzon Press, 1995), p. 198.

6. Genesis 1:7, 9, 14.

7. Maimonides even applied this idea to moral values, when he said there was no love or justice or goodness or mercy in the beginning—only God. This will be discussed at length within the context of the Trinity in chapter 11.

The idea that God might not be here at times is found through-out Scripture whenever God appears on earth, as he does when he dwells in the Israelite camp. If God enters the tabernacle, then logic dictates that he must not have been there before, at least not in the same way. This does not mean there are places where God is not present. It simply means God has different ways of "being," some of which are universal or omnipresent, and some of which are not.

So once again the Jews of Chever Torah have led me to a rev-elation: God is indeed limited in at least one way. He is the Cre-ator, which means he cannot be the creation. He must withdraw, or limit himself, to give us space to exist.

I do not mean to imply that God is limited in the way I am.

My limitations are mostly a function of my status as a creature confined to time, space, matter, and energy. I did not choose to be limited in these ways. I am limited by my very nature. But God, who is unlimited by his nature if the Shema is to be be-lieved, has *decided* to be limited in order to scale himself down to my level. If I walk very slowly while holding a toddler's hand, I do it for the child's sake, not because I am slow on my feet. In the same way, amidst all this talk about a limited God, I must never forget that the Master of the universe has merely deigned to slow down enough to walk beside me.

When thinking about the idea that God had to accept limita-tions as a prerequisite for the universe's creation, I find a related concept arriving hard on its heels. God began with all the power, but the moment he chose to give some power to humanity (spe-cifically a kind of power we call "free will") God's power monop-oly ceased.

Even though the dealer at a card game may own every card in the deck, she must follow the rules until the very end of the game, otherwise it is not a game at all since the game exists *because* of the rules. In the same way, even if God controls the universe and exists outside of the constraints of time, space, matter, and energy, the universal rules or laws that he has created must still be binding, even on himself. If God should ever decide to change the rules in the middle of this hand that he has dealt, the entire game would be off.

To understand this, I imagine myself in a room with two doors. I am told I may freely choose to exit through either door, but when I grasp the handle of the first, it is solidly locked. Simply because the owner of the room says I have freedom of choice in such a situation does not make it so, because anyone who has just one choice really has no choice at all. Free will depends upon the existence of at least two options.

Thinking along these lines, I find the following in the Talmud:

> Without the Evil Impulse, man would feel no satisfaction in his labor and no joy in his Torah.
>
> —Midrash ha-Neelam, I, 138a

In other words, I could take no joy in righteousness if evil did not exist to be denied. This thought is a corollary to the idea that evil and good must both exist if I am to have genuine free will. Unless I am willing to live in a deranged *Alice in Wonderland* kind of world where open doors are simultaneously locked, I cannot be free without the option to choose good *or* evil, even if that means other people use their free will to choose evil on the scale of the Holocaust.

If the Hebrew Scriptures are to be believed, at the heart of the paradox of free will and predestination stands a loving God who desires love in return.[8] But love must be given freely. Therefore, a loving God must allow human freedom of choice. Unfortunately, we abuse this freedom, causing untold pain and suffering with our choices. Of course, while I deplore the evil that we do, I also demand my own freedom to choose evil. Not all of the bad things that happen in this world are due to human choices here and now. There are hurricanes and earthquakes and diseases, after all, and I will discuss those later on. But when it comes to

---

8. Deuteronomy commands us to love the Lord at least seven times, the Psalmist mentions God's love for us dozens of times, and in Exodus 34:6 God himself describes his love as "abounding."

stopping the evil that humans do, it seems to me God has just four unpleasant options:

First, since I want some people to have the freedom to choose good or evil (these people with freedom of choice would include me, of course), and I want others to have their freedom removed, God can grant my wish by removing the universal law of logic and letting utter chaos reign.

Second, if I do not want chaos, but I still wish for only good behavior by all people, God can remove everyone's freedom of choice and allow us just the one option to choose good.

Third, God can obliterate all creation as we know it and begin again, establishing a different kind of universe with different rules of logic.

Fourth, God can continue with his current strategy, allowing both human freedom and human evil to continue in spite of the pain we inflict on every living thing.

There is no fifth possibility. God cannot grant us free will *and* control our wills *and* maintain a logical universe, because within the laws of logic even God cannot simultaneously allow and deny complete freedom to choose. So I have arrived at yet another divine limitation:

In a logical universe, even God cannot make sense of nonsense.

It has been one week since the Chever Torah debate on the relationship between Jewish suffering and God's omnipotence. Now I am back and we are discussing the meaning of holiness. I have already learned that God is indeed limited on at least two levels: as a necessary prerequisite for the act of creation itself, and for the coexistence of human logic and free will. I am about to find a third divine limitation.

The Torah teaches that God is holy, but what does this mean, exactly?[9] I have always assumed "holy" and "good" are synonyms, but today Rabbi David Stern explains that the Hebrew

9. Leviticus 11:45.

word for holy is *kadosh*, which literally means separate, or set apart. The word "holy" does not necessarily mean good.

In its most literal sense, "holy" simply means "pure."

According to the *American Heritage Dictionary*, the word "pure" is defined as "having a homogeneous or uniform composition; not mixed." So God's holiness depends upon his separation from the unholy. In fact, the English synonyms for "holy," "consecrated" and "sanctified," both include the idea of being set apart from, or not mixed with, anything that is profane. This is consistent with what I have already learned about God from the Shema, which teaches that he is pure and perfect in his essence, ("homogenous or uniform" in the dictionary's terms). In other words, the existence of anything in its pure state requires a separation from everything else.

Holiness requires boundaries, or limits.

Since God is pure and perfect in his essence, each thing that defines what the Lord is also defines what the he is not. This means all manifestations of God's goodness—manifestations that include his immutability, omnipotence, omnipresence, immortality, righteousness, justice, love, grace, and mercy—all imply a limitation on him.

So this is the third way that God is limited: his oneness/perfection requires that he be separate from anything that could dilute his essential being.

In spite of these apologetics, when the news is filled with some particularly heinous crime or when the subject of the Holocaust arises, the people of Chever Torah insist that God should stop the madness, and I feel exactly the same. My mother, my dear, sweet mother, will probably die a horribly slow and painful death as I stand helplessly by. And I am not alone in my grief. Everyone who ever lost someone they loved has felt this gut-wrenching sorrow, this impotent rage. All around the world, our hearts cry out together for an end to evil.

But what would it look like for the Lord to answer our entreaties and enter human history to stop all evil?

God says: "If by one step I overstep and transgress justice, I should set everything on fire; immediately the whole world would be consumed."

—Tanhuma, Buber, Tazria, 11

Here, the rabbis teach that God's justice must be perfect. As with his holiness or any other manifestation of his essence, anything less than perfect justice would pollute the ongoing Source of all justice, and thereby obliterate the basis for *any* justice. But perfect justice cannot coexist with this particular universe. In Genesis 18:25 Abraham asked, "Will not the Judge of all the earth do right?" and the rabbis of the Talmud imagined God responding this way:

. . . if it is a world You want, then strict justice is impossible. And if it is strict justice You want, then a world is impossible.

—Bereshit Rabbah, 49:20[10]

The rabbis knew God's "strict justice" is too pure for planet Earth, meaning we are too impure to survive it. Therefore, God has suspended strict justice here among us. He has limited himself, or withdrawn, for our protection.

You are not a God who takes pleasure in evil; with you the wicked cannot dwell. The arrogant cannot stand in your presence; you hate all who do wrong.

—Psalms 5:4–5

As Maimonides said, if the Shema is true and the Lord is one, then he is pure in every way. That absolute purity means his justice must be perfect, which in turn means no injustice can be allowed in his presence. None. That's what purity and perfection mean. They are absolute terms that limit God's ability to interact with an impure, imperfect creation.

In civil law, I am judged according to something called a "reasonable standard." This means my actions are compared to what most people would do under similar circumstances. On the

10. As quoted by Avivah Gottlieb Zornberg, *The Beginning of Desire, Reflections on Genesis* (New York: Doubleday, 1995), p. 110.

other hand, if God is without flaws, and if he took the place of my human judge and jury, the standard would shift from what is reasonable in human terms to what is reasonable in godly terms. Genocide, murder, rape, and assault would be out of bounds of course, but with the absolute standard of God's holiness and oneness, suddenly there can also be no exceeding the speed limit, no telling white lies, no little bits of "harmless" gossip. My everyday sins may be on a different part of the sin spectrum from those of a mass murderer, but they are sins nonetheless; they exist on the spectrum. That means the "wrong" and "evil" that Habakkuk said God "cannot tolerate" includes even the wrongs and evil I have done, no matter how small they may seem to me.

The Torah supports this view quite strongly. For example, in at least four places, Abraham's descendants are ordered to be holy, but not in a "reasonable" or "only human" way. They are told to be holy because *God* is holy. The holiness they must maintain is compared to God's absolute standard of perfection.

But is that really fair?

Like Pontius Pilate asking, "What is truth?" I am sometimes tempted to gauge justice on the scale of my self-interest. Anticipating this, the Torah's definition of justice reveals an uncompromising requirement of absolute balance between wrongs and redress, but first it warns me not to confuse justice with emotion:

> Show no pity: life for life, eye for eye, tooth for tooth, hand for hand, foot for foot.
>
> —Deuteronomy 19:21

Those first three words, "show no pity," speak volumes about the Lord's absolutely perfect standard of justice. Again, I wonder what would happen if God ever decided to enforce such a standard. As it happens, the Torah describes a time when God did just that: he entered history to halt human sin in a uniform, evenhanded way with perfect justice for everyone. In other words, we

all got what we asked for. The result was a universal horror
called the flood.

> The Lord saw how great man's wickedness on the earth had be-
> come, and that every inclination of the thoughts of his heart was
> only evil all the time. The Lord was grieved that he had made man
> on the earth, and his heart was filled with pain. So the Lord said,
> "I will wipe mankind, whom I have created, from the face of the
> earth—men and animals, and creatures that move along the
> ground, and birds of the air—for I am grieved that I have made
> them."
>
> —Genesis 6:5–7

I suspect the flood was the unforeseen answer to a million
foolish prayers. Imagine one fellow kneeling before his idols
with a neighbor in mind, praying, "Gods, I am sick of the way he
treats me, please put an end to him." Meanwhile his neighbor is
kneeling too, asking for the very same thing. Eventually, this
begging achieves results. God answers with the flood, destroying
absolutely everyone on the sin spectrum from people like Adolf
Hitler to people like those of us at Chever Torah.

Why such a harsh reply?

God the lover would rather have it that way than remove our
free will, because he knows existence without freedom would be
even worse than death. Patrick Henry expressed this idea more
eloquently than I ever could:

> Is life so dear or peace so sweet, as to be purchased at the price of
> chains and slavery? Forbid it Almighty God! I know not what
> course others may take, but as for me, give me liberty or give me
> death!

Some at Chever Torah have suggested that God was unfair to
flood the earth. Ironically, many of them are the same people
who suggested earlier that it was unfair for God to choose Israel
as his treasured possession without doing more to protect them
from evil. They are, I think, a representative sample of humanity
at large, trying to have its cake and eat it too. Their lament finds
a sympathetic ear among many Christians. We also sometimes
suffer for our faith. We also pray for deliverance and protection,

especially those of us enduring persecution in so many countries around the world today much as Jews have suffered so many times before in Christian lands. Humanity's violence has caused people of all religions to curse God from time to time for refusing to remove such evil from the earth.

Yet we object to floods.

As with everything else, God anticipates this reaction. After the deluge, he makes a promise: "I establish my covenant with you: Never again will all life be cut off by the waters of a flood; never again will there be a flood to destroy the earth."[11] Having demonstrated what would happen if he enforced strict justice on the earth, God now takes the next step. He voluntarily enters into a covenant with humanity and seals it with the promise *not* to impose perfect justice on earth, but to find another path. The Creator did indeed isolate himself out beyond the stars somewhere, but he did it so I could survive. It is yet another divine limitation, accepted for my sake.

A moment ago, I noticed that Genesis says God was "grieved" by the evil rampant on the earth before the flood.[12] This reminds me of the moment when Jesus wept on his way to the tomb of Lazarus.[13] It makes me think that God's self-limitation must be akin to self-sacrifice. It actually causes him pain. Throughout the Hebrew Scriptures there are hints that the cost of God's self-limitation runs deeper than I ever imagined. For example, the Lord warns that "no one may see me and live," yet he seems to yearn for exactly that. When Moses asks to see God's glory, he places Moses in the cleft of a rock, covers him with his "hand" and comes as close as possible.

God is Cyrano de Bergerac in the shadows, aching to reveal his love to Roxanne. He is Odysseus in rags, in love but unknown at Penelope's banquet. How deeply the Creator longs to commune with me, how frustrating this delay! The cost of God's self-limitation cuts right through to the core of his essence:

11. Genesis 9:11.
12. Genesis 6:6–7.
13. John 11:35.

Oh, that their hearts would be inclined to fear me and keep all my commands always, so that it might go well with them and their children forever!

—Deuteronomy 5:29

When I first read this verse, seeing it in my new Chever Torah way, I stop in amazement. Here is the Creator and Ruler of the universe expressing an *unfulfilled desire!* God's self-limitation costs him dearly. He is like a rich man deliberately going hungry in sympathy for starving people.

But to whom is this unfulfilled desire expressed? To Moses ostensibly, but Moses can do nothing about the hearts of Israel. Only God can respond to such an entreaty. So on a deeper level it seems that God is speaking to himself, offering up a kind of prayer. This is an idea straight from Chever Torah.

It is thus that God prays: "May it please Me that My mercy may overcome My anger; that all my attributes may be invested with compassion and that I may deal with My children in the attribute of kindness, and that out of regard for them I may omit judgment."

—Berakhot, 7a

Here, the rabbis agreed that God limits himself by withholding judgment, at least for a while. But another kind of limitation is implied in the Torah and the Talmud's surprising suggestions that God sometimes speaks—or prays—to himself. It is a radical concept for an evangelical Christian, but upon further reflection, I find it builds my faith because:

Jesus often withdrew to lonely places and prayed.

—Luke 5:16

Some might point to Jesus' prayers as evidence that he was not divine. After all, if Jesus is God, why bother to tell himself what he already knows? But the God of the Hebrew Scriptures grieved before the flood and expressed an unfulfilled desire for Israel's obedience. He is a self-limited God because of his love for us. And when the love of humanity limits the Father, why should I be surprised that humanity itself limits the divinity of Jesus?

Does human prayer make any more sense? After all, the prayers of my heart also tell God what he already knows, yet he wants me to pray so that my needs will be satisfied. This is like sacrifice, another religious ritual that makes no sense on the surface of it. As the Bible says:

> I have no need of a bull from your stall or of goats from your pens, for every animal of the forest is mine, and the cattle on a thousand hills.
>
> —Psalms 50:9–10

In the Torah God requires his chosen people to bring the first-born of their flocks to offer on the altar as if the animals were their own possessions, though the Lord provided the animals in the first place. Then in the Psalms he tells them that they missed the point. In the strictest sense, no human being has ever offered a sacrifice to God. Since everything we have comes from the Lord, all offerings *to* him are a kind of self-sacrifice *by* him. Unless this is kept in mind I am merely God's unwitting servant facilitating the ceremony, like a Roman soldier pounding spikes.

So why involve humanity at all?

I believe there is a reason God wants prayer for things he already knows we need, a reason God wants me to bring the sacrifices he himself provided, a reason God prefers to work through me to heal the wounds of the world rather than doing that work directly. I believe it is one reason he came to earth in a manger.

The Bible says I cannot see God's face and live.[14] My choice to disobey the Lord has reduced me to a state of spiritual fragility that cannot withstand the intensity of direct divine intervention. In other words, the Great Physician operates at arm's length through weak human beings *because* we are weak. My mother and I cannot survive more radical surgery.

Still, the distance between the Lord and me does not change my desire to be close to him. Like a moth drawn inexorably to-

14. Exodus 33:20.

ward the flame, I spend a lot of time and energy trying to break down the boundaries between us. Fortunately, the Bible teaches that God shares my desire to rebuild our relationship. In fact, "relationship" is too weak a word for what God wants. The Lord inspired Hosea and other prophets to present the bond between Israel and him as similar to marriage in order to teach that he wants to experience that kind of intermingling with our essence, that sense of oneness, of losing ourselves in each other.

I want more of God.

God wants *all* of me.

It makes sense, because the Torah says God loves me and I was created in God's image, and closeness is something I want too when I am in love.[15] Love wants more, at almost any cost. And the more I love, the more I am willing to sacrifice for those I love. For some very special people, I would even change my basic personality if I could. Since I am willing to go so far, surely God could do the same. Since nothing is beyond his power, why, oh *why* won't he come down here to dwell with me and protect me, even if it means giving up his precious holiness and justice?

The answer remains in Habakkuk's lament: "Your eyes are too pure to look on evil; you cannot tolerate wrong." But now I notice something new: God *cannot* tolerate wrong. I have been thinking theoretically here in terms of a God who is self-limited, but these are much stronger words.

God cannot.

Although the words feel heretical, there they are in the Bible. And as so often happens, once my eyes have been opened to this new way of understanding, I suddenly find the same idea elsewhere in the Scriptures. For example, the apostle Paul made note of God's limitations in an easily overlooked aside to his protégé, Timothy:

> If we are faithless, he will remain faithful, for he *cannot* disown himself.
>
> —2 Timothy 2:13 (emphasis mine)

I have never fully understood Paul's meaning before, but now I think I do. Paul means that if God is truly "one" he must be per-

---

15. See Deuteronomy 7:7–9.

fectly faithful, otherwise he would cease to be "God" as defined by the attribute of faithfulness. In other words, allowing himself to ignore any faithlessness in those who approach, allowing such flaws to pollute his presence even for the sake of love, would be tantamount to divine suicide.

Of course I cannot really pollute God's presence. In my examination of the Shema I learned that it is impossible for the creature to change the Creator, just as a flea cannot budge the sun. My thesis stands on the "cause, then effect" assumption that God's oneness cannot be diluted by anything in the universe. His very nature precludes his ability to change for me, in spite of how strongly he loves me. He cannot be unfaithful to what he is. It is the lesson of Nadab and Abihu, the priests who approached God with "alien fire" and were burned alive. The sun will incinerate the flea every time.

But what if—hypothetically speaking—I could somehow force myself upon the Lord and pollute his presence with my imperfect state? What would happen if God became something less than holy?

Christianity and Judaism alike teach that God is the force that binds the universe together. This belief stems from the Torah's statement that ". . . man does not live on bread alone but on every word that comes from the mouth of the Lord."[16] That verse may also be the basis for this remarkable comment in the Talmud:

> Were it not for the Torah, the world would not stand.
>
> —Nedarim, 32

I used to think the word "torah" meant simply the Pentateuch or first five books of the Bible, but at Chever Torah I learn that "torah" is also a Hebrew word for "teaching." Many rabbis of the Talmud equate it with the "wisdom" discussed in Proverbs.[17] If

16. Deuteronomy 8:3.
17. Cohn-Sherbok, *Popular Dictionary of Judaism*, p. 183. See also the further discussion of this topic in chapter 8.

they are correct, this torah/wisdom is more than just a collection of true and good ideas; it is the very stuff of existence:

> By wisdom the Lord laid the earth's foundations, by understanding he set the heavens in place.
>
> —Proverbs 3:19

Elsewhere in Proverbs, this torah/wisdom is presented as existing "from the beginning, before the world began," and functioning during creation itself as "the craftsman at his side."[18] The belief that God's torah precedes creation and was an instrument of the creative act is also found in the opening lines of the New Testament Gospel of John:

> In the beginning was the Word, and the Word was with God, and the Word was God. He was with God in the beginning. Through him all things were made; without him nothing was made that has been made.
>
> —John 1:1–3

Compare this to the following concept from the Talmud:

> God created the world by a Word, instantaneously, without toil and pains.
>
> —Bereshit Rabbah, 3, 2

So when the Talmud says, "without the Torah the world would not stand," it means the universe depends on God's word for its daily existence. Similarly, Rabbinic Judaism often refers to God as *Ha-Makom*, which means "the Place." Jews have given God this name partially in order to underscore the idea that the Lord is not only omnipresent, but he actually forms the framework of everything. The idea of God as the universe's framework does not imply the pantheistic notion that the universe and God are identical. Rather, it means that God is the ongoing external source of both the "everything" within the universe, and of the "nothing" beyond our mind's capacity to imagine. This concept is elegantly expressed in the following Talmud quote:

18. Proverbs 8:22–31.

God is the place of the universe, but the universe is not his place.

—Midrash Tehillim to Psalm 90:1

The New Testament expresses the same idea this way:

He is not served by human hands, as if he needed anything, because he himself gives all men breath and life and everything else.

—Acts 17:25

I note with interest that both of these statements are in the present tense. God's role as the giver of life was not finished after the first six days of creation, or with the "Big Bang." The Lord is still at work today, molding the cosmos by guiding its ongoing changes.

Many people visualize God as something akin to a child who has spun a top and then merely sits back to watch it wind down. But if the Lord is truly all-knowing (as I must believe if I accept the Shema), then he knew every possible ramification of his creative act right from the beginning. This means God is still the source of the change I see everywhere, whether he is causing change right now or whether all change was consciously predetermined when he set the universe in motion all those years ago.

Furthermore, the spinning top analogy ignores the fact that God exists outside of time. Because all time is here and now for God, he alone can have it both ways: causing all change with one creative act "in the beginning" *and* maintaining a personal involvement here and now.

So finally I return to the question left hanging a while ago: If—hypothetically speaking—the perfect Lord allowed himself to be polluted by contact with something less than holy, if God let himself be changed by my impurity, what would happen?

Theoretically, since all created life depends on change and all change must have an external cause, if the cause of all change became merely one more changing thing himself, then the universe as we know it would cease to exist. And as usual, once I think my way through from Chever Torah question to answer, I find the Scriptures have been there before me.

I the Lord do not change. So you, O descendants of Jacob, are not destroyed.

—Malachi 3:6

The Lord does not change, because—in the words of Paul and the prophet Habakkuk—"God *cannot* change." But that is a limitation he has voluntarily accepted for my free will and my very survival. So once again a "blasphemous" Chever Torah question has distilled new faith from doubt:

"God, are you limited?"

"Yes, I am limited for love of you."

It is a horrible answer indeed, which doomed six million Jews and five million Gentiles to death in the Nazi Holocaust. It has doomed my mother, and me, and every other created thing. But it is also the loving foundation of life itself, because in the words of the Talmud, had God imposed "strict justice" on the Nazis, we would have no world at all. Either the universe would drown beneath a tidal wave of perfect objectivity, or God would compromise himself by absorbing our imperfections, thereby committing divine suicide and forever shattering the foundation of all existence.

And yet. . . .

This is all so hypothetical. Although I now understand God's self-limitations to some extent, my heart stubbornly contends that a God who is truly the Master of the universe could find *some* way of fixing what is wrong with my mother. All this theory feels like irrelevant sophistry when it comes to real life, where cancer strikes those we love the most, babies are born with birth defects, Jewish children are shot in American daycare centers or blown to bits on Israeli busses, and madmen crash airliners into skyscrapers or open fire on Christians as they sing to God in churches. In the face of so much pain, I need something more than hypotheses and explanations. I need a God who is big enough to figure out a solution. So a Chever Torah kind of question remains:

Is anything really impossible for God?

Could he not devise some loophole, some method, some way to allow me to draw near in spite of my imperfections? Wouldn't a perfect God's love be so pure that he would be willing to do *anything* in order to allow me to approach . . . even to the point of self-sacrifice? After all, in the Bible God does sometimes set aside the rules of logic and nature in certain cases. Think of all the miracles, from the Tower of Babel to the resurrection . . . .

And with that final word I feel as if I have rounded a corner after searching through the night, only to find myself back home again by accident.

Tragedy is the fertile soil of miracles. I cannot recall a single miracle in the Torah that does involve affliction. Barren wombs lead to miraculous births. Joseph is sold into slavery and the result is one of the greatest examples of forgiveness in human history. Cruel bondage in Egypt culminates with the miracles of the Exodus and the Promised Land. In the same way, Jesus' gruesome death on a cross led to his resurrection, and eventually, to my mother's miraculous love affair with God here and now, in the midst of her suffering. It seems the way to deal with the evil of the world is not to pretend to go around it, but to plunge right through.

Why this connection between suffering and salvation?

I believe sometimes bad things happen to good people so we can watch God turn the greatest tragedies into the purest love. This is no theory. I lived it on the day before my father died of leukemia, while I carried soiled rags to a trash can after my mother had used them to wipe his bottom. It was the saddest moment of my life up to then. My father—the strong man at the center of my life—was reduced to no more than an infant, babbling incoherently and messing himself. It left me completely numb. I was not praying. I was not reaching out to God. I was in survival mode, with all emotions shutting down in self-defense. Then, as I crossed the room, a sudden warm and shining sense of perfect joy came without reason, filling me from head to toe. Words cannot describe the sensation. Maybe it was a tiny taste of heaven. It was the pinnacle of my spiritual life: standing there as my earthly father died and my heavenly Father spoke to my aching soul, saying, "Fear not. I am with you."

That was the most terrible moment of my life, but it was also the most wonderful . . . at least until the other day when it happened again.

When there was nothing more the doctors could do, we brought my mother home. Her pain was intense. I could not understand why God would let her suffering continue. I asked him right out loud to explain himself. And in the midst of that prayer, suddenly it hit me: "She's still got things to do." I could not imagine what in the world an emaciated, bedridden old woman could possibly accomplish for the Creator of the universe, but stranger things have happened, and I felt some comfort when this answer came, because it seemed so certain.

Little did I know she was living on for me.

I awoke the next day at 5 A.M. and crossed the hall to sit beside her bed. She was just the same as she had been at midnight: comatose and breathing shallowly and very rapidly, like a sprinter trying to get back her wind. I slipped a few drops of water from a soda straw into her open mouth and put some balm on her lips and sat down beside her bed to pray. "Lord, what are you waiting for? What possible good can come from letting her suffer this way?" My mother kept up her ragged breathing. Watching her open mouth as her hollow chest rose and fell, it occurred to me how easy it would be to send her on her way. Just cover her mouth and pinch her nose for ten or fifteen seconds and her suffering would stop. She would be in paradise.

We had a baby monitor on her bedside table, with speakers in the different rooms where my brother and the hospice nurse were sleeping. I could not turn it off without waking them because their speakers would roar with static when the microphone went dead on my end. But Mom might struggle a little bit—I didn't think so, since she was so far gone, but it was possible—and that could wake them too. I would have to lock the door in case the others heard and tried to intervene.

I rose to do just that.

Then I thought, "You shall not murder."

I sat back down.

But she was in so much pain.

I thought, "Honor your mother."

I rose.

Then, remembering "you shall not murder," I sat again.

Suddenly, Abraham came to mind, leading Isaac up Mt. Moriah for a sacrifice. By obeying God, he was disobeying him. How does a believer balance, "you shall not murder," and "kill your only son"? Like Abraham, I was damned if I did and damned if I did not. So I prayed, "Lord, I want to love you with all my heart and soul and mind, but I also love my mother as myself, and if it was me on that bed, I would want someone to stop my suffering. Still, as much as I love her and want to save her from this pain, I trust your ways. I'll wait."

Immediately after saying that prayer—and I mean *immediately*—my mother's ragged breathing changed. For the first time in twenty-four hours she seemed at peace, breathing normally, like a healthy person having a nice nap.

God had my full attention.

This was no longer solely about my mother's passing. Now somehow it also had something to do with me. I sat up straight and watched. My mother's chest rose and fell normally about ten more times. Then she was gone. I rose to my feet beside her bed and lifted my hands to heaven, praising the Lord, smiling, and crying all at once.

So, it turns out I was my mother's last mortal assignment for her maker, the reason she remained alive those last few painful hours. My mother and I were very, very close . . . so close that, for a moment, I was prepared to commit murder for her. I am convinced she struggled through those last few hours precisely so that I would have to make that choice. And like Abraham, in choosing to trust God's ways, my faith was strengthened—which was exactly what I needed to survive my precious mother's death.

Who else but the Lord could use my mother's death to prepare me for her death?

What perfect, awesome symmetry!

If I had not trusted God in that moment of decision, if I had not allowed my mother's suffering to continue, I might never have learned this valuable lesson: God can be trusted to do the right thing. Yet I did trust him, I did choose to plunge right through the tragedy instead of pretending to go around, and the Lord taught me a lesson in faith I will never forget. Without my trust, my mother's final day of suffering would have seemed pointless. With my trust, she had the opportunity to leave me with one final priceless gift. Sometimes God intervenes to stop human suffering. Sometimes he does not. Either way, there is always a good reason. Sometimes we are blessed to understand the reason in the end, as I was, and sometimes we are not. But the reason is always there, because God can always be trusted. He is good!

> The crucible for silver and the furnace for gold, but the Lord tests the heart.
>
> —Proverbs 17:3

Within fifteen minutes of learning she was dying, my mother began trying to think of ways to use that experience to tell the world about Jesus. One day as she lay in her hospital bed unable to rise, I heard her greet the morning with the whispered words, "This is the day that the Lord has made; I will rejoice and be glad in it." Another time I found her awake and staring out the window. Fearing she was dwelling on the worst, I said, "A penny for your thoughts."

She smiled weakly and said, "I was just counting my blessings."

My mother and I had no doubt that the Lord is up to something wonderful in the midst of our tragedy. We were treading sacred ground, that fertile soil of miracles. We believed with all our hearts that God is good, and he loves us, and he will bless us beyond our wildest imaginings if we will only cling to him in the good times and the bad.

> However, as it is written: "No eye has seen, no ear has heard, no mind has conceived what God has prepared for those who love him."
>
> —1 Corinthians 2:9

If my mother could type these words, she would say our family's grief is nothing compared to the underlying peace that we have, because Jesus, who is God, has been here before us. He is God, but he is also a man, dying willingly on a cross in the ultimate self-sacrifice—the ultimate self-limitation—for those who neither understood nor cared. Centuries before Jesus' birth, Isaiah expressed the reason for my family's joy better than I ever could:

> But he was pierced for our transgressions, he was crushed for our iniquities; the punishment that brought us peace was upon him, and by his wounds we are healed.
>
> —Isaiah 53:5

Because Jesus, who is God, felt human pain personally, I know God understands. He grieves with my family today just as he grieved for the world before the flood, and with all Israel during the Holocaust. And because God and I grieve together, I can also rejoice that the seeds of the solution to evil do indeed rest in humanity; they rest in the man who is God. The Master of the universe wants me to know he feels my pain, but he cannot be unfaithful to himself. So a human heart must lift the prayer. Human hands must bring the sacrifice. It is both a mystery and a revelation that God has invited human participation in every stage of his universal drama from Eden until today. In perfect accord with that mystery, Jesus' human hands were nailed to the cross to remind me that pain is a shared experience between my heart and God's. But the Lord never does one thing at a time. So in a world where evil cannot be avoided, he also used the cross to show that the way to defeat tragedy is to plunge right through. Because of Jesus' suffering on the cross, I am spared from the one grief beyond human endurance. Somehow—it is impossible to understand how—in this ultimate expression of divine self-limitation the man who is God endured spiritual separation from *himself* so that I could rejoin my maker in his place.

When the very worst thing happened to the very best person, God turned that greatest of all tragedies into the purest of all loves, and he did that just for me.

The New Testament book of James tells me to consider everything joy, even the most painful tests of life, because through those tests God makes my faith complete.[19] Knowing full well

---

19. James 1:2.

that very bad things do happen to people like my mother and me, I used to wonder if my faith was up to this challenge. How could anyone face life's pain and suffering, yet consider it all joy?

Now I know the answer.

four

# Yes and Yes

These words neither help nor hurt my arguments.

—Y. Taanit, 2, 12

Rabbi Zimmerman is away this Shabbat morning, so Rabbi David Stern leads Chever Torah in his place. Rabbi Stern is young, handsome, and possessed of a lightning quick wit. He wears his hair in the style made famous by J.F.K. His energy is contagious. The morning's discussion accelerates as he asks a question worthy of Rashi, then paces back and forth in front of the hall grinning with delight as we answer and respond with questions of our own. But a few minutes later the rhythm flags inexplicably and we sit silently, staring at our Torahs. Rabbi Stern fires off another question. No one answers. He offers a provocative observation—something controversial to stir the pot. Still, we are silent. Finally in frustration, he exclaims, "Come on people! Somebody disagree with me! How can we learn anything if no one will disagree?"

We laugh. But it occurs to me that Rabbi Stern has offered the most profound observation of the day, and it is a very Jewish idea.

Unfortunately, most theological conversations I have had in church have been the self-reinforcing kind: a group of people sitting around telling each other what everyone already believes. If some brave soul interjects a radical new idea or questions one of the group's firmly held views, it is usually an unpleasant experience. We shift in our seats uncomfortably until someone rises to the bait. The discussion remains civil, but it seems that any challenge to the groups' theology must be corrected, so all comments are solidly aimed at that one goal: arriving at a preconceived answer.

Chever Torah has no such agenda. Or perhaps I should say all discussions have the same agenda: to explore the possibilities—*all* the possibilities. That is both a benefit and a problem. After many months at Chever Torah, it has finally sunken in that God welcomes honest questions. Far from betraying a doubting heart, the rabbis and the Jews at temple have taught me that my questions demonstrate my faith, prove my love, display trust, and remove doubts by leading to answers I can use to help others on the path to the Lord. In fact, I now have an entirely new problem. In response to every question I send speeding up to heaven, God sends a shower of answers back to earth, and sometimes the answers seem contradictory.

For example, with my new freedom to question God, I have already learned that the Shema means he is all-powerful. When I questioned him again, I learned that he is limited in several ways. An all-powerful God who is limited? How can I understand such a paradox? I am not a prophet like Moses, with whom God spoke face to face. Moses' life was filled with "Mt. Sinai moments" of guidance direct from the Lord. What about me? This Saturday morning, when I'm still rubbing sleep from my eyes and the main thing on my mind as I enter temple is getting to the coffee urn, what should I do with these paradoxes of the Bible?

Like most everything else, the answer can be found in the Torah.

Abraham's grandson Jacob has been a very bad boy. He used trickery to steal his brother Esau's inheritance then fled to another country to escape Esau's wrath. There, Jacob married four women and became wealthy. Now he is returning to the land of his father after twenty years in exile, hoping to make peace with Esau. Along the way one of the most enigmatic events in the Torah occurs.

As Jacob nears Canaan, he sends advance groups of servants and animals as gifts to defuse his brother's potentially murderous anger. Having also sent his wives and children ahead, Jacob finds himself alone beside the river Jabbok, where, with no preamble or explanation whatsoever, the Torah says "a man wrestled with him until daybreak." The struggle lasts all night. When dawn looms on the horizon, the "man," unable to extract himself from Jacob's grip, "touches" Jacob's hip and throws it out of its socket. Still, Jacob clings to him,

> Then the man said, "Let me go, for it is daybreak." But Jacob replied, "I will not let you go unless you bless me." The man asked him, "What is your name?" "Jacob," he answered. Then the man said, "Your name will no longer be Jacob, but Israel, because you have struggled with God and with men and have overcome." Jacob said, "Please tell me your name." But he replied, "Why do you ask my name?" Then he blessed him there. So Jacob called the place Peniel, saying, "It is because I saw God face to face, and yet my life was spared."
>
> —Genesis 32:26–30

If I was too sleepy and preoccupied with coffee to come up with questions before, now questions seem to leap from the pages of the Torah, demanding answers. Why am I not told who the "man" is? Why did the man want to know Jacob's name? Why did he refuse to tell Jacob his own name? And most of all, what about that last verse, where Jacob seems to be saying that the "man" was actually God? How is that possible?

At Chever Torah I learn that there are homonymic undercurrents of deeper meaning in the Hebrew words of this brief story. The name "Jacob" (*Ya'aqob*), the river "Jabbok" (*Yabboq*) and the Hebrew word for "struggle" (*abaq*) all sound very similar in spoken Hebrew. *Ya'aqob. Yabboq. Abaq.* A man. A place. An action. Could there be some connection between these things, some hidden message?

Suddenly it occurs to me that all of these questions may be the fundamental reason for the story. For thousands of years an entire people have been called Israel, which means "struggles with God," because of this enigmatic episode. I have already seen that names are important in the Torah. When God wants to initiate a new level of intimacy with Moses, Elohim reveals his personal name, allowing the Hebrew people to call him *Yahweh*—I Am. When God wants to initiate a deeper relationship with Abram, he changes his name to Abraham. And now, this "man/God" has done it again. But what a name he has chosen for Jacob!

Israel.

"Struggles with God."

It is almost as if God has challenged Jacob to continue their wrestling match.

Ideas are flying faster now. I sense yet another level in the narrative. Could there be a connection between the name, Israel, and the paradoxical events of the story itself? Could it be that these things are described in this way because God *wants* me to be confused? Could these incomplete clues be placed here deliberately, because I am supposed to cast around for answers?

Could the paradox in this story be God's invitation to wrestle with *me?*

A moment ago, I was reading about a literary character's struggle with God in an old book. Now, somehow, I have been drawn into that struggle myself—really drawn in, right here, right now. In an instant, five thousand years have disappeared and I am there on the riverbank with Jacob and the "man," there with the sand and stones and the grunts and sweat and the barest glimmer of a golden dawn on the horizon. I have him in my grasp, this enigmatic man; the sinews of his shoulders strain against me, but I have him. He will tell me now. I am sure of it. He will tell me what I need to know.

Then, with a touch, he is free; the class is over and I lie panting for breath beside the river.

I close the Torah and stare at the cover, overwhelmed. What is this thing that lies before me? It looks like a book, but what is it really?

How did it *do* that?

In the following week, I cannot stop the memory of that tantalizing moment when I seemed to leave this world and step into another. The intensity of that feeling fades, but something permanent remains. I have a new, intimate understanding of how the Bible works. God has spoken to me through his Torah in a way I've never experienced before, and his message is clear:

"Struggle with me."

Like Jacob with his limp, I am forever changed. Before, I saw a few questions in the Bible. They seemed like inconsistencies, and they frightened me. If the Bible is inconsistent, how can I justify my faith? But now I see something shining just beyond the questions. I see paradoxes every time I open the book, and rather than feeling fear, I am excited, because I know each paradox is another invitation to return to that wonderful wrestling match with God—to that feeling of being *right there with him.*

Readers who have not yet found the Bible's paradoxes or who have trained themselves to ignore them for the sake of their peace of mind may doubt that I encounter them almost every time I read the Torah. Perhaps they would benefit from a few examples, so here is a brief list. For the sake of future reference, I will give each of them a name:

*The Paradox of Fertility.* God commands Adam and Eve to "be fruitful and multiply," but when he later selects a woman, Sarah, to be the mother of his chosen people, she is barren, unable to fulfill his command. This paradox is repeated with a barren Rebekah and a barren Rachel. A nation born of barren wombs— What could be more paradoxical?

*The Paradox of Obedience.* I alluded to this in the previous chapter: Abraham is commanded to commit the horrible evil of human sacrifice by killing his son Isaac, but this command to vi-

olate God's law against murder *comes* from God. The paradox
rises again when the Israelites are condemned for melting their
golden jewelry and building a golden calf—a violation of the
commandment against "graven images"—yet they are later commanded to melt their golden jewelry to make a pair of cherubim
for the ark of the covenant, and later still are told to fashion and
look upon a bronze serpent in order to survive snake bites. I find
this paradox another time when God commands the Israelites
not to seek "revenge," then orders Israel to destroy the people of
Midian in the name of "vengeance."[1] To obey is to disobey. How
is that possible?

*The Paradox of the Promise.* God promises to give Canaan to
Abraham, but Abraham must pay dearly for a burial spot in that
land for Sarah, and later the Israelites must fight and die to take
it. How can the Promised Land be considered a gift when it must
be bought with gold and lives?

*The Paradox of Blessing.* God promises Abraham that "all peoples on earth will be blessed through you and your offspring," yet
just before they enter the Promised Land, God commands Abraham's offspring to completely destroy the pagan people living
there. If anything, the Canaanite people were cursed by Abraham's offspring, so how can it be true that "all peoples on earth"
will be blessed?

*The Paradox of Omnipresence.* God is said to be omnipresent,
yet he is often described as visiting a certain place in a manner
that implies he was not previously there.[2] If he is omnipresent,
why is the Torah filled with descriptions of him coming and
going on earth?

*The Paradox of the Red Heifer.* Throughout Mosaic law people
must be "ceremonially pure" *before* they can bring sacrificial offerings to the tabernacle, and priests must be purified *before* they
can offer those sacrifices. Also, Torah is clear that offerings can
be made at the tabernacle altar and no place else. But with the
"red heifer sacrifice" of Numbers 19, the offering is not made at
the altar; it is made outside the camp. Also, the priest must be purified *after* making the offering, and the people are actually puri-

---

1. Compare Leviticus 19:18 and Numbers 31:1. The same Hebrew word, *naqam*, is
translated as "vengeance" or "revenge" in both verses.
2. See Genesis 17:1 and 18:1 for examples.

fied as a *result* of the offering. Why this reversal of everything else the Torah teaches about sacrifice?

*The Paradox of Justice and Mercy.* The Torah defines justice as "Show no pity. Life for life, eye for eye, tooth for tooth. . . ."[3] It is an unforgiving standard, yet elsewhere the Hebrew Scriptures tell us we should ". . . act justly and love mercy. . . ."[4] How can we simultaneously uphold the strict justice described in the Torah's *lex talionis* or "law of retaliation," and also love mercy?

The Hebrew Scriptures are not the only ones filled with paradox. Throughout the New Testament Jesus loves to use paradox to entice me to wrestle with the Lord. For example, Jesus says, "But many who are first will be last, and many who are last will be first." In a similar reversal of the usual wisdom, he also says, "For whoever wants to save his life will lose it, but whoever loses his life for me and for the gospel will save it."[5] Jesus was always saying self-contradictory things like that. Indeed, one of his most frequently discussed teachings cannot be understood in any other context. I call it the Paradox of Love.

In Matthew 22:37–40, Jesus explains that the greatest commandment is to love God with all of our heart, soul, and mind. Then he says the second most important commandment is like the first, namely, we are to love each other in the way we love ourselves.[6] But if I have given all of my heart, soul, and mind over to loving God, where will I find the capacity to love my neighbor as myself? For that matter, if I must love my neighbor in the same way that I love myself, obviously I must first love myself to some extent. Yet to the same extent that I love myself, I must withhold part of my heart, soul, and mind from loving God. The paradox deepens when I observe that in spite of this high-minded commitment to love, Jesus also made the following remarkable statement: "If anyone comes to me and does not *hate*

---

3. The *lex talionis*, or "law of retaliation," is found in three of the five books of the Torah: Exodus 21:24; Leviticus 24:20; Deuteronomy 19:21.

4. Micah 6:8.

5. Matthew 19:30; Mark 8:35.

6. Deuteronomy 6:5; Leviticus 19:18.

his father and mother, his wife and children, his brothers and sisters—yes even his own life—he cannot be my disciple."[7] Love God wholeheartedly, but save some love for yourself and your neighbor. Love your neighbor and love the Lord but hate your family and your life.

How can anyone obey these teachings?

The last few pages have contained just a tiny portion of the many paradoxes in the Bible. I hope I have listed enough to convince the skeptic—be she a believer or unbeliever—that they do indeed fill the Scriptures. Yet because of Chever Torah, I have learned that none of these examples constitutes an inconsistency, much less a contradiction. On the contrary, I think biblical paradoxes are closer to the truth than any clear and simple statement could possibly be. If I am correct, it is the height of irony that throughout the centuries Christians and Jews have argued with each other and among themselves about the answers to these riddles. Both religions have divided into denominations over them. Churches and synagogues alike have split over them. Wars have been fought and people martyred for them. Everyone seems to think it is vital to understand "the truth" about these things—the one and only truth. But now at Chever Torah, armed with my new freedom to doubt and question, I read the story of Jacob's wrestling match with the "man" on the shores of the Jabbok river, and a startling train of thought begins.

What if God placed these paradoxes within the Scriptures to *cause* me to struggle for the truth? What if it is the *struggle* he desires as much as the truth itself? Could it be that the truth lies not in one of the seemingly opposed answers to the paradox, but in between them, within the paradox itself? Could it be that uncompromising stances on the paradoxical teachings of the Scriptures are foolishness, no matter how important the doctrine or belief in question, because such dogmatic posturing misses the point entirely? Could it be that the answer to these either/or questions of paradox is neither this nor that, but simply, "Yes" and "Yes"?

7. Luke 14:26 (emphasis mine).

I read somewhere—it may have been in something by C. S. Lewis—that the devil's favorite trick is to get people to focus on one truth to the exclusion of another.

When I was five years old my father took me to a fishing barge on a lake near our home. There, he showed me how to bait a hook and throw it into the water. Watching the bobber for nibbles, I began to learn an important lesson about patience. But I did not learn it well. Soon the bobber dove beneath the surface, and with my father's help I caught my very first fish. As my father dealt with the unlucky beast, I reeled in my line, placed the pole on the deck, and told him I was ready to go. When he asked me why I wanted to leave so soon I replied, "Because I caught the fish."

The fish was real enough; I could see that for myself. But one little word in my answer—"the"—skewed the truth about that fish, making it something it was not. And just as I assumed there was only one fish, I have often made the mistake of assuming there was nothing left in the pool of knowledge after reeling in a single truth. To find out how this phenomenon transfers to matters of God I will apply the idea to a few of the paradoxes already listed.

Consider the Paradox of Omnipresence. In the moment that I focus exclusively on God's omnipresence, I find myself ignoring the fact that he is personally here, within my little life. Conversely, in the moment I try to fit him in my life according to some preconceived idea of who and what he is, I fail to appreciate his omnipresent majesty. God is both in everything and beyond everything, yet he is also here watching over my shoulder as I type these words. To worship the one without the other is to worship something less than God. He is neither a dear friend I can confide in nor an impersonal force of nature. Or, more precisely, he is both at once, and when I try to limit him to either, he slips away altogether.

Now consider the Paradox of the Promise. When I revel in his promised gifts, I fail to see the work required to prepare me to receive those promises. When I focus on the work required, I forget that my very ability to do the work is itself a gift. It is true that a proper relationship with God is "the gift of God—not by works, so that no one can boast,"[8] but it is equally true that only he who does the will of the Father will receive that gift.[9] It is true that "faith without deeds is dead,"[10] but deeds without faith are just as dead. This is the quintessential riddle of redemption, and it is folly to pick one side over the other.

The Paradox of Love also fits the pattern. If I try to love God with all of my heart and soul and mind to the exclusion of everything else, I exclude love of my neighbor and risk viewing her as a distraction, a *thing* that interferes with my devotion to God. This is the mistake of pious hermits and those of us who prefer churches or synagogues to soup kitchens. But if I center all of my attention on loving my neighbor as myself and forget about loving God, I find it impossible to maintain that neighborly love because I am no longer connected to the Source of love itself. This is the mistake of secular humanists. True love must flow from God through me to everyone else. I am merely the conduit. Therefore, I cannot love God with all my heart without passing that love on to my neighbor, and I cannot love my neighbor as myself unless I first accept God's love. So is "love the Lord" the greatest commandment, or is "love your neighbor"?

The answer is "yes." And "yes."

By now, some may suspect I am making a case for moderation in all things, a favorite theme of Judaism and Christianity. But even moderation can become sinful if I ignore the fact that sometimes it is good to be wholehearted.

Moderation has been created a virtue to limit the ambition of great men, and to console undistinguished people. . . .

—La Rochefoucauld[11]

8. Ephesians 2:8–9.
9. Matthew 7:21.
10. James 2:26.
11. *Maxims*, trans. Leonard Tancock (New York: Viking, 1982).

So moderation alone is not the secret to a virtuous life. I need more than that, because moderation itself is merely one virtue among many and can be perverted just as easily as all the others.

I have learned that God uses the paradoxes of Scripture to ease me back toward the middle between the truths, because only from there can I keep all truths firmly in view. To live righteously, I must somehow find a way to love God *and* my neighbor. Faith *and* works are both important. Justice *and* mercy are required. My actions are somehow free *and* predestined. God is somehow everywhere *and* uniquely here. Both halves of each paradoxical statement are equally true, and in each case I must apply them to my life wholeheartedly, not in moderation, but to the greatest extent possible. Yet each half without the other becomes a distortion and a barrier on the way from here to my Creator. I must somehow find a place where the truths of each paradox mix and mingle harmoniously. There, in that delicate balance, lies the path of righteousness. And at the end of that path stands God.

> The Torah is like two paths, one of fire and the other of ice. It is best to walk in the middle course.
>
> —Y. Haggigah, 2, 1

Unfortunately, the human mind—or at least the Western mind—or at least *my* mind—finds it impossible to hold two paradoxical truths simultaneously and equally, much less all the virtues that exist. My new insight into the need for balance—for something the rabbis called *tsedakah*—is helpful as a goal, but it doesn't really tell me how to manage the seemingly impossible task of reaching that kind of balance in my life. For that, I need to turn to the Scriptures for guidance.

At home in my study, I am reading the Torah. God has just commanded Abraham to sacrifice his son Isaac. I pause for a moment, remembering that this is a perfect example of the Paradox of Obedience. God commands Abraham to sacrifice his son, yet God has also said it is wrong—a capital offense—to shed human blood.[12] Abraham is quite literally damned if he does and damned if he doesn't because to obey is to disobey.

What is Abraham to do?

I return to the story.

Abraham does what he has been told to do; he ascends Mt. Moriah with the knife and wood for Isaac's sacrifice. He does not know how things will work out, but he seems to believe God will provide a middle way between his command not to murder and his command to kill his son. This becomes clear when Abraham tells his servants to wait at the base of the mountain until he *and* Isaac return.[13] Of course, Abraham knows this thing he has been told to do is wrong, yet he also knows not to do it is just as wrong. Trapped between the apparently opposed truths of a bitter paradox, he resists the impulse to focus only on one truth to the exclusion of the other and proves his faith by his action, pressing onward up Moriah, believing God will provide a solution. His faith is rewarded when God delivers a ram in substitution for Isaac and a renewal of the covenant for Abraham and his descendants.

Abraham found the way through the paradox, but how? I look deeper, and a few weeks later I find this strange little tale:

The Israelites are attacked by poisonous snakes in the Sinai wilderness. It is the Paradox of Obedience all over again, as God commands Moses to forge a bronze serpent, put it on a pole, and tell Israel to look at it for deliverance. Surely the Israelites must wonder if this is a cruel trick. Thousands of them were killed the last time they looked to a man-made image for help (the golden calf they built in violation of one of the Ten Commandments). Yet the fabrication of the bronze snake is a direct order from God. Although the Israelites are now trapped between the horns of Abraham's paradox—to obey is to disobey—they too pass the test. They follow God's command and look at the man-made image when the snakes attack. They are saved from death.[14]

How did they cling to the middle ground between God's commandments?

I decide to look at the Hebrew to see if the original words offer a stronger hint. Studying the terms that seem most impor-

---

12. Genesis 9:6.

13. Genesis 22:5.

14. Numbers 21:6–9.

tant in the bronze snake incident, I find nothing to explain the paradox. In fact, I am ready to give up the search and assume this is one of those questions God has chosen not to answer. But then I look into one last Hebrew word, the term *nes*, which is translated as the "pole" upon which the bronze serpent is mounted. Right away I realize this word is not as simple as it first seemed.

In other Scriptures, *nes* is translated as "example" or "banner."[15] In Isaiah 33:23, the word is translated as "sail," and another word entirely is used for the pole or mast upon which the sail hangs. In fact, I can find no other place in the Hebrew Scriptures where anything else was mounted on a *nes*. Except for the bronze snake it is always the other way around. The *nes* is never the pole; it is always the object lifted up on the pole. But here at the story of the serpents in the wilderness, the bronze serpent is mounted *on* the "banner" or "example"—the *nes*.

In other words, here in this enigmatic little story I find a *symbol* (the bronze serpent) hung upon an *example* (the *nes*, or pole).

Suddenly, I feel goose bumps rising on my arms. Could it be that this word has been deliberately chosen to hint that it was not the serpent Israel must look to for deliverance, but the One *behind* the serpent? Could it be that the graven image on the pole is a test to see if the Israelites can see the Truth *behind* the truth? As if in answer to that question, I flip back through my Chever Torah notes and find a remarkable statement made by Rabbi Stern. This word, *nes*, has yet another meaning.

It is the Hebrew word for "miracle."

Too excited now to remain still, I rise and pace my study. The Torah is doing it again: showing me it is more than a mere book, using the words themselves to communicate something beyond mere words, with layer behind layer behind layer of truth. I am certain that these stories of Abraham and the Israelites have given me the key to holding two truths in sight simultaneously. Could the key lie in looking past the paradox to focus on the truth behind it? And with that thought, I stop dead in my tracks.

Of course!

The key is faith.

15. See Numbers 26:10 and Psalm 60:6 (JPS).

Today's Chever Torah session is over, and almost everyone has left the meeting hall, some to get on with their Saturday morning, others to attend the worship service down the corridor. Meanwhile, Mort, a scientist and Torah scholar, sits at my table shaking his head good-naturedly. He and Margie are discussing the sacrifice of Isaac. (Jews call this story the *akeda*, or "binding," of Isaac.) Mort is explaining his perspective on the story:

"The man almost killed his son. Imagine the psychological damage that must have done. It's the worst kind of abuse."

"But the Torah says God told him to do it!" responds Margie.

"If you take it literally, as history." Shaking his head again. "There's no proof of that."

"I don't need proof. I have faith."

It is as if a veil has dropped before Mort's eyes. "I don't accept things on blind faith."

Many liberal Jews and Christians today share Mort's distaste for blind faith. I don't blame them. Blind faith is the "my country right or wrong" kind of belief that causes wars and bitterly divides families, congregations, denominations, and religions. Blind faith is arrogant. It is well communicated by a bumper sticker that used to be common in my town, which read, "God said it. I believe it. That settles it." Take away the middle sentence and I agree completely. But with that middle sentence in place, the real message is this: "*I* have chosen to believe this thing and *I* will never change in spite of what may come, because this is what *I* have chosen."

Blind faith is based on something much too small: me.

If Abraham had that kind of faith in the pagan gods of Ur, he would never have obeyed God's call to sacrifice Isaac. If the Israelites had that kind of faith, they would not have left their idolatrous calf-worshiping ways behind and learned to see beyond the serpent. But the faith of Abraham and the Israelites was not blind; it had a solid basis in facts external to themselves.

At Chever Torah, I have learned that true faith is open to new facts, even when they threaten to change my beliefs.

Abraham's faith was grounded in the fact of Isaac—a miracle baby given to an elderly man and his barren wife seventeen long years after God had promised to make them into a great nation. But Abraham also knew what it was to doubt God. Tired of waiting on the Lord, he had tried to preempt the divine promise, having a child out of wedlock with Sarah's servant and suffering devastating family divisions as a result. So when the command to sacrifice Isaac came, Abraham responded with a well-informed faith, a faith based on the history of blessings God had already given and the mistakes he himself had made.

Israel's faith flowed from blood in the Nile and on their doorposts and lintels, from standing walls of water and a thunderous voice atop Mt. Sinai. Israel's faith was also instilled with a plague and the sword. When Moses took too long to return from the top of Mt. Sinai, they fashioned the golden calf and suffered death as a result. Like Abraham, Israel had seen the tragic results of failing to trust God for the resolution of intolerable situations, intolerable paradoxes. Israel and Abraham learned these lessons and proved their faith with the tests of the binding of Isaac and the bronze serpent, so God rewarded them with the deceptively simple answer to divine paradox: if I am to escape the warped perspective that turns virtues into vices, I must refuse to choose between the truths and focus instead on the Almighty Truth between the truths.

Many Christians seem to fear paradox for all the same reasons we fear questioning God. How ironic! Christianity is founded on paradox and would not exist without it. Indeed, many of the paradoxes already mentioned speak directly to me of Jesus. For example, I already mentioned the Paradox of Fertility, which stems from the fact that Adam and Eve were commanded to "be fruitful and multiply," but the Lord selected a barren woman, Sarah, to be the mother of his chosen people, even though she was unable to fulfill his command. This paradox is repeated with a barren Rebekah and a barren Rachel. Why would God command fruitfulness, yet establish the Jewish people through women physically unable to obey that command? Always before, I have assumed this odd contradiction was simply a message about faith. These men and women were chosen in part because they believed the Lord could do the impossible. But as I have observed before, God never does one thing at a time, and now, after thinking about this paradox in terms of Jesus, it occurs to me that Sarah, Rebekah, and Rachel may have also been God's way to prepare his chosen people to accept the virgin birth.

Then there is the Paradox of Blessing. Before, I could not reconcile the notion that all humanity would be blessed through a group that gained its foothold on the planet by wiping out other nations. But then I thought of this in terms of Jesus. He was a descendant of Abraham, as were his first followers. Christianity flows directly from the religion of Moses, which in turn traces its roots back to the Lord's promise to Abraham. If Jesus is the path to an intimate relationship with God, as over one billion people from virtually every nation on earth believe (including many descendants of the Canaanites), then this paradox is transformed into a prophecy that has already been fulfilled.

(This same notion explains something that often puzzles the Jews of Chever Torah. On the one hand, God told Abraham that his offspring would be "as numerous as the stars in the sky and as the sand on the seashore."[16] On the other hand, Jews have always been a tiny minority of the world's population. But this paradox is perfectly explained if one thinks of billions of Christians as the spiritual inheritors of Abraham's blessing, right alongside Jews.)

Earlier, I mentioned the Paradox of Omnipresence, which arises from the fact that "God is said to be omnipresent, yet he is often described as visiting a certain place in a manner that implies that he was not previously there." With the Trinity this difficulty simply evaporates. God can be everywhere yet uniquely here because he is omnipresent as the Father and uniquely here as the Spirit and the Son.

A final riddle I identified earlier is called the Paradox of the Red Heifer, which involves the fact that in all the Bible, no other sacrifice is made outside the camp, no other sacrifice causes impurity in the priest who offers it, and no other sacrifice is intended to purify those who are ceremonially impure. For millennia the rabbis puzzled over the red heifer, arriving at many complex explanations for what appears to be a contradiction to

16. Genesis 22:17.

everything else the Torah has to say about sacrifice. But I believe there is a simple explanation. Like the red heifer, Jesus was killed "outside the camp," that is, beyond the walls of Jerusalem. And surely the execution of Jesus—who was innocent of all wrongdoing—brought guilt upon the Jewish and Roman men directly responsible, just as the sacrifice of the red heifer caused impurity in the priest. Yet Jesus' death and resurrection brings perfect atonement to all who believe and place their trust in him, just as the red heifer's ashes cleansed everyone and everything they touched. So once again I find that faith in Jesus has turned unexplained paradox into fulfilled prophecy.

For me, these and other paradoxes of the Hebrew Scriptures provide reasons to believe in Jesus. But of course Jesus himself is the greatest paradox of all. Like all Christians, I believe he is both fully man and fully God. The New Testament leaves no room for choice between one or the other, but demands that I see him as both simultaneously. Yet how can the created be the Creator? How can the Immortal die on a cross? How can the Omniscient have the limited mind of a man? It is as if I have been asked to believe that the flea is the sun, and the sun the flea, while both remain fully "sunnish" and "fleaish." It defies all common sense, and I believe that is exactly as it should be.

The idea that an entity could be both man and God is beyond my ability to understand. The idea that an entity could be both three distinct individuals and one omnipresent individual defies logic, yet these paradoxes are what Christianity would have me believe. And I do believe, in part because the one idea of Jesus answers so many of the bothersome enigmas in the Torah. But paradoxically, I also believe in part because the puzzle of a God/man defies all human logic. It seems obvious to me that any God capable of creating the universe must be an unsolvable riddle for a finite human mind. So I believe in Jesus precisely because he is pure paradox, and on a certain level, only paradox can reveal the divine. Although Maimonides would disagree with my conclusion, he certainly supported the underlying concept:

> Praise be to him who is such that when our minds try to visualize his essence, their power of apprehending becomes imbecility; when they study the connection between his works and his will, their knowledge becomes ignorance; and when our tongues desire

to declare his greatness by descriptive terms, all eloquence becomes impotence and imbecility.

—Maimonides[17]

Given what the Torah has taught me about God, I am no
longer surprised that the Paradox of Jesus makes no common
sense. In my earlier exploration of why bad things happen to
good people, I learned that God has limited his involvement in
the cosmos for the sake of human free will and logic. But that
limitation is tied to the *human* inability to combine paradoxical
attributes—it implies no similar inability on God's part. Perhaps
there are other reasons not to believe in Jesus, but in light of the
many paradoxes in the Bible, the idea that God can never be a
man is not one of them. God can be anything he pleases. In fact,
if Jesus' man/God nature or the Trinity were completely understandable, I would abandon Christianity precisely because of
Maimonides's point. Any attempt to fully understand the Lord
does indeed lead to imbecility. Given that fact, all true explanations of God's nature must openly include paradoxical concepts
my mind cannot grasp.

Thus it is with the Paradox of Jesus. If I focus on Jesus as man,
I miss Jesus as God. If I focus on Jesus as God, I miss Jesus as
man. Is he God or is he just a man? As with all paradoxes of the
Bible, the answer is "yes." And "yes."

17. *The Guide of the Perplexed*, trans. Chaim Rabin (Indianapolis: Hackett, 1995),
p. 82.

# five

# The Beautiful Terror

Blessing is to be found only in a thing hidden from the eye.

—Taanit, 8

I am at Emily's Bat Mitzvah, and against all odds I am wearing a tie for the second time in six months. When the ceremony begins, there is much rising and sitting down again (and rising and sitting and rising and sitting). Many words are spoken, some in English, some in Hebrew, all from the Reform Movement's *Gates of Prayer*, which has the familiar heft and cloth bound cover of the Southern Baptists' *Broadman Hymnal*. I read along with everyone on the English parts and try to follow the transliterated version of the Hebrew, feeling foolish for pronouncing the sounds with no idea of their meaning. This up and down reading business quickly becomes boring. I turn my attention to the architecture. The sanctuary is built of brick and glass block, a soaring three story cylinder atop a square ground-level plan with a gently curved dome, gold and azure in the mortar, and radiant stained glass. It is a magnificent space, but still, after half an hour, I am ready to leave.

Then Emily mounts the platform steps and everything changes. She is the daughter of my friends Philip and Barbara. For the next hour and a half, I will bask in the reflected glow of their awesome love for her.

Bar and Bat Mitzvahs are one of Judaism's finest achievements. At the threshold of those terrible years when children's soft skin erupts with acne, when enchanting boys and girls become convinced that they are ugly and unpopular, when they seem to sink beneath a tidal wave of lust, when they turn to a desperate denial of their pain, their awkwardness, their vulnerability, and even denial of their love for family—at the threshold of all that, these marvelous Jews take such a child and teach her a little Hebrew and stand her up in front of dozens (or hundreds) of friends and family and listen to her read Torah, and they join her on the platform and there in front of everyone they tell her just exactly how deep, wide, long, and tall is the size of their love for her, and they celebrate what is happening to their beloved daughter/sister/friend, affirming the struggle of her metamorphosis from child to woman in ways that clearly say, "We love you as much as life itself, because for us, that is what you are. You are the future and the life of our people. You are important. You are needed."

Everybody cries, including me.

After the ceremony Emily's family throws a party for her and a couple hundred of their friends and family. I know Philip has been saving money for this all year. I should be enjoying myself. It is a grand affair. But it is also my first social situation with the Jews at temple and, unlike at Chever Torah, here I cannot hide in silence. Fortunately the small talk never touches on matters of religion, so my secret remains safe. In fact, Barbara takes me aside, her beautiful eyes twinkling, and tells me that her father (one of the few who knows I am not Jewish) has asked if I converted.

We laugh, but a small voice within whispers that I am a coward.

A few minutes later, this accusation is confirmed at the buffet line, where I am trying to select a dessert. Someone steps up beside me. I turn. It is Rabbi Zimmerman himself. He offers a perfunctory nod and begins dishing food onto a clean plate. I select a nice piece of cake and take a step back toward my table, but he stops me with these words:

"You're Philip's friend."

"Yes, Rabbi."

"You come to Chever Torah."

"Yes."

He nods and returns his attention to the kosher buffet. At first, as his hands busy themselves with the food, I think he is done with me. Then without looking my way again he says, "You should speak up more." Something in the rabbi's tone makes me wonder if Philip has told him I am a Christian.

That was a week ago, and I have been thinking about Rabbi Zimmerman's words ever since. An invitation? A command? I only know that I have not been as anonymous as I thought. And now, entering the hall for another Chever Torah session and remembering Emily's beautiful day, I smile and nod at one or two people I met at her Bat Mitzvah. They still do not know about my religion, but I feel less concerned with that and more comfortable here than ever before. I feel this way because of what I saw these wonderful people do for Emily.

After I am seated, Rabbi Zimmerman enters the hall. We have announcements. We say the Hebrew blessing for Torah study. We begin another fascinating Chever Torah session. I listen anonymously as usual for almost an hour, then the rabbi suddenly directs our thoughts to the Christian doctrine of original sin. He compares it to the Jewish doctrine of the good and evil impulses. He says Christians believe babies who die can go to hell.

"Now."

It is as if someone has whispered in my ear.

"Now."

I cannot ignore this inner voice, and so, for the very first time at Chever Torah I tentatively raise my hand. Apparently, this is just what Rabbi Zimmerman has been waiting for. Ignoring all the others already holding their hands in the air, he points straight at me.

"Straighten us out," he says with a smile.

I swallow. I begin at the beginning, with my credentials.

"I'm a Christian, and . . . ."

*Everyone* turns to look at me.

Painfully aware of a hundred pairs of eyes searching my face, I mumble something ineffectual about a person's age of accountability superseding the doctrine of original sin. The Rabbi thanks me and moves on. A few of the others continue to stare at me, even though someone else is speaking now. Then one of them, an old man, smiles and nods.

Bat Mitzvahs, rabbis encouraging my participation, old men taking the trouble to empathize with someone who feels horribly out of place—these are just a few examples of the enormous capacity for love that I have found at Chever Torah. It is genuine, and it is consistent. Just last week as my mother lay in the hospital fighting for her life, a rabbi from the temple came to visit, and another day a Jewish fellow I have never met at Chever Torah came to offer comfort. Last Friday, a woman from temple arrived with a small bag containing a bit of *challah*—the special bread Jews eat on the Sabbath—a little bottle of grape juice, and a couple of tiny candles . . . everything we needed for a traditional Sabbath meal, should we be so inclined.

Now, after all these years, when I enter temple I immediately feel enveloped in a blanket of protection. Here, the hard, cruel world cannot intrude. Here exists the real possibility of a life surrounded only by friends. These Jews draw me close with acceptance; they entice me with respect. I often find myself wishing I were one of them. I am sometimes even tempted to convert . . .

Whenever those feelings rise to the fore, I am struck by the fact that most of us—one Christian and a hundred Jews—study the Scriptures together at Chever Torah for the same reason. Although this Jewish community has built a warm cocoon of human kindness, it is not enough. If it were, we would not study Torah; we would simply come together. But here we are with open Bibles, because things are somehow not quite as they should be between ourselves and our neighbors, and between ourselves and God, and we believe the Torah can help us find out why. The existence of Bat Mitzvahs and my fear of rejection at Chever Torah speak volumes about a fundamental human need that the Scriptures take great pains to address. We are all searching for a depth of relationship beyond the ordinary. In our heart of hearts, all of us—even atheists—want a love affair with the Lord. Failing that, we will take whatever we can get.

A fortunate few will question the idea that everyone feels a need for harmony with God. Some may even question the idea that they have been isolated from the Creator. Such a person may be living a fulfilling life, in a good romantic relationship, building a promising career, parenting happy children, and so forth. But I have lived long enough to know these pleasant diversions will not last. I have been fired unjustly from a job I worked eight years to get. People I trusted have stolen large amounts of money from me. My father and my mother both died torturous deaths. One day, even my devoted wife will pass away, leaving me alone (unless I am fortunate enough to die first). When these transitory people and things have trickled through my fingers, I am left with the fact that what little peace I thought I had was never here inside my heart, but was always out there somewhere, in a place I never quite reached. That is what Solomon tried to say with these words:

> "Meaningless! Meaningless!" says the Teacher. "Utterly meaningless! Everything is meaningless."
>
> —Ecclesiastes 1:2

A person who is "on top of the world" may be convinced that the harmony and peace of his life is authentic simply because it feels that way, but that is an unreasonable argument. One might as well say an emotional response to a drama can make the characters come to life. I cry genuine tears when a tragically separated couple finally reunites, or cheer with real enthusiasm when the good guy triumphs over evil, but when the book is finished and the show is done, I am still myself. And even a person like me, rich in friends, family, health, and possessions, has moments when the loneliness shows through.

Every novelist and playwright knows that the heart of drama is tension. It is easy to gain the undivided attention of a reader or an audience. Take a character, place her in terrible trouble, and make it look as if she has no way out. The audience is captured every time. But why? The answer is not that I enjoy seeing the protagonist squirm. (I am not as depraved as that.) On the contrary, I long to see her problem *solved.* I long for something called the *denouement,* the resolution to her conflict, the moment when peace returns to her life at last. But again, why? Her problems are not my own; she is fiction after all. In fact, just to enter into her drama I must engage in something Coleridge called "the suspension of disbelief."[1] But in truth I must go further; I must pretend this fictional protagonist's problems are my own. I must empathize with a fantasy. And when the heroine gets her man in the end or captures the bad guy or finds some other reason to go on living, my reward for playing this little mind game is the momentary illusion that her fictional peace is my own.

Would I be this interested in borrowing the peace of a fictional character if I fully enjoyed the real thing?

Some will say I have missed the point of drama. Some will say my pleasure comes from the escapism that drama offers, the ability to step outside my own reality and enter another, to exchange my world for one that is more interesting. Others will point to wildly popular novels, plays, and motion pictures that have no peaceful resolution and say the reward for audiences and readers comes from sharing the protagonist's angst. But these are just different ways of making the same point. The fact that I seek escape speaks volumes about what I wish to flee. I would no more want to escape from a completely satisfactory real life into fiction than I would trade a loving flesh and blood friend for a doll. As for those plays and stories with unhappy endings, clearly I do not enjoy them because they leave me feeling depressed and empty along with the protagonist. (Again, I am not as depraved as that.) Rather, I enjoy them because they whisper the beautiful lie that I am not alone. I love to cry along with the heroine pre-

---

1. Samuel Taylor Coleridge, *Biographia Literaria* (1817; reprint, Princeton: Princeton University Press, 1985), ch. 14.

cisely because I cry *along with* her. Unhappy endings provide the fleeting illusion of companionship in my isolation. The universal attraction of such stories, the universal need for such camaraderie, is one more proof of all humanity's aching sense of isolation.

It is not felt solely through such lofty things as drama and literature. It also whispers to me while I haggle for a purchase at the flea market or negotiate a business deal over a conference table. Why do I sometimes feel an almost irresistible urge to simply agree to the other person's terms? This desire can be so intense I am driven to pay exorbitant prices or accept unfavorable conditions just to end the bargaining and achieve harmony with the one across the table. Even the most seasoned negotiator has walked away wondering why on earth she said yes. Could the answer be found in an intense desire for companionship on a level I have never known?

At other times, I think perhaps someone else could complete these undone parts of me. I seek new relationships, trying them on for size as I would a new suit, but always comes the moment when I wonder if I might feel more complete with that person over there instead of this one. How many lonely couples part, yearning for something no human heart can provide? How many friendships and marriages crumble because we feel driven to seek another without knowing why? Even if I successfully resist this urge, I am plagued by a need for friends and family to conform themselves to me. Although I know they were made in the image of God, I find that image frightening and infuriating. I try to recast everyone, to remake them in a smaller image, one I can understand and control—my own. So I seek to dominate, or I agree at any cost (the result is much the same), but in my heart I know my proposed improvements to the human race are doomed to failure. Even if I managed to reduce everyone to my own image (forbid it Almighty God!) nothing here inside of me would change. And it is here, in my mind or heart or spirit— whatever I choose to call this center of myself—it is here that the real problem lies. In rare moments when I manage to turn and see the truth before it fades, I find it is akin to the most devastating of human emotions, something Joseph Conrad captured with a question:

Who knows what true loneliness is—not the conventional word
but the naked terror?

—Joseph Conrad[2]

I know what true loneliness is. It is the naked terror of standing alone at the chasm between God and me, knowing I cannot
cross over.

As I said earlier, there are some who deny all of this. They deny
the loneliness. They deny the separation from God. But every
Sabbath at Chever Torah when we come together with open Bibles, I think most of us are there because in our heart of hearts
we are seeking answers to the same important questions:

Why are we isolated from God?

What can we do about it?

The Scriptures say we cannot cross the chasm because God
will not abide our sins.[3] This leads to yet another question: If sin
separates me from God as most Christians and Jews believe, and
if my separation does not end, what will be the result? The New
Testament holds that "the wages of sin is death."[4] Some at Chever
Torah have said that this idea was merely a concoction of the
apostle Paul, but I have found the idea in many places in the Hebrew Scriptures. For example:

Consider, all lives are Mine; the life of the parent and the life of
the child are both Mine. The person who sins, only he shall die.

—Ezekiel 18:4 (JPS)

The Torah states that part of Adam's curse for his disobedience
is death, and of course, just as everyone sins, everyone dies.[5]

What can I do about it? There are many other places in the Hebrew Scriptures that promise life in return for fidelity to God. In

2. *Under Western Eyes* (1911; reprint, New York: Modern Library, 2001).
3. See Habakkuk 1:13, for example.
4. Romans 6:23.
5. See Genesis 3:19 (". . . to dust you will return . . .").

fact, I need look no further than the end of this same chapter in Ezekiel:

> Rid yourselves of all the offenses you have committed, and get a new heart and a new spirit. Why will you die, O house of Israel? For I take no pleasure in the death of anyone, declares the Sovereign Lord. Repent and live!
>
> —Ezekiel 18:31–32

But this leads once again to paradox. On the one hand, I have the obvious fact that everyone dies, no matter how devout or sincere our repentance might be. Yet here the prophet says, "Repent and live." How is this possible? What can it mean?

Christianity understands the death caused by sin in two ways: the physical death we all experience, and a spiritual death that, if true, is eternal banishment to Conrad's "naked terror" of loneliness, a permanent isolation from the presence of God. There are countless references in the Hebrew Scriptures to the life that can be gained through a proper relationship with God. Since everyone dies physically, I believe these verses can only mean that the spirit may live or die separately from the body. That is why Christianity teaches that people can die twice—and be born twice.

To understand how this is possible, I return to Chever Torah.

Rabbi Stern is leading us today in a discussion of a "Mt. Sinai Moment" in which Moses asks God to teach him his "ways" and to show him his "glory."[6] The rabbi explains that "ways," or *derek* in Hebrew, may mean either a path or road, or a condition of being. He also tells us that "glory" in the original Hebrew is *kevod*, meaning wealth or weight. Rabbi Stern points out that the connection between "weight" and "glory" is perfectly logical, since the ancients had no money as such, but bought and sold with clumps of silver or gold that were weighed to determine their value. With this in mind, rabbinic tradition holds that *kevod*, or glory, when applied to God, means his full value. Were God hu-

6. See Exodus 33:18–20.

man, we might say his glory is the thing that makes him worthwhile, his essence, or his "inner self."

Back on the mountain, God responds to Moses' request by warning him that "no one can see My face and live." "Face" in the Hebrew is *paniym*, which in this case is apparently a synonym for *kevod* since both are used to mean God's essence. *Paniym* is also often translated as "presence," as it was when Adam and Eve "heard the voice of the Lord God walking in the garden in the cool of the day: and Adam and his wife hid themselves from the presence [*paniym*] of the Lord God amongst the trees of the garden."[7] Regarding that experience, Rabbi Stern points out that before the description of Adam and Eve's expulsion from the Garden, Genesis is careful to say "the man and his wife were both naked, and they felt no shame."[8] But the first thing the Torah mentions after the expulsion—the immediate effect of their disobedience—is that they suddenly realize they are naked; furthermore, this fact makes them fear God for the first time. So it seems there is some connection between the idea of "knowing" nakedness, and being unable to commune face to face with God.

As the rabbi makes that final observation, I have a Mt. Sinai moment of my own, when it occurs to me that here is a way of understanding the paradox of life and death in the Tanakh.

> If there is a natural body, there is also a spiritual body.
>
> —1 Corinthians 15:44

With these words, Paul sums up the Christian idea that Adam and Eve's choice to sin divided their state of existence into at least two parts. These parts can be thought of as their body and soul, or metaphorically, as their "nakedness " and "presence." They are two halves of a disconnected whole, neither of which can survive for long alone. Before the fall, these human components were so perfectly interwoven that they could not be distinguished from each other, hence the first people "were naked, and they felt no shame." But after Adam and Eve disobeyed God, a fundamental division occurred within their essence and

7. Genesis 3:8 (KJV).
8. Genesis 2:25.

suddenly they were outside themselves looking in, aware for the first time of their bodies as something separate from their consciousness. They were not only locked out of the Garden; they were banished from themselves. The fig leaf was the world's first disguise, predecessor to all the things I hide behind today. I once mistakenly assumed it was meant to conceal Adam and Eve from God. Now I know that movies, books, family, friends, jobs, and possessions are the temporary distractions I use to hide myself from me. Conrad's "naked terror" cuts much deeper than the simple fact that I am alone. I am worse than alone; I am undone, and nothing could be lonelier than that.

Most of the angst of life can be explained if I visualize my existence as a relentless swinging back and forth between the physical and spiritual "selves" in a never ending struggle to reunite the two. Apparently, some Jewish thinkers would agree. Consider this Talmudic parable on the soul and the body:

> [Rabbi Judah said] "To what is it like? To a human king who possessed a beautiful orchard in which were the choice first fruits; and he set two watchmen over it, one lame and the other blind. . . . The lame man mounted the blind man and they took the fruits and ate them."
>
> —Sanhedrin, 91a, b

I believe this means that neither spirit nor body can sustain itself alone. When they were separated, both were doomed to die. To "know nakedness" is to focus on my physical existence to the exclusion of my spiritual life. The pendulum has swung too close to that which is animal within me, and the result is the death of my soul. This is what happens when I commit the worst of all possible sins, something Jesus warned against when he said, ". . . everyone who speaks a word against the Son of Man will be forgiven, but anyone who blasphemes against the Holy Spirit will not be forgiven."[9] C. S. Lewis understood this to mean that those who disregard the Lord's spiritual presence have no hope of establishing a personal relationship with him. In Lewis's interpretation, a single-minded focus on the physical world to the

9. Luke 12:10.

exclusion of the spiritual is the only unforgivable sin.[10] Even a single-minded focus on *halacha*, the laws of Torah, can threaten my soul if it is not counterbalanced by deep-seated spiritual concerns. Theologians have a word for the adoration of the Bible in the place of God. They call it "bibliolatry," a combination of the words "Bible" and "idolatry."

On the other hand, to "see God's face" is to immerse myself in the spiritual to the detriment of the physical. The pendulum swings so near to the Creator that the creature is destroyed as the mortal fabric comes too near the fire. In the Sinai, this result was dramatically illustrated in the destruction of Nadab and Abihu, who approached God without making the necessary physical preparations. Today this error often appears when preoccupation with philosophical or religious thought obliterates concern for the intended sanctity of the physical world. For example, justice and mercy, when studied long enough, can become ideas instead of obligations. This is what James had in mind when he wrote:

> Suppose a brother or sister is without clothes and daily food. If one of you says to him, "Go, I wish you well; keep warm and well fed," but does nothing about his physical needs, what good is it? In the same way, faith by itself, if it is not accompanied by action, is dead.
>
> —James 2:15–17

Action and faith, body and soul—however I choose to express this division within human nature (which of course is fundamentally inexpressible), I find the back-and-forth division of self particularly obvious when entering the realm of paradox. Indeed, paradox only exists because of the unnatural separation inside me. For example, the tension between justice and mercy originates with the fact that they are so intertwined that one cannot be had without the other, yet my divided mind is incapable of embracing both concepts simultaneously. Justice is anchored in the practical, physical world, while mercy springs from spiritual roots. Whenever I try to grasp them simultaneously, I find myself too narrowly focused on one or the other to see the Source of them both.

10. C. S. Lewis, "Man or Rabbit?" *God in the Dock* (Grand Rapids: Eerdmans, 1970), p. 111.

Another way to express this idea is to say that the division of body and soul has lowered my focus from God to me. Suddenly I am looking down at my nakedness instead of up at God. He knows this, of course. The fig leaf is a poor disguise; in fact it is a dead giveaway. And in spite of his warnings ("Sin is crouching at your door"), this irresistible self-interest leads me directly to loneliness and death.[11]

So where can I turn for company to escape this naked terror of loneliness? At Chever Torah, I find a clue in these words:

> Then I will remove my hand and you will see my back; but my face must not be seen.
>
> —Exodus 33:23

Here is God describing himself in human terms; he has hands, a back, and a face. Elsewhere in the Scriptures God is described as having nostrils, feet, a waist, and so forth.[12] How comforting it would be if that were true! How accessible such a God would be! But of course, the Creator of the universe does not consist of human body parts. In providing this anthropomorphic imagery, the Tanakh simply meets me where I am, unnaturally divided between the physical and spiritual, unable to remain focused on the Truth between the truths. It makes perfect sense that God would work within my limitations by meeting me in those same terms, which is yet another reason why I believe in Jesus.

The huge space between the Creator and me is most clearly felt when I witness a beautiful sunset or watch an eagle soar above a mountain valley. I am not referring to those inspirational moments when my spirit soars along with the eagle or rises with the sun. I mean the other times, when I allow my heart to soar just a little too high and find I have begun to fall, when I sense myself being drawn outward into something so vast I know it will swallow me without a trace. Sometimes the sight of snow-capped mountains spanning the horizon or the gentle curve of a

11. Genesis 4:7.
12. Exodus 15:8, Exodus 24:10, and Ezekiel 8:2, respectively.

calm sea meeting the sky fills me with an awe that is indeed the root of something awful. Like a starving man who has been served a sumptuous dish too hot to eat, I am attracted and repelled simultaneously.

I seldom discuss this feeling with anyone. I wonder why? Is it too difficult to put the emotion into words? Am I afraid no one else feels this strange sensation? Or do I wish to avoid seeming ungrateful for the all-too-rich meal of creation? Whatever the reason for my silence, when twilight paints the clouds with rosy fingers and others wax poetic about the ecstasy they feel at sunsets, I sometimes watch the divine pyrotechnics and feel my heart sinking with the sun. I stand in an exquisite place, overcome with a strange desire. I watch the hand of God at work upon the world, and in that perfect moment I am most aware of what is missing.

In the midst of all this beauty, I long for . . . beauty.

Strangely, not all beauty affects me this way, as I learn today while my wife and I visit a traveling Monet exhibit at a local museum. She and I view art at different paces, so we split up, she hurrying ahead, searching for that special painting, while I linger behind, drinking in each and every canvas. One painting, a landscape scene, is different. As I stand before it, something glorious happens. I become transfixed. My heart is drawn directly into the painting. In spite of hundreds of people crowding all around, I feel as if some part of me really does leave my body to enter the world of a nineteenth-century hillside. Just for a moment I completely forget who I am. When I come back to myself every hair on my arms stands on end. I shiver. It is the deepest response I have ever had to a painted work of art. It leaves me feeling raw joy, on the order of a spirit-filled moment in my church.

I hurry away to tell my wife what has happened. The crowd is thick, and she is small. It takes some time to find her over in a far corner, gazing at another Monet, this one a study of a sunset on a Venetian canal. Still filled with wonder at what happened, I approach her from behind and touch her arm. She does not seem to notice. I touch her again, and she gives a little jump, turning quickly. Tears are flowing down her cheeks.

Monet has done it to us both.

I have never shivered that way at the beauty of a real life pastoral scene. I pull back too soon from the glorious dread I feel at sunsets. Yet I was completely drawn in by a painted imitation. What a bittersweet paradox! I am a drunkard choosing the easy alcoholic glow instead of doing the hard work required to find genuine wellbeing.

I am in denial.

Earlier I said that I feel lonely in moments of almost irresistible beauty, but it is more accurate to say I sometimes feel as if I am falling away from myself into an abyss of loveliness my heart cannot survive. The closer I get, the larger God becomes, and the smaller I am by comparison, until I know I will disappear completely if I move another step. So I stop at the edge before the connection is complete. I shiver and look away, heeding Einstein's warning to the little girl: I am not properly suited up for heaven.

Perhaps that is why Orthodox Jews will not speak the name Yahweh except in limited circumstances (while studying the Torah). To refer to God in daily conversation, they have developed the habit of saying "the Name" (*ha Shem*) instead. Orthodox Jews will not even say the word "God" in reference to the Master of the universe. They will not even write the letters down. They spell it "G-d" instead.

They understand.

He is too awesome for words.

The psalmist and the apostle Paul both state that the natural creation reveals God.[13] But Paul is not describing something comfortable and welcoming in the perfect sunsets. It is God's "eternal power and divine nature" he sees revealed up there. How vast God is, how terrifying. How insignificant I feel within his world. "No one may see me and live," said the Lord to Moses,

13. Psalm 19; Romans 1:18–20.

and I think that's just as true of his better work on earth.[14] Although I long to dive right in, I dare not go too far. I feel my spirit being drawn outside my body, an elastic band stretched to the limit, and I fear my soul will snap. As Jesus said, "The spirit is willing, but the body is weak."[15] Think of the language of photography and paintings: I "frame the view," as if it were too large, or "capture the scene," as if it were the enemy. I pave nature, log it, fence it, and ignore it. Although I pretend not to hear, the smallest blades of grass and grains of sand whisper, "he's God and you're not," frightening me on a level I cannot even properly express. And if the least of God's creations reveals such intimidating majesty, how can I ever hope to be comfortable in his presence?

I believe this is yet another reason God came to earth as a baby in a manger.

In our eagerness to express a joyful connection with the Father, we Christians have been known to speak in rapturous terms of "hearts entwined with him," but the truth is somewhat less ambitious. The gulf between Yahweh and me is too wide to bridge with heartfelt connections like the one I felt with Monet. It is the height of immodesty to pretend otherwise. This is why before there was a single human sin on the earth, when it was just God and Adam, even then the Lord said, "It is not good for the man to be alone."[16] What can this mean except that Adam was lonely even before he sinned, even when he was still able to walk with God in the Garden in the cool of the day?

This is not blasphemy. I do not say God was not enough to keep Adam from loneliness. I say instead he was too much.

Still, lonely as Adam was, at least he got to walk with God. If I approach too close alone I am consumed with fire like Nadab and Abihu. Yet as a Christian, when I gaze into the beauty of creation through Monet's eyes, I see the wonder of God as I believe it was intended to be experienced—in union with another

14. Exodus 33:20.
15. Matthew 26:41.
16. Genesis 2:18.

human heart. Just for an instant the line between the physical and the spiritual is blurred, and I can delve deeper into the glory of the Lord because the company of that other, that painter or writer or maker of films, gives me courage enough to lift the veil and see the fearful Artist behind the art. I am no longer consumed by the naked terror of loneliness in the face of all this beauty, because Monet is right there with me, in the moment, in my heart. The company of another human soul, seeing what I see, feeling what I feel, adds a sense of connection to God's glory that is too overwhelming for me otherwise.

In short, my heart alone is not bold enough to sing his praises, but two hearts together are a step in the right direction.

Remembering that Jesus said "love your neighbor as yourself" is like "love the Lord with all your heart," I believe God has interwoven our love for each other with our love for him in a way that is mutually supportive.[17] In the fifth chapter of his Revelation, the apostle John relates perhaps the most beautiful vision in the Bible: the angels and every other creature in the universe are all together, hearts in perfect unison, praising God in song.[18] Imagine all of us and the angels and even our favorite dogs and cats, singing for joy together! But it is not the Father we will honor in that moment of consummate ecstasy. We do not have the words to praise a God so vast. The wisest among us will not even speak his name. Instead, John saw us singing praises to the Lamb—the God of the universe whose heart *can* intertwine with ours precisely because he is the God who is also man.

Many Christians report that their most momentous spiritual experiences occur while standing among the pews, lifting their voices to God in song together. Most of my own moments of raw spiritual joy have come in that way. I feel a deeper connection at those times for the same reason I feel an almost overwhelming desire to meet a shop owner in the middle when I haggle, for the same reason I hope to fit in at Chever Torah although I am a Christian.

"Cognitive dissonance," the psychologists call it.

They might just as well say, "It is not good for man to be alone."

17. Matthew 22:36–39.
18. Revelation 5:13.

> Blest be the tie that binds
> Our hearts in Christian love;
> The fellowship of kindred minds
> Is like to that above.
>
> —John Fawcett[19]

My shivers and my wife's tears were not a response to Monet's artistic technique. This is not a case of the perfect touch of a brush or a picturesque composition of a canvas. It was the legacy of an artist brave enough to bare his torn-asunder spirit to the world. Ours was a soul-deep call to the divine in the company of his little Monet, that wide-alive Frenchman who captured a glimpse of the glory of "what has been made." I was there beside his easel looking on. I felt brave enough to gaze into the reflection of God's face because another human heart was looking too. There was no vastness between my soul and Monet's. When his heart spoke to me in his painting, I felt attracted by the nearness, not repelled by an insurmountable distance. Instead of that lonely sense of losing myself in something far too lovely, I felt a comfortable fit, as if our spirits were interlocking pieces of a puzzle, sliding into places custom made for them by the hand of the divine.

Unfortunately, for all of its ecstatic joy, that soul connection was over in an instant. Imagine how much more I could experience, how much deeper my connection could be, if God himself would somehow find a way to hold my hand as I fly into the heart of all creation. Monet did it for a fraction of an instant, but if God did it, could the connection go on and on and on?

Of course it could.

There is no vastness between my heart and that of Jesus. He is God, but he is also man. He is my Creator and my brother. There are often walls between us (all mine), but when I meditate upon the love of Jesus I feel the opposite of loneliness. I feel completely connected with the Lord. I feel myself coming back together again.

I am not speaking here of Jesus as a mediator between God and me. (That will come later.) I am speaking of Jesus in a lesser

19. "Blest Be the Tie," from *The Broadman Hymnal* (Nashville: Broadman Press, 1940), Hymn 239.

known role: as my companion on the journey. I believe this is one of many reasons the Word became flesh and dwelt among us.[20] Christianity teaches that Jesus came to die for my sins, but he also came to live, to establish a connection with me on a level the Father cannot. The New Testament says Jesus understands my weaknesses because he knows what it is like to be tested.[21] And what was his first recorded test? The *loneliness* of forty days in the wilderness. Just like me, he has endured the grandeur and vastness of nature without another soul for company. His was a loneliness much like what I feel when I see the Great Artist's work in a sunset. Jesus understands Conrad's "naked terror," because Jesus felt it too.

> For we do not have a high priest who is unable to sympathize with our weaknesses, but we have one who has been tempted in every way, just as we are—yet was without sin. Let us then approach the throne of grace with confidence, so that we may receive mercy and find grace to help us in our time of need.
>
> —Hebrews 4:15–16

Holding Jesus' hand, I can approach God's throne of grace. But that is just a part of what Jesus did for me. The New Testament says he rose again to prove death's hold on me is broken. For many years, I understood this doctrine in the obvious way: Jesus rose from the dead, therefore death has no power over him or his. But now I think I see another dimension to the victory. Jesus did not rise to resume the same existence, divided into body and soul as it was before the cross; rather, Jesus rose to assume a new state of being, or perhaps I should say the most ancient human state of all. He rose to restore the possiblity of an unknowingly naked life, recombining body and soul, restoring what should have been all along.

The Christian Scriptures teach that Adam "was a pattern of the one to come," a preview of the perfect spiritual and physical unity of Jesus.[22] Then, with his first sin, Adam was transformed into the prototype of the divided man. There was no "first, then

20. John 1:14.
21. Hebrews 4:15.
22. Romans 5:14.

second" in Adam's existence before the expulsion from the Garden, no confusion about paradox. He was naked, yet he did not know, because his attention was wholly consumed by being in God's presence. There was no distracting inner debate about whether God or Adam himself should occupy the central position in his life. Adam's every thought was of God. He spoke to God with righteous freedom. He was holy, set apart, as no man since has ever been . . . until Jesus.

According to Paul, I will return to that same state of existence someday because of Jesus' return from the grave. His resurrection makes it possible to reverse forever the division Adam caused.[23] One sinned in the Garden and went down to death a divided man; another rose undivided and sinless from a garden tomb. Thus, the possibility of balance reentered the world. Christianity teaches that my body and soul can also be reunited if I accept Jesus' death and resurrection as a gift from God to me. And if I do, I will not abandon my humanity in favor of something more. Rather, I will find real humanity at last. Then, like Adam in the beginning, I can forget my nakedness, see God's face, and live.

23. 1 Corinthians 15:45–53.

# six

# Spiritual Suicide

No man sins for someone else.

—Baba Metzia, 8.

At Chever Torah this morning, Rabbi Zimmerman explores the Jewish explanation for sin. He says Rabbinic Judaism teaches that human evil is caused by something called the *yetzer ha-ra*, or "evil impulse," and human goodness is the result of a "good impulse," or the *yetzer tov*. Then Rabbi Zimmerman spends several minutes comparing these ideas to "original sin," which is the Christian explanation for human evil. It soon becomes clear that there are significant differences between these Christian and Jewish ideas. But not everyone cares. An attractive young woman near the front raises her hand; a half-dozen slender bracelets slipping down her forearm as her fingers languidly stretch for the ceiling. The rabbi pauses to call on her.

"What difference does it make whether we believe in the good and evil impulses or original sin?" asks the woman. "I mean, everyone sins, right? Does it really matter why?"

It is exactly what I have come to expect from these Chever Torah Jews: an excellent question, even if it is a bit irreverent. Strangely, the rabbi does not answer, choosing instead to lead Chever Torah deeper into the Jewish conception of human good and evil. He says Rabbinic Judaism also teaches that I was born with a pure or neutral soul. From birth I am perfectly free to choose either good or evil, therefore only my choices determine whether I incur the guilt of sin or whether I live as a righteous person. I will later learn that this is by no means the only opinion voiced in the Talmud. There, one can also find the theory that humans are born with only an evil impulse, then acquire the good impulse when the Torah is accepted upon reaching adulthood.[1] But the concept that we are born completely pure with no predisposition toward sinful behavior is the reigning Jewish doctrine. Also, according to Rabbi Zimmerman, if I choose to follow my evil impulse, I can correct my guilty situation by confessing my wrongdoing, making reparation as best I can, and repenting. Judaism calls this process *teshuvah*, or "returning," because it is said to return me to my prior state of moral neutrality or purity.

With that the rabbi dismisses us, hurrying off to officiate at some lucky boy's Bar Mitzvah. The discussion of the Jewish concepts of the good and evil impulses was interesting, but as I head for home, I find myself wishing the rabbi had answered the young woman's question.

I climb the stairs to my study, once again determined to search for an answer. Deciding that the best way to begin is probably to look for the biblical basis for the Jewish doctrine of the good and evil impulses, I bury myself in several books on Jewish theology. Soon it is obvious that almost everyone agrees the rabbinic term "evil inclination" was originally drawn from the following verse:

1. R. J. Zwi Werblowsky and Geoffrey Wigoder, eds., *The Encyclopedia of the Jewish Religion*, (New York: Holt, Rinehart and Winston, 1966), p. 409.

The Lord saw how great man's wickedness on the earth had become, and that every inclination of the thoughts of his heart was only evil all the time.

—Genesis 6:5

Here, both *yetzer* ("inclination") and *ra* ("evil") are found together in a verse that recounts God's assessment of human nature before the flood. The words "ra" and "yetzer" are next found together when God observes that humanity remains fundamentally unchanged by the flood experience.[2] But although the word "yetzer" occurs twice in the flood narrative, the Hebrew Scriptures actually use the term quite rarely. It appears in just nine verses, few enough for me to quickly determine that there is no verse in the entire Tanakh that speaks of a *yetzer tov*, or good impulse. God does call the universe "very good" after the creation of humanity, but that is before the first human sin—a vital distinction. Each time I find the term *yetzer* in the Bible, it is always used in one of three ways: to simply affirm that we have inner motivations, to express a desire that our inclinations might become favorable toward God in the future, or (most often) to underscore the idea that our motivations do not meet with God's approval.[3]

People do wonderful things throughout the Bible, but again and again I find evidence that is well communicated in the following quote from the Talmud:

The Good Impulse is poor and weak, and has nothing tangible to show as a reward for obedience. The Evil Impulse is strong. Whatever the Good Impulse is able to acquire through tireless labor, the Evil Impulse snatches away easily by holding forth the immediate rewards of worldly pleasure.

—Pesikta Rabbati, 9, 2, and commentary

Since the *yetzer ha-ra* and the *yetzer* tov have no direct parallels in Christian doctrine, a Christian theologian would express this idea differently. But if the Talmud quote above is representative of predominant Jewish thought, our religions can agree upon the

2. Genesis 8:21.
3. 1 Chronicles 28:9; 29:18; Deuteronomy 31:21.

main point: the evil within us seems to be much stronger than the good. Perhaps that is why I am able to find so many more biblical hints of humanity's inherent sinfulness than I can find for a good impulse. In all the Torah only one man, Noah, is described as perfect, and of course that was before he got so drunk he passed out cold after the Flood—hardly the behavior of an upstanding citizen. The patriarchs were no better. Abraham and Isaac were both willing to give away their wives in return for their own safety.[4] Jacob swindled his brother for his birthright and took his father's blessing through fraud. Even Joseph—the Torah character most often praised as a paragon of virtue—was guilty of ruthless opportunism during a time of extreme famine when he sold the people of Egypt their own grain (which he had earlier seized from them as taxes) in return for their freedom. Thus, although Joseph was a recently freed slave himself and therefore should have known better, he placed an entire nation in bondage on his Pharaoh master's behalf.[5]

Try as I might, I am unable to find a single person in the Torah who always chooses good over evil. As the psalmist wrote, "no one living is righteous before you."[6] This begs the question: Since I can find no direct biblical reference to a good impulse, why does Rabbinic Judaism lay so much emphasis on it?

At Chever Torah, the rabbi provided the following as one source for the idea of *teshuvah*:

> But if a wicked man turns away from all the sins he has committed and keeps all my decrees and does what is just and right, he will surely live; he will not die. None of the offenses he has committed will be remembered against him.
>
> —Ezekiel 18:21–22

Obviously, this "wicked man" must have some reason for turning from his misbehavior. That reason could be explained by the rabbis' theory of a good impulse. It does seem that God rewards *teshuvah* with complete reconciliation. In fact, the word *teshuvah* shares the root word translated above as "turns." Reading

---

4. See Genesis 20:2; 26:9.
5. See Genesis 47:18–21.
6. Psalm 143:2.

these verses within the context of the entire eighteenth chapter of Ezekiel, I begin to wonder if the rabbis are right: perhaps sincere repentance and a return to obedience really are all God requires in order to be reconciled with him. If that is so, then reaching harmony with God is simply about obeying my good impulse.

But upon further reflection, it occurs to me if that is true, then God doesn't really care about justice as it is defined in his own Torah. Simply promising "I won't do it anymore" will not restore things to the way they were before I sinned. Yet the Torah says in several places that justice requires a perfect balance, or "eye for eye, tooth for tooth, life for life." This is the *lex talionis,* or law of retaliation, that I mentioned before. And in several other places God clearly says he *does* care about that kind of justice. For example:

> It is mine to avenge; I will repay.
>                     —Deuteronomy 32:35

Back at Chever Torah a week later, I am discussing this subject with Karen, a psychologist, feminist, and Torah scholar. I propose the possibility that the *lex talionis* "eye for eye" teaching of Torah may mean God desires either perfect behavior on our part, or perfect justice. In response, I receive a skeptical look accompanied by another typical Chever Torah question:

"Why would God ask for the impossible?"

Clearly Karen does not believe he would, and since I have yet to live even a single day without succumbing to my own evil impulses in some way, I know her question is important. Yet my religion teaches that God does indeed demand absolute perfection of me. Part of the basis for that idea is this:

> I am the Lord who brought you up out of Egypt to be your God; therefore be holy, because I am holy.
>                     —Leviticus 11:45

The conventional Christian interpretation of this command is that God wants me to be as holy just as he is holy; in other words, he wants me to be perfect and pure. It is one of those ubiquitous, fundamental canons of the faith, so widely assumed that I never thought to question it before. But now I notice that the verse does not actually say, "be perfectly holy." And because I am not perfect, I find myself hoping Karen's skepticism is well founded, hoping God does not really expect perfection of me after all, hoping that the old Christian doctrine is in error. As I talk this through with her, a new uncertainty rises within me, impossible to ignore. So although I have yet to learn whether it matters why I sin, now I must add another Chever Torah question:

Does God really expect me to be perfect?

I begin yet another exploration by turning to the Jewish sources, and soon realize this question has its roots in a debate between Rabbinic Jews and Christians going all the way back to Jesus. At the heart of the disagreement lies the definition of holiness itself. It seems that many Jews (although not all) believe the idea of holiness in the context of "be holy for I the Lord am holy" applies only to ritual purity, and therefore has nothing to do with ethics or morality:

> The issue of "purity" does not concern ethics, does not intersect with ethics, and does not stand in tension with ethics when one has attained "acceptability in the holy place" even though guilty of a lack of mercy. . . .
>
> —Rabbi Jacob Neusner[7]

The concept of purity is inseparable in Torah from the idea of holiness, so here is a glimmer of hope for those of us who are well aware that we are far from perfect. It is true I cannot live a single day without violating some standard of ethics or morality, but if Rabbi Neusner is correct, that does not necessarily mean I am too impure to be in harmony with God. If holiness simply means observing purity rituals, and if, as the rabbi says, "purity

7. *A Rabbi Talks with Jesus* (New York: Doubleday, 1993), p. 121.

does not concern ethics," maybe I can be both imperfect *and* holy as God is holy after all.

But when I turn to the Christian sources on my shelf, I find that Jesus' position in the New Testament contradicts Rabbi Neusner's view:

> For out of the heart come evil thoughts, murder, adultery, sexual immorality, theft, false testimony, slander. These are what make a man "unclean"; but eating with unwashed hands does not make him "unclean."
>
> —Matthew 15:19–20

In this case, the subject under discussion is the tradition of ritual hand washing before eating. The Pharisees believe it is required to maintain ritual purity, which in their opinion is identical with holiness. But here, Jesus disagrees with that last idea and uses their tradition to teach that purity is based on our inner condition, not on observance of exterior rituals or traditions. In direct contradiction to Rabbis Neusner's comment, Jesus is saying that ritual purity does indeed "concern ethics . . . intersect with ethics, and . . . stand in tension with ethics." In fact, according to Jesus, there is no difference at all between ethics and purity.

Many Jews today also believe "uncleanness" and "sin" in the Torah are not necessarily the same thing. They observe that one had to be purified of uncleanness in order to approach the sacrificial altar, but it was the sacrifice itself that purged the guilt of sin. Judaism says these are two different acts to deal with two different conditions. Christians disagree with that conclusion, maintaining that purification and sacrifice are two parts of a single ritual, both intended to deal with the same issue. We say this in part because the Torah equates uncleanness with "guilt" in many places, and "guilt" is a word used elsewhere to describe the results of sin.[8] Also, speaking of a person who has become unclean unawares, the Torah specifically says, "he has sinned."[9]

Of course, this debate will not be settled here. But while Jews and Christians may not agree that "sin" and "uncleanness" are much the same in Torah, surely we can all acknowledge the To-

8. Compare the use of the word *asham* in Leviticus 4:27; 5:2.
9. Leviticus 5:5, in reference to Leviticus 5:2–4.

rah's consistent teaching that both conditions separate us from God. If I were drowning I would not waste time wondering whether I had too much water or too little air. In the same way, since the goal of life is harmony with God and since both sin and uncleanness destroy that harmony, any distinction between them is immaterial to my main point: I am out of touch with God, not only because of my choices but also because of my condition.

I keep looking, and things get worse.

In another place Jesus says: "Be perfect, therefore, as your heavenly Father is perfect."[10] Because of the obvious parallel between his phrasing and the admonition in Leviticus to "be holy because I am holy," it seems I must pay particular attention to the word "perfect," which Jesus has substituted for "holy."

"Perfect" in this New Testament verse is a translation of the Greek term *teleios*, meaning "complete." This definition reminds me of the Hebrew word *tamim*, which, like teleios, is also translated as "complete," "blameless," or "perfect."[11] *Tamim* is used in reference to Noah, who was "blameless [*tamim*] among the people of his time," and in reference to Abraham, whom God commanded to "walk before me and be blameless [*tamim*]."[12]

Since Noah is described this way, and Abraham is given this command, apparently the Torah would have me believe it really is possible to be *tamim*, or blameless. Jesus builds upon that fact to teach that God expects me to rise to that standard. But Noah and Abraham were unique individuals, towering men of faith. Surely there is some mistake; surely God does not really expect that level of commitment from everyday folks like me.

Unfortunately, just as this thought arises, I find the following:

You must be blameless [*tamim*] before the Lord your God.

—Deuteronomy 18:13

The Jewish Publication Society translation interprets *tamim* as "wholehearted" in this verse, but either way it seems the Torah is making Jesus' point again, phrased as a command to the entire

10. Matthew 5:48.
11. See Leviticus 23:15, for example.
12. Genesis 6:9; 17:1.

Israelite community: be perfect; be complete; be wholehearted. I have been hoping that the answer to Karen's question is, "God does not expect the impossible." It seems there is no way out. God does indeed demand moral perfection.

But wait. What if God is thinking of "perfection" in the sense of a perfect gymnastic performance, when the athlete is so brilliant that the judges all give the highest possible score? After all, perfection here among mere mortals does not necessarily mean perfect in the absolute sense. For example, if a machine were designed to make the same gymnastic moves, it would almost certainly be more precise, more technically perfect. But the judges are not comparing the athlete to a machine's standard of precision. They are judging her on a human level. When they judge her performance to be "perfect," they mean no *human being* could do better.

Is that God's standard too? Is he is simply saying, "Be as good as you can be, given the limitations of your nature?" After all, the Torah does not say, "be as holy *as* the Lord is holy." It says, "be holy *because* the Lord is holy."

What hope this new idea creates!

I cannot be technically perfect, but if I try very hard, perhaps I can be as perfect as anyone else can be—not absolutely perfect as God is, but perfect enough. Here is something I might be able to accomplish, and I am eager to get started. So how do I go about attaining this kind of holiness?

The way to become *tamim*—complete, perfect—is found in the law of Moses, near the beginning of a section that theologians call the "holiness code." There, I again find the commandment to "be holy because I, the Lord your God, am holy."[13] After this, the Scriptures list many laws, most of which relate back to the original Ten Commandments. When read in context, the command to be holy is an introductory remark intended to explain the reason for the commands that follow. So it seems being

13. Leviticus 19:2.

holy is about observing those commandments to the best of my ability.

This blends right in with the idea of the good and evil impulses and the idea of *teshuvah*—returning—as the fundamental component of forgiveness. If I want to be reconciled with the Lord, I must repent and begin doing my best to obey his laws. As I have already seen in Ezekiel: ". . . if a wicked man turns away from all the sins he has committed and keeps all my decrees . . . he will surely live." I am on a comfortable path shared by both Rabbinic Judaism and Christianity. A primary theme of Rabbinic Judaism is observance of the 613 commandments of Torah, and the apostle James taught that ". . . faith by itself, if it is not accompanied by action, is dead."[14] But then I read the Ezekiel verse more closely, and my comfort level drops dramatically. The verse describes the one who "turns" as the one who "keeps all my decrees."

And there's the catch, right there in the middle: that small word, "all."

In Hebrew, that word is *kol.* It is much overlooked in sermons and books on the Mosaic Law, which is odd, because it is present in the vast majority of Hebrew verses that command obedience to God's will. Again and again—more than fifty times by my own rather hurried count—the Hebrew Scriptures say I must obey *all* of God's commandments. Lest I respond again that this kind of perfect obedience is unrealistic, the Torah has this to say:

> Now what I am commanding you today is not too difficult for you or beyond your reach. It is not up in heaven, so that you have to ask, "Who will ascend into heaven to get it and proclaim it to us so we may obey it?" Nor is it beyond the sea, so that you have to ask, "Who will cross the sea to get it and proclaim it to us so we may obey it?" No, the word is very near you; it is in your mouth and in your heart so you may obey it.
>
> —Deuteronomy 30:11–14

My newfound hope has vanished.

These words are an indictment, because in my heart of hearts, I know they are true. I could indeed be perfectly obedient in the

---

14. James 2:17.

most stringent technical sense if I really wanted to be. There are a lot of laws to follow, but not too many to learn if I make it a priority. And once I learn them all, technically speaking, I could follow them all—kol—just as, technically speaking, a well-trained gymnast really is capable of turning out a performance as perfect as that of any robot.

But it hardly seems fair of God to expect absolute perfection, knowing full well that no human being has ever met that standard. And if God is perfectly just, shouldn't he be perfectly fair?

Just as I begin to take solace in the sour grapes notion that God is not fair, it occurs to me that I am indulging in a little bit of hypocrisy. The truth is, I also sometimes expect absolute perfection of people.

> We all have our own standards in business or academic life—our own points at which errors begin to bother us. It is good to get an A in school, but it may be OK to pass with a C. We do not maintain these standards, however, when it comes to our personal life. If we did, we should expect to be shortchanged every now and then when we cash our paycheck; we should expect hospital nurses to drop a constant percentage of newborn babies; we should resign ourselves to going home to the wrong house periodically, by mistake. We as individuals do not tolerate these things. We have a dual standard. . . .
>
> —Philip B. Crosby[15]

Mr. Crosby's point is made in the course of demonstrating that it is reasonable to establish an absolutely perfect record of turning out top quality business products. But does his idea also hold true in the moral realm of life? Is it reasonable of God to expect me to be a morally perfect person all of the time? I decide to use Mr. Crosby's method to find out. For example, is it acceptable for someone to refrain from murder *most* of the time? No. Of course I expect my friends and family to maintain a perfect record in that regard. Does this example seem too extreme? What if I

---

15. *Quality Is Free* (New York: McGraw-Hill, 1979), p. 201.

phrase it this way: Do I have a right to expect my wife to refrain from extramarital sex at all times, with no exceptions? Still too extreme? Well then, is it acceptable for my coworker to steal from the petty cash drawer some of the time, or the postman to read my mail some of the time, or the cashier to pocket my change some of the time? Still my answer is, "No, no, and no." Even when moral issues involve mere postcards or pennies, I feel I have the right to demand absolute moral perfection, and I protest when I do not get it. I am made in the image of God, after all, and share many of the same desires. Like him, I want love and fidelity and commitment. Like him, I feel impatience with moral imperfection.

Yet when God expects the same perfection of me, I object that he asks too much.

It might be said that I am unenlightened. If I were more mature I would not take offense at such minor peccadilloes as opened mail or a stolen penny or two. And knowing the truth of this, I often accept people's shortcomings without comment. But even as I let the little daily affronts of life go by unchallenged, even as I grin and bear it, I am still disappointed and very often angry in my heart of hearts at the imperfection of my fellow human beings. Something inside me always seems to say, "This is not right. Things are not supposed to be this way."

And according to Christianity, I am quite correct. Things are not right at all.

The Torah's commandments are clear, concise, and readily available to be read and understood. None of them require supernatural powers to accomplish. They are not too difficult. I could do them all—*kol*—and yet I do not.

Why is that?

It occurs to me now that the answer to this question explains why it really does matter whether disobedience to God is caused by original sin or the *yetzer ha-ra*. Christianity agrees that God did indeed create humanity in a pure or neutral state, just as Judaism asserts. After all, the Torah says the first humans were created in God's own image, and God is pure and perfect, according to the Shema. Genesis teaches that some time later a human being exercised his or her free will by choosing to disobey God. According to the New Testament, the guilt of this first sin penetrated that first person's soul, and ever since then our desire to sin (our evil impulse) has been much stronger than our desire to be good, as the Talmud says. But that is where the doctrines of the *yetzer ha-ra* and original sin part ways, because unlike Rabbinic Jews, Christians believe the damage done to our spirit by our disobedience cannot be purged simply by "returning."

We believe this for two reasons. First, as I already discussed, if my behavior has caused alienation between God and me, then simply saying "I'm sorry" is not enough. Basic justice requires the damage done to our relationship to be repaired somehow. Wrongs must be righted.

So far, most Jews would agree, but Christians and Jews disagree on what can repair the damage done by our sins. Many Jews believe that God will accept reparation in the form of Torah study, prayer, fasting, and a renewed commitment to obey the Law of Moses. This is the path of *teshuvah*—returning. But Christianity teaches that this is not a truly balanced way to right the wrong; it is not really an "eye for an eye" kind of justice. And even if it were, Christianity teaches that *teshuvah* is humanly impossible. That is the second reason why Christians believe repentance alone is not enough, and is the basic idea behind the doctrine of original sin. We believe we cannot obey the Law of Moses because sin has caused a fundamental change in us, and that fundamental change means the evil impulse will always have the upper hand.

The foundation of the doctrine of original sin is not that I inherited Adam's guilt, as is sometimes inaccurately said, but more precisely that I inherited his condition. In other words, while Judaism sees sin mainly as a choice, Christianity sees it also as a state of being. Like the chemical change caused in our brains when we become addicted to alcohol, Christianity teaches that sin leaves an intense desire for itself in my soul. Once an alcoholic, always an alcoholic, whether one drinks or not, and it is much the same with sin. So while the Talmud teaches that people are free to be good after returning to their former state of moral purity or neutrality, the New Testament teaches the exact opposite. The first humans permanently abandoned that free-dom to be good when they committed the original sin, and as a drug addict's baby is born craving drugs, so the urge to sin was passed on to their descendants.

How then do I explain all the good people in the world?

> Accordingly, he who is the servant of sin is free to sin. And hence he will not be free to do right. . . .
>
> —Augustine[16]

Here Augustine cannot mean that people are not free to do good things, because of course he saw people doing good things in his time, and of course Augustine was no fool. Instead, I think he means that even the most benevolent deeds are flawed—however slightly—by self-interest at their core.

Some will object that selfless acts are indeed possible. They will point to those who sacrifice everything for the sake of others, like the man in a foxhole who throws himself on a grenade to save his comrades at arms. But I wonder if such actions are really selfless, or if they arise from a sense of duty, which in turn stems from a need for self-respect.

> If I hand over my body so that I may boast, but do not have love, I gain nothing.
>
> —1 Corinthians 13:3 (NRSV)

Someone as selfish as I am might possibly die for someone I love, but how much of my motivation comes from fear of being alone, or fear of guilt for surviving? In truth, if I were to sacrifice myself that way, my motives would rise from maintaining self-respect or the ability to face myself in the mirror. Self, self, self . . . even the most sacrificial and loving of acts seems to be done at least partially for the sake of me. But Christianity teaches that a truly good act, a *perfectly* good act, would be to die for someone I hate, or for someone who hates me, and who is capable of that? It is impossible. Yet that is what Jesus demands of those who follow him:

---

16. *Enchiridion on Faith, Hope and Love* (Washington, D.C.: Regnery, 1961), p. 37.

Love your enemies, do good to them. . . .
—Luke 6:35

Try as I might, I cannot pass this litmus test. Pure, undiluted goodness means sacrificing for the sake of others even when there is no hope of receiving a benefit in return. But I cannot bring myself to love my enemies without expectation of getting something for my trouble: a pat on the back, the admiration of my peers, a little self-respect—*something*. I suspect this is true for everyone. There is an unrelenting focus on self that taints even our most altruistic behavior.

Of course, self-interest is not synonymous with sin. I eat because of hunger and drink because of thirst, and both of these are perfectly acceptable sensations even though they are self-centered at their core. God created me to desire my own survival. But whenever self-interest controls my moral or spiritual decisions, it begins to blur my motives for obedience to God, because I base my decision on a self-centered viewpoint. Although I might appear to be living for the Lord, if I do so with my own fulfillment in mind, I have placed a little me at the center of my universe. And of course, we have a word for putting something in that particular location.

It is "idolatry."

Probably, the prophet Habakkuk had precisely this point in mind when he wrote:

Of what value is an idol, since a man [*yetzer*] has carved it? Or an image that teaches lies? For he who makes it trusts in his own creation; he makes idols that cannot speak.

—Habakkuk 2:18

Habakkuk's use of the term "yetzer, " which the translators render as "a man," is a telling bit of wordplay. In yielding to the evil inclination to carve a religious idol, the man himself becomes the very thing to which he has surrendered. In modern terms this means that although I might appear to be a good religious person, so long as even a hint of self-interest motivates my obedience to God, I have merely made an idol out of me. Note this well: Habakkuk's man does not *have* an evil inclination to carve an idol; he *is* that inclination. This is the prophet's way of saying that sin is not a choice; sin is a condition that causes sinful choices.

I often hear strong counterarguments at Chever Torah. The Christian doctrine is too hard, placing me in a lose-lose position with my sinfulness preprogrammed rather than under my control. Or it is too easy, offering a justification for sinful behavior as a kind of inherited condition rather than a conscious choice. Sometimes I am tempted to throw out this awkward bit of Christian theology in the interest of Judaism's optimistic belief that all I have to do to live a righteous life is make righteous choices. But Habakkuk's observation to the contrary forces me to deal with the idea of original sin, especially since it is just one of many such statements in the Hebrew Scriptures. Another comes early in Genesis:

> This is the written account of Adam's line. When God created man, he made him in the likeness of God. He created them male and female and blessed them. And when they were created, he called them "man." When Adam had lived 130 years, he had a son *in his own likeness, in his own image*; and he named him Seth.
>
> —Genesis 5:1–3 (emphasis mine)

Three times the Torah has already said Adam was created in God's image and likeness. That idea is one of the reasons Christians believe God loves us in spite of our sin. But here the Torah uses those words a fourth time in a new way when Seth, who carries on Adam's bloodline to Noah and thus to all humanity, is said to be created not in the image of God but in the image of Adam. The words, "in his own image, in his own likeness" are used of only those two individuals in the Torah. Since the first use clearly describes God's spiritual endowment to Adam, it seems to me that the second should be interpreted a similar way. If Adam was created in the Lord's morally perfect image, then Seth was created in Adam's sinful image. From there it seems only logical to assume that Seth's children were created in his sinful image, and they passed it on to their children, and they to theirs, and so on and on and on. After all, if Judaism is right and Seth was indeed born with a perfectly neutral soul like Adam, it seems to me a just and righteous God should have given Seth (and me) a fresh start in the Garden. In other words, if my soul was perfect when I entered life, fully capable of choosing obedience and righteousness, why was I born into *this* life, where evil so often holds sway over good? Why not enter life as Adam did, in the presence of God, in the Garden, in paradise? If sinfulness is simply a matter of choice, why was I not given my own chance to pluck the forbidden fruit— or not—and so obtain for myself the destiny I deserved? Instead, all the other conditions of Adam and Eve's punishment continue today. Death, pain in childbirth, survival at the cost of grueling work, and the natural world's inherent opposition to human creature comforts were all part of the curse, and here we are today, still suffering all of these same penalties. Why is that?

I can think of only two possible explanations. First, I might have been born with a pure spirit and then cursed in this way unfairly because God is unjust or does not love me. But as Maimonides said, a God who is one must therefore be pure, and everything that flows from him or returns to him—including justice—must also be pure. This is also true of God's love for me, which does not change in spite of all my sins, because God never changes. So if the Shema is true, this first explanation must be false. That leaves only one other possibility: I was born into Adam's curse because I inherited the reason for that curse. But does the Torah really support the idea that I can be cursed as a result of someone else's sin?

No sooner is the question asked than my mind is filled with examples of exactly that. In the story of the Passover, the firstborn offspring of all the Egyptians are killed because of the stubborn refusal of one man—the Pharaoh—to obey God. Something very similar happens again after Joshua takes over as leader of Israel, when just one man, Achan, keeps the spoils of war in violation of God's will, yet all of Israel is held accountable upon pain of death.[17] And then, following a vague memory, I flip back through my Torah and find this:

> If the anointed priest sins, *bringing guilt on the people,* he must bring to the Lord a young bull without defect as a sin offering for the sin he has committed.
>
> —Leviticus 4:3 (emphasis mine)

If one priest can sin and "bring guilt on the people," if a Pharaoh's sin—or even the sin of a common Israelite man like Achan—can cause so many others to be condemned even though they did not personally take part in that sin, it seems possible to me that the sin of one man can also corrupt the spirits of his descendants. But still, after months of hearing the Jewish viewpoint—that I was born with a pure soul and corrupted only by my deliberate choices—I wonder if a single act of disobedience in the Garden is really enough to contaminate all future generations. Then, remembering something we studied long ago, I turn back and forth through the Scriptures. After a few minutes there it is: a warning in the Torah that the idolatrous thoughts of a single man can lead to severe punishment for an entire nation.[18]

This man's sin begins in his mind, when ". . . he invokes a blessing on himself and therefore thinks, 'I will be safe, even though I persist in going my own way.'" But the Torah warns that such thinking ". . . will bring disaster on the watered land as well as the dry." A note in the margin of my Bible taken at an earlier Chever Torah lesson reveals that this last phrase is an ancient Hebrew expression meaning "everywhere," in the sense of the English phrase, "coast to coast." So the Torah is saying this man's sinful thoughts can spread out until they corrupt absolutely everything. Reading this now, I wonder . . . can it mean this man's sin actually influences the land itself?

Apparently the answer is yes.

In the next series of verses describing the result of this man's sin, God says, "Your children who follow you in later generations and foreigners who come from distant lands will see the calamities that have fallen on the land and the diseases with which the

---

17. See Joshua 7.
18. For the Torah quotations that follow, see Deuteronomy 29:18–28.

Lord has afflicted it. The whole land will be a burning waste of salt and sulfur—nothing planted, nothing sprouting, no vegetation growing on it." The devastation caused by this one man's thoughts becomes a warning to those who ask, "Why this fierce, burning anger?" and are told, "It is because this people abandoned the covenant of the Lord. . . ."[19] The corruption beginning as a hidden thought in one man's mind is so contagious it ends with a curse not just upon humanity but even upon the soil and plants! Suddenly it seems the Torah is treating sin not as a mere choice, but as a disease, a highly contagious, full-blown plague upon the earth.

I turn back to the Torah portion of the morning and try to refocus my attention on the rabbi's lesson, but these discoveries refuse to release their hold upon my imagination. In fact, I cannot help believing there is an even deeper connection here.

Earlier, when I explored the Christian explanation of why bad things happen to good people, I found part of the answer in the notion that God allows evil to exist for the sake of human free will. In other words, I must have a true choice between good and evil if I am to be held accountable for my behavior, therefore evil must exist as a choice. Now, sitting at Chever Torah surrounded by Jews who were personally scarred when the Holocaust's flames touched friends and family, the connection between evil and human freedom is never far from my thoughts. But what about the bad things that happen without any human decision, the so-called "natural" disasters that have caused at least as much suffering as Nero, Vespasian, the crusaders, Stalin, Hitler, and Pol Pot combined?

"Your children who follow you in later generations and foreigners who come from distant lands will see the calamities that have fallen on the land. . . ." With passages such as this, the Torah seems to suggest an answer. Could Adam's curse be so contagious that it not only spans human generations, but also actually transforms things outside the human race?

19. Deuteronomy 29:24–25.

In light of the idea that sin is actually contagious, I begin to think of other Scriptures in new ways. I am reminded of the Torah's teaching that simply touching holy things such as Mt. Sinai, the tabernacle altar, or the offerings presented at the tabernacle altar could cause a person to become holy.[20] The Torah says physical contact with a specific piece of real estate, a portable piece of furniture, or a slaughtered animal could make a person holy under the right circumstances. There is no stronger argument for the contagious nature of spiritual conditions. Unfortunately, I believe the Torah also strongly implies that this spiritual contagion flows both ways. For example:

> Anything that an unclean person touches becomes unclean, and anyone who touches it becomes unclean till evening.
>
> —Numbers 19:22

In another place it is written that emitting the fluids associated with the reproductive process causes men and women to become unclean, and contact with those fluids can transfer that uncleanness to inanimate objects such as a bed or a chair.[21] So the Torah teaches that a spiritual condition can be passed from people to inanimate objects, like beds or tents. It can even be transferred to the very land itself. And if that is true, why should the spread of sin's corrupting influence stop there?

According to Christianity, it did not.

The New Testament teaches that the corruption Adam and Eve released upon the universe has also infected the animals, atmosphere, oceans, and land.[22] This explains disease, hurricanes, and earthquakes. The Scriptural basis for this is first found in the Garden of Eden, where the Torah describes an environment so benign that clothing is not required and all animals are vegetarians. We are in such perfect harmony with our Creator that we feel no fear of him, no need to cover ourselves. But after the expulsion from the Garden, the Torah describes spiritual perversion spreading like wildfire. Cain becomes a murderer. Humanity challenges God with towers up to heaven. The climate be-

---

20. See Exodus 19:12, 23; 29:36–37; Leviticus 6:18.
21. Leviticus 15:16–24.
22. Romans 8:20–22.

comes capable of producing a worldwide flood. Humanity and animals descend into violence and carnivorous behavior.[23] Life spans in the Bible become shorter with each passing generation from Noah to David due to the expanding influence of violence and disease. The effect of sin upon creation continues to worsen with time, right up to now. Today it takes all our knowledge, machines, and medicines to keep people alive into their seventies and eighties, and those in third-world countries without the benefit of medical technology routinely perish at half that age. I believe these are signs of a pollution rippling out from the first sin, corrupting everything it touches.

Some will say the stories of the fall and tower and flood are merely fables. They will point to evidence that predatory dinosaurs lived long before us and infer from this that carnivorous behavior did not arise from human choice. But who knows what science may learn about the chronology of men and dinosaurs in years to come? Perhaps Adam's fateful choice warped time itself, imposing violence and evil upon nature in his past as well as his future. Throughout recorded history, the scientific discoveries of each generation have radically challenged the beliefs that went before. We are no different; indeed, we do not know half so much as we think. In the last century, an "extinct" fish was pulled from the depths of prehistoric times to thrash alive upon the deck of a Japanese fishing boat. The tumbled walls of Troy and Jericho, long thought to be ancient fantasies, were found beneath the sands. Fables are stories designed to teach a larger truth. Sometimes the details themselves are also true, and sometimes the truth they tell is so profound it makes the details immaterial. In the case of the expulsion from the Garden and the flood and all the rest, Christianity understands that truth as this: The world is not supposed to be this way. Something is wrong here; something is out of balance, and it has corrupted absolutely everything. In the face of such a monumental idea, to me it seems beside the point to debate the details.

If sin exists as a kind of plague upon the world, then I would expect the Scriptures to mention that it can come without warning, like a bad case of the flu. And sure enough, in Leviticus I find many references to sacrificial ritual in response to *unintentional*

23. See Genesis 1:29–30; 9:3–4.

sin.[24] Leviticus also says an Israelite can become unclean, "even though he is unaware of it."[25] In these passages, the Torah says quite clearly that isolation from God is not always about the choices I make. Sometimes I am unacceptable simply because of my contact with the environment. In a logical universe, I cannot wade through slop without becoming filthy. In a logical universe, even God cannot make sense of nonsense.

This helps me reconcile a loving God with the horrors of disease or natural disasters, but I believe it is also important because if I can sin or become unclean unintentionally, then apparently my choices alone cannot control evil. I cannot simply choose to return—teshuvah—to harmony with God, any more than I can conquer influenza with a positive attitude.

Digressing just a bit, earlier I noticed that contact with the fluids associated with reproduction causes uncleanness. Men become unclean because of a discharge of semen, and woman because of their menstrual flow. In another place the Torah says a Hebrew mother must bring a sin offering after giving birth.[26] Now I wonder: If a baby is born with a pure soul as the rabbis say, why is this necessary?

The Song of Solomon attests to the fact that sex between a husband and wife is a glorious gift from God, but the more I study Torah the more it seems that everything physical associated with procreation has some connection with guilt or sin. Pain in childbirth is part of Eve's curse for the original sin, and God chose to symbolize his covenant with Abraham and all his male descendants with circumcision, an act that leaves a permanent scar on the male reproductive organ. (The Hebrew word for "circumcise" was also chosen by the Psalmist to mean "broken," "blunted," and "cut off.")[27] This scarred part of a male Israelite priest's anatomy had to be covered at all times at the tabernacle upon the altar steps, lest he "incur guilt and

24. Leviticus 4:2, 22, 27.
25. Leviticus 5:2–3.
26. Leviticus 12:6.
27. Psalms 58:7; 118:10–12.

die."[28] Yet Adam was created in God's perfect image, with no scars and nothing to hide until after the Fall. This question may offend some Jews, and for that I apologize in advance, but within this context it simply must be asked: Could the hidden disfigurement of circumcision symbolize the idea that the priest—representing all the people—had something to hide, just as the fallen Adam did? Similarly, could a new mother's uncleanness come from her part in bringing another sin-addicted soul into the world? And could a woman's pain in childbirth—which is unnatural according to Genesis—be intended to remind us of our loving God's pain at the other end of life, at our death, which is also unnatural?

> For I take no pleasure in the death of anyone, declares the Sovereign Lord. Repent and live!
>
> —Ezekiel 18:32

Every painful birth heralds an eventual death, and both are part of the curse that Adam and Eve received as the result of the original sin. As with birth, the uncleanness caused by death is highly contagious. According to the Torah, simply entering a tent where a person has died makes one unclean. Even open containers within the tent (and presumably their contents) become unclean because of the death that occurred nearby.[29] How powerful is the force of this impurity! Apparently it is more contagious than any disease. It is passed along with both our birth and our death. It can be transferred just by touching something someone else once touched. It corrupts the inanimate objects and the animals around us, and a man's evil thoughts—merely his *thoughts*—can lead to the devastation of the very land itself.

I try to return my attention to Rabbi Robbins. I have learned much this morning, but surely not the lesson she intended. As she closes this week's Chever Torah session, I reflect upon two important facts I found in the Torah today. First, impurity, uncleanness, profanity—whatever I wish to call it—travels from person to person, and even from a person to an inanimate object or the land itself, and then back to another person. Second, the

---

28. Exodus 28:42–43; 20:26.
29. Numbers 19:14–15.

Torah takes great pains to link this unholy condition to the cycle of birth and death. This implies that spiritual conditions can span the generations, and indeed, I have seen that the merits of the fathers doctrine proves a positive spiritual legacy can be inherited. But so far I have not found a Torah passage that actually states this is true for negative spiritual effects.

I head home, wondering if such a Scripture exists.

Coincidentally, Rabbi Robbins is teaching again several months later when I get my answer. She is telling us about a Jewish doctrine called *zekhut avot,* or the "merits of the fathers." It seems that Isaac, the son of Abraham, has had considerable trouble in the land God promised to his father. Again and again he encamps in that arid country and digs water wells, only to have outsiders come along and falsely claim the wells as theirs. A peaceful man, Isaac always acquiesces to their unjust demands and moves on. Finally he reaches a place where no one comes to steal the fruits of his labor. There, God pronounces this blessing:

> I am the God of your father Abraham. Do not be afraid, for I am with you; I will bless you and will increase the number of your descendants *for the sake of my servant Abraham.*
>
> —Genesis 26:24 (emphasis mine)

The Lord loves us in spite of everything and longs to prove his love with blessings. But this, says Rabbi Robbins, is one of many examples of God's strange habit of blessing one person because of another. This is found throughout the Hebrew Scriptures. For example, when King Solomon's punishment for idolatry is postponed, and when King Hezekiah's reign is prolonged in the face of an apparently invincible enemy, these divine actions are undertaken for the sake of David who was long dead in both cases.[30] Why, asks Rabbi Robbins, did God say he would bless Isaac for Abraham's sake, or save Solomon and Hezekiah for

---

30. 1 Kings 11:10–13; 2 Kings 19:29–34.

David's sake, unless some sort of merit or divine favor can be inherited from one's father?

Suddenly my ears perk up.

If Isaac can inherit special dispensation due to God's blessing on his dead father, it seems to me just as likely that one could inherit the reverse. In other words, if a blessing can flow across the generations, why not a curse? To me it makes no sense to believe in one without the other. Instead, it seems more likely that *zekhut avot* and original sin are two branches of the same stream.

I am excited as today's Chever Torah winds down. I have searched the Hebrew Scriptures and found them filled with evidence on many levels to support the idea that I inherited an addiction to sin. When the rabbi departs to lead a Bat Mitzvah, I mention a few examples to the people who have stayed to talk. But of course my Jewish friends reject my interpretation completely, and like me, they believe they have the Scriptures on their side. One man suggests that I carefully consider these words:

> The soul who sins is the one who will die. The son will not share the guilt of the father, nor will the father share the guilt of the son. The righteousness of the righteous man will be credited to him, and the wickedness of the wicked will be charged against him.
>
> —Ezekiel 18:20[31]

Now I am confused. After all the Biblical evidence I have found for the inherited effects of Adam's original sin, I thought it was an airtight case. But the message of Ezekiel is simple, clear, and undeniable. Just as the Torah takes pains to tell me Seth inherited Adam's imperfections, Ezekiel now takes pains to tell me I will be punished only for my own sins, not for those of my predecessors.

"Why," asks my Chever Torah friend, "Would our Scriptures teach such contradictory ideas?"

31. See also Deuteronomy 24:16.

I think it over for a while before realizing that these things are not really contradictory at all. To return to an earlier metaphor, it may simply mean I was born addicted to alcohol, but God will only hold me accountable for actually getting drunk. Temptation itself is not sin. So when Ezekiel says "the soul who sins is the one who will die," he means my loving God will not punish me for inheriting the addictive effects of Adam's original sin; I am only judged guilty when I succumb to those effects. After all, the New Testament teaches that even Jesus was tempted, yet he was without sin.[32]

"Ah hah!" another Chever Torah Jew exclaims. "In that case, it really is about human choice, and not about an inherited condition."

And in a way she has a point. Most Christians believe if a human being were able to make every choice of her life in complete obedience to the will of God, she would be in perfect union with the Creator, reconciled with him forever.[33] But no mere human has ever managed to live a completely moral life, with the possible exceptions of Enoch and Elijah, which finally brings me back to the young woman's Chever Torah question, "Everyone sins, right? Does it really matter why?"[34]

Malaria was impossible to conquer until we realized it is contracted through mosquito bites. During the Middle Ages hundreds of thousands died because we did not know bubonic plague traveled by way of the rats infesting our cities. Similarly, if sinful choices are a symptom of a contagious condition, then sin's effect upon my spirit can never end until I have some understanding of the way it moves through the human population. So yes, it matters why I sin. It matters quite a lot, because knowing the source of my condition is an important milestone on the road to recovery.

32. See Hebrews 4:15 and Matthew 4:1–11.
33. See Romans 2:13 for righteousness through perfect obedience.
34. See Hebrews 11:5 and Lev. R. XXVII. 4 as quoted by Abraham Cohen in *Everyman's Talmud*, p. 73, for traditional Christian and Jewish views on Enoch and Elijah.

As a Christian, understanding sin as a condition and not merely a choice is the first step toward finding a way to face the pain of "natural disasters" (an oxymoron if original sin is true). It is a first step toward finding a way to endure the evil that men do without being drawn deeper into that same evil. It is also a step toward reconciling myself with God once and for all.

But what is the next step? I cannot simply stop sinning, because my sin-infected condition means the young lady was right: everyone sins, especially me. I cannot obey all—*kol*—of the Lord's commands, although his Torah makes that demand so many times. In fact, the universe has become so perverse that I must sometimes sin in small ways just to avoid sinning on a grander scale. That fact alone is a strong argument for sin as a condition if one thinks it through—after all, if everyone is given a chance to freely choose obedience over sin, why am I so often forced to choose the lesser of two evils? One cannot wade through slop without emerging filthy.

Some might ask, If this world is so awash in evil that I cannot possibly live a holy life on my own, what is the point in trying?

Others may wonder, If all I can do is to try my best, shouldn't that be enough?

These last two questions bracket perhaps the greatest misunderstanding between Christians and Jews that I have found in all my years at Chever Torah. I brought the Christian half of the misconception with me the first day I went to temple. It took almost a year for me to see that my preconceived notions were not true. And to this day, many of the Jews I meet each week at Chever Torah still labor under a seriously flawed understanding of what I believe. These mutual misconceptions have caused many needless divisions between Jews and Christians through the years, and the shame of it is, just a little education is all it would take to shed the burden of this load.

Perhaps it is time to look at what Christianity and Judaism really t￼ subject of what to do about human sin.

seven

# Pitching Tabernacles

Because of his very acuteness, he overlooked the point.

—Erubin, 90

One of the many facinating people I have met at Chever Torah is
Bobbie, an artist who often impresses me with the virtuosity of
her doodles on the paper tablecloth during Chever Torah. Each
week she casually tosses off one elegant sketch after another: a
fellow student's profile, a pair of clasped hands, or an abstract
border around a group of Hebrew letters like the frontispiece of
a meticulously illuminated manuscript. Sometimes I think she is
not listening, but I am about to change my mind about that. As
the Chever Torah Jews and I discuss the *parasha* or "portion" of
the Torah named for Jethro, Moses' father-in-law, the portion of
Exodus that contains the Ten Commandments, the rabbi poses
this question: Why does the Talmud teach that Jews should
begin counting the commandments with "I am the Lord your
God, who brought you out of Egypt," instead of beginning with,
"You shall have no other gods before Me" as the Protestant

Christians do?[1] After all, this Jewish version is not really a commandment at all; it is more a statement of fact. Many excellent reasons are offered, but only one is powerful enough to make me decide on the spot to count the Ten Commandments as Jews do from now on. It comes when Bobbie lays down her pen and raises her hand. When Rabbi Stern calls on her, she says, "I think they began counting the Commandments with that verse because it reminds us we couldn't get out of Egypt by ourselves."

As usual, Rabbi Stern immediately understands. "Good point," he says, "And isn't that what the Torah means in the previous chapter, when God says, 'I carried you on eagles' wings and brought you to myself'?"

It is a simple observation, but to a Christian it stands at the heart of belief about atonement, forgiveness, and reconciliation with God. In fact, as a Christian, I believe one of the most important truths in the universe is hidden within this brief exchange between artist and rabbi. Still, what I think I heard just now runs counter to everything I have learned in the church about Judaism. Perhaps I am reading too much into this.

A few weeks later I have just about succeeded in writing the whole thing off as a misunderstanding on my part when the same idea is thrust upon me as I enjoy a cup of coffee with Alan, a talented advertising man and one of the most articulate members of Chever Torah. Although Alan might not phrase it this way, we are talking about a topic Christians usually call "grace and works."

At first, mine is the typical Christian attitude. Since Alan is a Jew, I assume he believes in working his way into God's good graces. I am determined to show him the futility of trying to please God through obedience to his commands. "We can't reach up to God," I say. "He has to reach down to us."

Alan's attitude is equally stereotypical. He seems to think I believe I can ignore God's will now that I have been saved by God's grace. He insists that I have no right to brush aside God's commands simply because I believe the Lord has reached down to me.

I respond to Alan's point by observing that I do not ignore God's laws (at least no more so than a typical Reform Jew). In

1. Exodus 20:2–3.

fact, my relationship with God inspires me to obey, whereas before I was reconciled with God I felt no such desire. It is a question of motivation: I do not obey to *reach* harmony with God; I obey because I *am* in harmony with God. The first is works, and is hopeless. The second is grace, and is the only way to God. I tell Alan what I have learned in my study of the Hebrew word *kol:* the Torah insists again and again that God expects me to obey *all* of his commands if I am to work my way into harmony with him, yet that is something no human being can do.

Alan responds that he is well aware that he cannot obey every bit of the law, but that fact does not relieve him of the responsibility to do his best. What kind of a message would he be sending to God if he simply said, "I can't do this because I'm only human, so I'm not even going to try?"

To that, I reply in a slightly contentious tone that Alan is not listening. Didn't I just say I try to obey the will of God? I just do it for a different reason. I obey as best I can *because I love God,* not to earn his love.

Now Alan tells me that I am the one who is not listening. Why in the world would he do his best to obey a God he doesn't love? In fact, the only reason he's doing his best is *because he loves God* and God loves him!

Suddenly, Alan and I stare at each other with wonder. It has dawned on us that we are saying exactly the same thing: we both obey *because we love God.* In other words, it is the love of God in us that leads us to obedience. God leads. We follow. And whether you are a Jew or a Christian, that is grace.

The word "grace" in religious contexts means "undeserved favor." It is the idea that God takes the initiative in establishing a peaceful, harmonious relationship with me in spite of the fact that I do not deserve his forgiveness. Grace is related to the concept of mercy, but it is different, because mercy involves simply withholding a punishment I deserve, while grace combines mercy with the gift of a blessing I do not deserve.

On the other hand, in the Christian lexicon, "works" is the idea that I can reach reconciliation with God by being good enough or obedient enough to earn his forgiveness.

The reason it took Alan and me so long to realize we actually agree with one another is that Christians have long perceived Judaism as a "works-based" religion, and since Talmudic times Jews have perceived Christians as so focused on grace that we do not bother to obey God's commandments. In my earlier study of holiness, I learned that the first moments of this controversy are recorded in the Gospels, where Jesus and the Pharisees debate the meaning of "ritual purity." Jesus taught that purity depends upon the condition of the heart, while some of the Pharisees of his time taught that purity is strictly a matter of observing external rituals. Large sections of the New Testament were written in response to this issue, as the early Jews who believed in Jesus struggled to find the correct path between the doctrine of grace and works. Like most Christians, I used to think the Pharisees in my New Testament were typical of all Jews. But now, after hearing Alan's motivation for obedience to the Torah, I am not so sure.

Is Alan's apparent grace-based faith normal in Judaism, or is he a rare exception?

I decide to keep an eye out for Jewish texts that support Alan's position, and sure enough, the following quote from Martin Buber soon turns up. Buber's status in twentieth-century Jewish theology and apologetics can be compared to the Christian work of C. S. Lewis or Francis Schaeffer. In the following quote, he paraphrases an old Hasidic saying:

> In the psalm we read: "How long shall I take counsel in my soul, having sorrow in my heart by day." As long as I take counsel in my soul, there must be sorrow in my heart all day. Only when I know of no further counsel that can help me, and I give up taking counsel, and know of no other help but God, will help be vouchsafed me.
>
> —Martin Buber[2]

2. *Martin Buber's Ten Rungs: Collected Hasidic Sayings* (New York: Citadel Press, 1995), pp. 19–20.

I think Buber's "sorrow in my heart" corresponds to Conrad's "naked terror of loneliness." It is the sorrow of being separated from God. And for this malaise, Buber acknowledges there is "no other help but God." Since that sounds suspiciously like an acknowledgment of the need for divine grace, my confusion about the ancient Judeo-Christian grace-versus-works debate merely deepens. If Judaism is truly a "works-based" religion, why would such a widely respected Jewish scholar write in support of the idea that God will only help me when I admit that I cannot help myself?

To confuse matters even more, I soon find this midrash in the Talmud:

> When all the materials of the tabernacle and its appurtenances had been got together, the Israelites tried in vain to set it up. They then asked Moses to set it up, but he was unable to do so. He then turned to God and said, "I do not know how to set it up." "Try again," God replied, "and before long you will find that the tabernacle will set itself up, as it were."
>
> —Tanhuma on Exodus 39:33

Setting up the tabernacle is a brilliant metaphor for obedience to God, a humanly impossible task—something even Moses cannot do—which becomes possible only after help is sought from God himself. Indeed, after asking God for help, the tabernacle seems to set itself up. This is a remarkably apt explanation of the importance of grace.

Grace, then, is not an exclusively Christian idea. Judaism teaches it too, which is not really surprising when I notice that even a casual reading of the Torah turns it up again and again. For example, consider the Lord's explanation for choosing Israel:

> Understand, then, that it is not because of your righteousness that the Lord your God is giving you this good land to possess, for you are a stiff-necked people.
>
> —Deuteronomy 9:6

Bracketing these words are a number of verses stating that Israel is being given the Promised Land because the people living there are evil, yet here God says that Israel is not righteous either, in fact they have a serious pride problem (they are "stiff necked"). So why did God choose Israel instead of one of those other peoples? Did he find some admirable characteristic in them that the others lacked?

No.

On the contrary:

> The Lord did not set his affection on you and choose you because you were more numerous than other peoples, for you were the fewest of all peoples. But *it was because the Lord loved you* and kept the oath he swore to your forefathers that he brought you out with a mighty hand and redeemed you from the land of slavery, from the power of Pharaoh king of Egypt.
>
> —Deuteronomy 7:7–8 (emphasis mine)

So God saved Israel not because of anything they did, but simply because he loved them. That is grace.

It seems my friend Alan's perspective and Martin Buber's wisdom are not unique to these modern times, but have deep roots in the Torah and in ancient, traditional Judaism. Consider this:

> . . . you will find that our father Abraham only inherited this world and the World-To-Come by virtue of faith; as it is said, "he believed in the Lord, and he counted it to him for righteousness."
>
> —Talmudic commentary on Genesis 15:6[3]

Here are these supposedly legalistic Jews going out of their way to say that God bestowed the World-To-Come on Abraham not because of his obedience to the law, but because he had faith enough to believe in the Lord. Again, that is a perfect example of grace. Ironically, the Christian Scriptures make precisely the same point using precisely the same scriptural example more than once.[4] And in a stroke of even higher irony, the Christian Scriptures also use the same verse to underscore the importance of *works*:

3. *Everyman's Talmud,* p. 79.
4. See Romans 4:3–5 and Galatians 3:6–9 for examples.

You foolish man, do you want evidence that faith without deeds is worthless? Was not our ancestor Abraham considered righteous for what he did when he offered his son Isaac on the altar? You see that his faith and his actions were working together, and his faith was made complete by what he did. And the scripture was fulfilled that says, "Abraham believed God, and it was credited to him as righteousness."

—James 2:20–23

How many sermons have I heard throughout the years about the legalistic Pharisees, concerned only with works? Yet now I find *their* descendants using Genesis 15:6 to proclaim the need for faith and grace, while *my* spiritual ancestors use the exact same verse to defend the importance of works! As has happened so often in my time with Chever Torah, the floor of my study is littered with fallen stereotypes. And lest I become tempted to think James has spoken out of turn, I recall these words of Jesus himself:

Not everyone who says to me, "Lord, Lord, " will enter the kingdom of heaven, but only he who *does the will of my Father* who is in heaven.

—Matthew 7:21 (emphasis mine)

So where is the famous debate between Judaism and Christianity over grace versus works? The Talmud's statement "Abraham only inherited this world and the World-To-Come by virtue of faith" is hardly indicative of a legalistic Jewish religion. And Jesus' declaration "only he who does the will of my Father [will go to heaven]" is hardly the teaching of a man in favor of abandoning the Torah for grace alone. In fact, reading on in the New Testament, I find Jesus warning his followers again and again that we are expected to live obedient lives. For example:

Jesus replied, "If anyone loves me, he will obey my teaching. . . ."

—John 14:23

When Jesus spoke about his "teaching" here, he probably used the Hebrew word *torah* or its Aramaic equivalent, since *torah* is the word for both "teaching" and "law." In other words, Jesus is saying, "If you love me, you will obey my Torah." But I have just noticed something else: Jesus stops short of saying obedience will reconcile me with God. On the contrary, the quote above expresses the idea that true obedience to God *follows* a loving commitment to him. James made much the same point by saying Abraham's "faith was made complete by what he did. . . ." In both cases, it is faith or love first, then obedience or action. To put it in the terms that Alan and I agreed upon just recently, we obey because we love the Lord, not the other way around.

Suddenly it occurs to me that this entire debate could hinge upon a matter of timing. What if Judaism teaches that obedience must come before God's grace, while Christianity teaches the opposite? Could that explain the centuries old "grace versus works" controversy between church and synagogue?

I turn to the Talmud to research this new theory, and sure enough, here is what I find:

> The Torah is like a goad because it serves to guide the students on their way.

> —Hagigah, 3

Ah, this is more like it. The idea that the Torah—the law—goads me on my way to God sounds suspiciously like the notion that I can reach God by obeying Torah. It seems my Christian teachers did not lead me astray after all. Judaism is a works-based religion.

But not so fast. . . . Something about that last Talmud quotation is familiar. Turning to my New Testament I find this:

> So the law was put in charge to lead us to Christ that we might be justified by faith.

> —Galatians 3:24

Paul seems to be saying the law *can* lead me to God, and since the Torah is the law, now it seems that Paul and the rabbis are in agreement! Once again, I feel caught in a maze of inconsistency. Does obedience lead to faith, or does faith lead to obedience? And which religion stands for which position?

Perhaps I can gain some clarity by considering the way Judaism and Christianity view the Torah itself.

Although the Talmud's simile for the Torah as a "goad" is hardly complimentary, I know that the rabbis uniformly view the books of Moses as a positive expression of the divine will, a guidebook to heaven so to speak, which, like all good guidebooks, also encourages the traveler to set out upon the path. In contrast, the New Testament takes a more pessimistic view of the Torah, teaching that one of the reasons it so uniformly stresses obedience to *all* commandments is to demonstrate the hopelessness of achieving that goal without the intervention of God.

> For whoever keeps the whole law and yet stumbles at just one point is guilty of breaking all of it.
>
> —James 2:10

Far from being a guidebook that encourages me to set out upon the path, the Torah is seen by Christians as a warning that the path is hopelessly steep. The logic goes like this: Since God obviously knew I could not obey all of the Torah's commands long before he caused the Torah to be written, the frequently repeated demand to obey all of its commands must exist for another purpose. That purpose is to instill the humility necessary to admit my helplessness in the face of sin, so I will accept God's graceful provision of a solution for the problem.

Imagine a novice sailor who insists he needs no compass to navigate across an ocean. "I have a well-developed sense of direction," he says. "I can find my way without it." He sets out with the charts, which tell him where he must go, but without the compass, which would tell him where he is. Eventually he makes landfall, but according to the charts, he is far off course. Christianity teaches that the main purpose of God's commandments in the Torah is to inspire "a broken spirit and a contrite heart."[5] Like the sailor's charts, the Torah tells me where I should go in life and warns me when I make landfall at the wrong location. But it does not guide me as I sail along. For that, I need the "compass" of God's grace.

5. Psalms 51:17.

In the Galatians quote above, Paul writes that the law will "lead us to Christ [God]," but he also writes that we are "justified by faith," meaning I am reconciled with God by placing my faith in him alone—not in anything I might do. So in Christian theology, the Torah shines the spotlight of true perfection on my imperfect efforts to live a righteous life without God's help, making my inadequacy impossible to ignore.

But I wonder . . . is there any practical difference between this idea and the Talmud's position that the Torah is a goad guiding me on the way to God? Or could these simply be two different ways of communicating the same truth?

I keep reading, and come across this:

> A man should study and perform Mitzvot [the commands of Torah] even with an ulterior motive, for in the end he will do so for the sake of the Lord.
>
> —Pesahim, 50

Based on what he wrote in Galatians, I think Paul would agree with this Talmud quote, so I begin to sense some equilibrium between these ideas. But it proves to be short lived, when I read Rabbinic Judaism's Scriptures further and find this teaching in another place:

> Only Torah serves to purify a man.
>
> —Zohar iii, 80b

I feel like I am in a whirlwind. As a Christian, I can heartily agree that the Torah goads me toward the Lord, but how can the Torah also purify? Put another way: if the Torah goads me toward God's graceful provision of forgiveness and purity, it seems a contradiction to state that the Torah actually provides those same things, somewhat like saying the menu is the meal.

This is indeed a paradox.

Fortunately I remember one of my first Chever Torah lessons: When faced with contradictory truths, focus on the truth standing in the middle. In other words, maybe it is time to admit I cannot understand this Torah God has given.

And therein lies the solution.

Be not afraid of a work which has no end, (such as learning Torah).

—Abbot de-R. Nathan, 27, 3

The Talmud I can never know all there is to know about the Torah—that humble admission is perhaps its greatest lesson. So in this sense, the Torah does indeed serve to purify me (the Jewish idea), and I am also back again to the proposition that the Torah's role is to inspire humility (the Christian idea). It purifies by instilling humility. And sure enough, it turns out this connection between the Torah and humility is a common theme in Rabbinic Judaism:

Words of Torah are not lasting except in him who is lowly of spirit.

—Taanit, 7

Before the Scroll of the Torah, all men are as the poor.

—Baba Batra, 43

As it was given in fear and awe, so it shall be read.

—Tanhuma Buber, Wayyera

So this is how it works: I begin my journey toward God with the delusion that if I work hard I can be "good enough," that is, I can reach him on my own. And since God loves me too much to remove my free will, he stands aside to let me flounder in the foolish pride of this ridiculous proposition. But eventually I notice that I always fall far short of the standard God has set in his Torah. Finally, when I admit I can never be obedient enough to enter God's presence on my own, when I "know of no other help but God," as Martin Buber so aptly phrased it, then the Lord rushes down to carry me up.

O Bush of Moses! Not because thou art tall, but because thou art lowly, did God reveal himself in thee.

—Shabbat, 67

In our coffeehouse conversation Alan alluded to a classic Christian mistake: If the Torah humbles me enough to admit that I am not up to the task of living a holy enough life for God, I may as well just relax and forget about trying to be obedient. After all, if I cannot obey to God's satisfaction anyway, why bother trying . . . right?

Wrong, of course.

Actually, this is the moment when obedience becomes most necessary. Jewish readers may wonder what it is that Christians feel they are obedient *to*, since we deliberately ignore many provisions of the Torah. I will address that question in the next chapter. Here it is enough to say I believe that if I have truly submitted myself to God's will, obedience becomes unavoidable, because my acceptance of the Lord's grace fills me with a compulsive desire to please him by obeying. Indeed, an ardently obedient life is a sure sign of a loving acceptance of God's grace. As Jesus said:

> If you love me, you will obey what I command.
>
> —John 14:15

To put a slightly different spin on my earlier discussion with Alan, we don't obey to *earn* God's love; we obey in *response* to God's love. And so, as with every biblical paradox, the truth stands in the center: it is not works *or* grace; it is works *and* grace, in a mutually supportive cycle.

First-century Jews who believed in Jesus felt the confusion of this idea hitting home with tremendous force. For centuries they had lived with the certainty of a covenant with God, an agreement that was sealed by one specific ritual at his command:

> You are to undergo circumcision, and it will be the sign of the covenant between me and you.
>
> —Genesis 17:11

Circumcision is the physical symbol of the Jews' special relationship with God. For a Jewish man, its symbolic power is akin to that of slipping on a wedding ring. No other action in a Jewish man's life holds quite the same importance. But even this most fundamental requirement of Moses' law—this most fundamental "work"—was called into question with the coming of Jesus:

> For in Christ Jesus neither circumcision nor uncircumcision has any value. The only thing that counts is faith expressing itself through love.
>
> —Galatians 5:6

The paradox of grace *and* works is something Paul surely must have recognized. After all, this same man who wrote that circumcision has no value was himself a circumcised Jew. Moreover, he was a circumcised Jew who had personally circumcised Timothy, his friend and recent convert to Christianity![6] So apparently, even after committing himself to Jesus, Paul saw a benefit to circumcision in some cases. But he also knew that a few Jews in the early church believed circumcision itself actually influenced reconciliation with God, as if it were a magic ritual that somehow forced God's hand. Paul understood how wrong they were. In his letter to the Roman Christians, he wrote the following:

> A man is not a Jew if he is only one outwardly, nor is circumcision merely outward and physical. No, a man is a Jew if he is one inwardly; and circumcision is *circumcision of the heart*, by the Spirit, not by the written code. Such a man's praise is not from men, but from God.
>
> —Romans 2:28–29 (emphasis mine)

Paul's point is that when it comes to lasting harmony with the Lord, just one kind of circumcision really matters: the cutting away of guilt for sin that only God can do. Is this a new theology that Paul invented on his own? Absolutely not. It is straight from the Torah:

> *The Lord your God will circumcise your hearts* and the hearts of your descendants, so that you may love him with all your heart and with all your soul, and live.
>
> —Deuteronomy 30:6 (emphasis mine)[7]

6. Acts 16:1–3.
7. See also Romans 2:25–29.

So what appeared to be a paradox is really a cycle. I go from law to grace to law again. But because I am still an imperfect person, I continue to disobey the law from time to time. That means I never cease to rely upon God's grace, and so the cycle continues.

> It can be proved by the Torah, the Prophets and the other sacred writings, that man is led along the road he wishes to follow.
>
> —Makkot, 10b

As I read those words, again it seems that Rabbinic Judaism and Christianity are far closer than I once thought. Christianity says if I love Jesus I will obey his teaching. Judaism says if I wish to follow I will be led along the road. In both cases, faith by the grace of God leads to obedience to God. On the other hand, if I rely on God's grace as if it were an excuse to disobey him, the Lord will stay far from me, which leads to even less concern about heartfelt morality and ethics, which leads to even more disobedience, which takes me even farther from God. One cycle spirals up, the other spirals down. I am free to choose the road I wish to follow and then I am led along it, either downward by my foolish pride or upward by the grace of God.

Obviously, I want to take the upward route and find the fulfillment only God can offer. But questions still remain. How do I get started? Is there a beginning to the cycle, or can I step into the loop through either portal: grace or law?

Because Paul said "the law was put in charge to lead us to Christ," and because the Talmud says the Torah "serves to guide the students on their way," at first I lean toward the theory that one enters this cycle through the law, or Torah. But then I stumble across these verses:

> I have no need of a bull from your stall or of goats from your pens, for every animal of the forest is mine, and the cattle on a thousand hills.
>
> —Psalms 50:9–10

Reading these words, I realize that the animals and grain on the tabernacle altar were not really offered by the people at all. Those sacrifices came from God and belonged to God all along.

When I go to the bank to withdraw my money, I do not owe the banker a debt of gratitude because he gives me what is already mine. Because I entrusted my money with him for safekeeping, it is his duty to hand it over when I ask. In fact, he should be grateful for my business, without which he would be unable to make a living.

In the same way, the people of Israel merely functioned as caretakers of the material blessings that God had gracefully provided. The foolish among them believed they were somehow buying divine forgiveness with the goats or bulls they brought to the tabernacle altar, much like a banker thinking he is purchasing my patronage by returning my own money. But there were wiser people in Israel who felt humble gratitude for the undeserved loan of the offering and returned it in a spirit of thankfulness.

The Torah's very existence is a gift from God. Therefore, even if the Torah guides me to a humble acceptance of God's grace as a result of my attempts (and failures) to obey the law, I cannot say my decision to obey the law was the first step in the process. The Lord first had to provide the gift of the Torah, or there would have been no law to obey. As the Torah says, "The Lord will circumcise your hearts . . . so that you may love him. . . ." So it is only by the grace of God that I feel such a strong instinct to search God out at all.

The timing of God's grace pops up when thinking about forgiveness as well. At Chever Torah, Rabbi Sheldon Zimmerman quotes the following story to explain a classic Jewish view:

> Two strangers, one rich, one poor, were traveling together. One took an immediate dislike to the other, and verbally abused him for the entire trip. When they arrived at their mutual destination, both made their ways separately to the same synagogue, where the abusive man was mortified to find that the poor person he had insulted on the road was a guest rabbi. After the service, the man approached the rabbi and begged forgiveness. The rabbi refused.

"But rabbi," said the man, "Aren't we required to forgive?" The
rabbi replied, "Yes, but I am not the man you insulted. Go apologize to a poor man on a train."

Rabbi Zimmerman explains the moral of this story: repentance
must be offered from a sense of genuine regret and humility,
never as a self-serving tactic. So far, I agree. But then the rabbi
goes on to say that until genuine repentance is offered, forgiveness *cannot* be given in return. The first steps toward reconciliation are up to the wrongdoer. The final step is in the hands of the
one who was wronged. That is the predominant Jewish position.

According to Jesus, however, this is not true when it comes to
God's forgiveness. If divine forgiveness depended on my confession, repentance, and reparation, that would make it something
to be earned, a quid pro quo arrangement, like paying a fee for
the banker's services. But when everything I possess is a gift from
God, I have nothing of my own to offer in payment. I am not a
cause; I am an effect—a creature, not the Creator. If the Lord de-
cides to forgive me, it will be for reasons of his own, not because
I purchased forgiveness with my actions, no matter how humble,
sincere, or benign.

Who has a claim against me that I must pay? Everything under
heaven belongs to me.

—Job 41:11

So although it may sometimes appear that I have taken the
first step toward God of my own free will, in reality he was there
all along, guiding me home. I am drawn to the Lord by his grace
alone—first, last, and always.

It goes before the unwilling to make him willing; it follows the
willing to make him effectual.

—Augustine[8]

This brings me to yet another reason why I believe in Jesus.

8. *Enchiridion on Faith, Hope and Love*, p. 40.

Most major religions suggest that intimacy with God can be obtained by following a specific teaching, such as the four noble truths of Buddhism, or the *dharma* (right way of living) of Hinduism, or the five pillars of Islam. But if a relationship with the Lord is possible only by virtue of God's grace, then the teaching of these religions simply cannot be true. Intimacy with God can never be "obtained"; it can only be received as a gift from God.

The importance of this idea becomes clearer when I realize that Jesus stands alone as the only founder of a major religion who said he was God. Buddha, Confucius, and Muhammad never made that claim. And of course, neither did Moses. Jesus' assertion that "no one comes to the Father except through me" has all the hallmarks of megalomania unless he and the Father are one and the same. If he were just another holy man founding a new religion, it would be an outrageous thing to say. But if Jesus is really the Creator of the universe, he was simply stating the obvious: the only way I can find intimacy with God is by the grace of God.

There was a time when I felt empty and alone, even among the best of friends and family. I did my best to be good enough for God, but I was a slave to pride and disobedience. Finally I realized that only Jesus—only God—could liberate me from my personal bondage in Egypt. Jesus alone carried me on eagle's wings and brought me to himself. To paraphrase one of his most hotly disputed statements: "No one comes to the Lord except through God." Today, in loving appreciation, I try to respond by obeying the Lord's Torah, but I also try very hard to always remember that even my meager obedience comes from him.

Jewish readers may wonder how I can say that I try to obey the Torah, when like almost all Christians, I do not observe many of the commands in the law of Moses. It is a fair question, which I will address in the next chapter. But before moving on, it is important to note that my friend Alan and I discovered something important today.

I was surprised to find that Alan agreed with the idea that grace is essential to faith, and he was surprised when I agreed that observance of the *mitzvot* of the Torah can inspire reconciliation with God. The fact that it took so many conversations before each of us really heard what the other was saying speaks volumes about the stubborn tendency of our religions to focus on preconceived notions instead of really listening to each other. But in the end, Alan and I learned a great deal about grace and works from each other. All of which makes me wonder, if I listened more and assumed less, what else could I learn?

eight

# The Small Print

Everything follows the intention of the heart.
—Tosefta Yebamot, 2

It is about one year since I discovered Chever Torah. I decide to teach a class on the Hebrew Scriptures every Sunday at my church, to try to transfer what I am learning at temple to a Christian venue. Soon, a Jewish man begins attending. In him I sense a kindred spirit, since he has boldly come to a church to learn the basis for Christian beliefs directly from Christians, just as I attend Chever Torah to learn about Judaism straight from Jews. One Sunday he approaches me after class and asks, "Why are some Torah commandments observed by Christians, while others are not?"

The question does not surprise me. It is essentially the reverse of a question I longed to ask when I first began attending Chever Torah: Why do Jews cling to so many ancient laws and traditions?

Both questions flow from the "grace versus works" debate discussed in the previous chapter. In view of the Christian belief explained there—that faith in Jesus leads to a heartfelt desire to obey God's Torah—many Jews wonder why Christians do not obey the Mosaic Law more rigorously, joining them in keeping kosher and so forth. For that matter, even Christians sometimes wonder why our tradition allows us to ignore many commandments in the Hebrew Scriptures. After all, Jesus had this to say on the subject:

> Do not think that I have come to abolish the Law or the Prophets; I have not come to abolish them but to fulfill them. I tell you the truth, until heaven and earth disappear, not the smallest letter, not the least stroke of a pen, will by any means disappear from the Law until everything is accomplished.
>
> —Matthew 5:17–18

But Christians also wonder why Jews have "added" so many traditions to the Torah with their Talmud, when the Scriptures themselves say we must not add to the Torah or subtract from it.[1]

These are valid and natural questions. Chever Torah kinds of questions. And in searching for answers I again learn that the differences between us are not as great as I once thought.

I can think of five reasons why Christians do not strictly observe large portions of the Mosaic Law. First, those commandments explicitly made in the written Torah must be separated from those in the oral Torah. The oral Torah is a group of verbal traditions handed down through the generations and eventually codified in the Talmud. Jews do not see the Talmud as an addition to the Scriptures; they see it as a divinely inspired elaboration on the sacred text. But while Judaism teaches that Moses received the oral Torah along with the Pentateuch on Mt. Sinai,[2] Christians do not agree, just as most Jews do not believe God in-

---

1. Deuteronomy 4:2.

2. According to an article entitled "Written Law" in *The Encyclopedia of the Jewish Religion*, p. 405, this belief is based partially upon Exodus 34:27 which can be literally translated: "Write thou these words, for according to the mouth of these words I have made a covenant . . . ." The idea of two Torahs, written and oral, is found in the phrases "write thou" and "according to the mouth."

spired the New Testament. So Christians do not follow the traditional rules contained in the Talmud because we do not believe they came from God. But we do believe the written Torah is of God, and try to obey its commands in our own way, as I will soon explain.

Second, both Jews and Christians do not observe many of the Torah's commandments because they can only be obeyed at the temple in Jerusalem, but of course that temple was destroyed about forty-six years after the crucifixion of Jesus. I have often pondered the timing of this event. For me it is yet another basis for Christian faith. I believe it is possible the temple was destroyed at precisely the moment in history when the news about Jesus' passion and resurrection was finally delivered to every Jew on earth. The temple was not destroyed earlier, since that would have breached the covenant between God and those Jews who had not yet heard the "good news." Conversely, if the temple remained in place beyond that moment, Jesus' claim to be the fulfillment of the rituals practiced there would ring less true, because it seems unlikely that God would allow the prophetic symbolism to continue when the thing symbolized had actually come.

This leads me to the third reason why Christians do not observe many of the Torah's commands. At Chever Torah, I learned about *mishpatim* and *chukim,* two terms often found together in the Torah, and translated as "laws" and "decrees."[3] Some of the Talmud's rabbis believed these corresponded to two distinct legal classifications: casuistic law and apodictic law.[4] Casuistic law is case law, the kind we live by in daily life, the kind that is derived in response to known circumstances. I must not steal, lie, or murder, for example, and the reason for these prohibitions is self-evident from long experience. But apodictic law is different. There is no clear explanation for such a law. It is simply ordered on the authority of God or the whim of a king or dictator, and I obey without understanding the rationale behind the command.

---

3. See Leviticus 18:4, for example.

4. Rabbi W. Gunther Plaut, *The Torah, A Modern Commentary* (New York: Union of American Hebrew Congregations, 1981), p. 566.

In the Torah, there are many such unexplained, incomprehensible laws, most of them connected directly with sacrifice or, like those in the so-called "holiness code," arising as prerequisites for the offering of a sacrifice. Jews from Moses to the time of Jesus obeyed these laws not because they understood them, but simply because God had so commanded. In an admirable demonstration of their reverence for the Lord, many Jews still obey some portions of the Torah without understanding the purpose of the commands. But Christians believe these laws were actually prophetic rituals laced with symbolism, designed to make God's identity more clear when he later entered human history as a humble Jewish carpenter.

Although they disagreed that the carpenter was the divine messiah, some of the Talmud's rabbis apparently also viewed these kinds of laws as temporary measures, pending a coming change:

> The ritual and ceremonial commandments will be abolished in the future that is to be.
>
> —Niddah, 61b

Christianity teaches that the prophecy contained in the sacrificial and holiness rituals was fulfilled with Jesus' death and resurrection. This is what Jesus meant when he said nothing in the law would disappear until everything had been accomplished. Since we believe those laws were really prophetic, and since the prophecy has now been accomplished, there is no longer any need to follow them. As I have already observed, symbolism becomes redundant when the real thing comes along.

The fourth reason why Christians do not observe many of the Torah's commandments in meticulous detail involves the fact that Jesus taught a different method to reach the same goal. From the very beginning of Jesus' ministry on earth, this has been a point of contention between Christianity and Judaism, but oddly enough it is actually an area that can bring us closer together when both positions are fully understood.

The rabbis of the Talmud, recognizing the extreme difficulty of observing all of God's commands, chose to defend against disobedience with an approach they called "a fence around the Torah." The phrase might be derived from idea that there was a fence around the Garden of Eden, because the Hebrew word *gan*, translated in Genesis as "garden," is also related to a word that means "fence" or "hedge." This Talmudic concept adds requirements and prohibitions not specifically found in the written Torah, with the intention of keeping a person far from any situation where it might be possible to violate the core Torah commands.

The metaphor of a fence is quite appropriate. At the zoo there are signs warning me not to climb the low fences surrounding the cages of dangerous animals. These signs are not intended to save me from falling off the low fence; rather, they exist to keep me from the danger of sharp claws that can be thrust through the bars of the next barrier, which is the cage itself. In the same way, the traditions of the Talmud, which sometimes seem extreme and legalistic to Christian minds, become more understandable when I consider their intention: to keep Jews from stepping close to the temptation of violating a Torah commandment.

For example, I used to be perplexed by the Talmud's "fence around the Torah" prohibition against using the same container to store or cook dairy and meat products. It seemed an unnecessary addition to the Scriptures. But the tradition began to make sense when I realized it is simply a way to ensure obedience to the Torah's command not to cook a baby goat in its mother's milk.[5] Most Christians observe similar "fence around the Torah" prohibitions. For example, so far as I know, the Bible contains no specific prohibition against watching a sexual act. But I have a personal "law" against watching movies with explicit sex scenes, because I believe watching them could eventually break down my inner barriers to adultery. If one takes the commandment against boiling a lamb in its mother's milk as seriously as the command not to commit adultery, then the Talmud prohibition against using the same pot for dairy and meat becomes similar to my decision to avoid risqué movies.

The controversy I mentioned earlier arose when Jesus taught a different method to improve our chances of obedience. In a way, his is the opposite approach. And just as Christians misunderstand the Talmud's intention, Jews frequently fail to appreciate the rationale behind the Christian system. It is simply this:

5. Exodus 34:26.

rather than propose a fence around the outside of the Torah, Jesus teaches that we should solve the problem from the inside out, by holding the beast back from the bars of his cage, so to speak. While the Talmud supplies many rules to avoid breaking one in the Torah, Jesus offers single commandments to summarize and replace many others. For example, he warns that "lust in the heart" is actually adultery. If I concentrate on refusing to think sexually about anyone other than my spouse, I need not concern myself with the many Torah laws that forbid sex with various other people. One command yields the same effect as a dozen or more. This is also true of the entire class of Torah commandments concerning conflicts between persons. Jesus teaches that unrighteous anger is equivalent to murder, and forbids me to allow such anger to control my actions. Thus, anything that engenders or flows from anger (physical or verbal fights, revenge, etc.) is forbidden on a de facto basis, and another large class of Torah law becomes redundant if this one command is obeyed.

But even these kinds of comprehensive commandments—no adulterous lust, no unrighteous anger—become unnecessary when Jesus sums up the law and the prophets by quoting the Torah's commandments to "love the Lord your God with all your heart, mind, and soul," and "love your neighbor as yourself." Here are strong parallels with Judaism. As I have already mentioned, Rabbi Hillel, one of the most famous teachers of the Talmud, agreed that the first of these commands summarized the entire Torah, and called the rest of the Scriptures "commentary" on this one command. By implication then, Hillel might also agree with the Christian notion that if I were successful in loving God wholeheartedly, I would not need to concern myself with the balance of the Torah's commands because my love for God would keep me far from all disobedience. In other words, if I love God wholeheartedly, obedience to the other commands will follow naturally.

Of course, few can live without feeling adulterous lust or unrighteous anger from time to time, and absolutely no one can live every day with a wholehearted love for God or their neighbor. But neither can a person live in perfect conformance to the Talmud's "fence around the Torah."

Which brings me to the fifth answer to the question of why some Torah commandments are observed by Christians while others are not. In the Tanakh, I find that God "puts" his Spirit "on" certain people (Joshua and David for example). The Holy Spirit also departs from some people, or is "on" them only for limited times and reasons.[6] But Jesus promises that those who trust in him will receive the presence of the Holy Spirit in a new and permanent way.[7] Christians believe the Holy Spirit now lives within our hearts in exactly the same way the Spirit or *Shekinah* once lived within the tabernacle in the midst of the Hebrew camp. We believe this "indwelling of the Spirit" changes us from persons who are comfortable with sin, into "new creatures" whose fundamental desire is now to be obedient.[8] This core change of our nature is what we mean when we talk about being "born again."[9] It is not a uniquely Christian concept, but has its roots in a promise found in the Hebrew Scriptures:

> I will give you a new heart and put a new spirit in you; I will remove from you your heart of stone and give you a heart of flesh. And I will put my Spirit in you to move you to follow my decrees and be careful to keep my laws.
>
> —Ezekiel 36:26–27

Just as the Shekinah's presence in the camp once inspired the people of Israel to obedience, Christians believe the Holy Spirit guides our obedience to God's will. This means another large class of Torah law became redundant for Christians: those laws that were intended to reinforce love for God and a sense of connection with him. If God's Holy Spirit is within my heart working to increase my commitment to him, no external command could improve upon his divine effort.

This further explains a paradox mentioned in the previous chapter: How can the New Testament say that circumcision no longer has any value one way or another, when the Torah re-

---

6. Compare for example, 1 Samuel 11:6 where Saul receives the Spirit for the second time (the first being 1 Samuel 10:10), and 1 Samuel 16:14 where the Spirit departs from him.

7. John 14:16–17.

8. Romans 7:6.

9. 1 Corinthians 3:16; 6:19; Ephesians 2:18–22.

quires it as a condition of covenant with God? Christians believe part of the answer is because Jesus fulfilled this prophecy:

> "The time is coming," declares the Lord, "when I will make a new covenant with the house of Israel and with the house of Judah. It will not be like the covenant I made with their forefathers when I took them by the hand to lead them out of Egypt, because they broke my covenant, though I was a husband to them," declares the Lord. "This is the covenant I will make with the house of Israel after that time," declares the Lord. "I will put my law in their minds and write it on their hearts. I will be their God, and they will be my people."
>
> —Jeremiah 31:31–33

Christians believe the Holy Spirit's effect on our hearts is an extension of the covenant of circumcision between Abraham and the Father, making physical circumcision unnecessary, much as the rituals of sacrifice and ritual purity are unnecessary, because again, when the real thing comes along, symbolism becomes redundant. And as a Christian, it seems to me Jeremiah's prophecy that the Lord will put his law in my mind and write it in my heart dovetails perfectly with Jesus' "inside out" approach to obedience, versus the Talmud's "fence around the Torah."

Most Jewish readers will disagree with that final thought, of course, and many Christian readers will object at first glance with the Talmud's "fence around the Torah" concept. But surprisingly, I have found that this is yet another area where Judaism and Christianity are closer together than I once believed.

For example, I have already compared the separate dairy and meat provisions of the Talmud to a Christian's common sense decision to avoid racy movies, but the parallels even extend to formal teachings in the church. Until twenty or thirty years ago, the Southern Baptist denomination of my youth had strict prohibitions against dancing and coed swimming. These rules were intended to build a fence around the Torah's commandments against adultery, exactly as the traditions of the Talmud do.

Similarly, the Christian idea that some laws are no longer appropriate for some people should ring true in Reform Jewish ears. One of the early thinkers in that movement, Abraham Geiger, proposed two concepts that have become pillars of Reform Judaism. First, he said that revelation is not static, but continues throughout the generations, right down to today. Second, Rabbi Geiger said this means Jews must be free to apply the knowledge of modern generations to their understanding of Rabbinic Judaism.[10] A fundamental tenet of Reform Judaism springing from Geiger's propositions is the idea that each individual Jew should select which *mitzvot* are appropriate for him or her, based on his or her own experience with God. This is an extremely close parallel to the Christian position that some laws are no longer applicable to our lives.

The similarities between our religions continue when I note that the rabbis of the Talmud often acknowledged the concept of sins of the heart, as in this quote:

> The first step in transgression is the evil thought.
> —Derek Eretz Zuta, ch. 6

It is worth remembering in this context that Rabbinic Judaism calls an entire class of human instinct "the evil *impulse*." While the degree of emphasis that Jesus and the rabbis placed on sins of the heart differs strongly, there is agreement on the concept. And Jesus' teaching reveals an underlying goal identical with the Talmud: both approaches focus on preemptive measures, heading off potential disobedience to the *mitzvot* of Torah long before the evil impulse is translated into action. This fact is particularly important to understand and explore in the area of our responses to the Mosaic Law, since misunderstandings on the subject have so often formed the basis of bitter divisions between Christians and Jews.

Given this new understanding, I often ponder the irony of the widely held Jewish notion that Christianity takes the easier path

10. Rabbi Ben Isaacson and Deborah Wigoder, *The International Jewish Encyclopedia* (Englewood Cliffs: Prentice Hall, 1973), p. 255.

by discarding much of the Torah's rigorous discipline. On the contrary, difficult as it is to act in accordance with the many rigorous laws of the Talmud, it seems to me a much more demanding thing to stop my nerves themselves from transmitting sinful impulses within my brain. Yet that is what Jesus commands in his famous Sermon on the Mount, which is essentially a commentary on the *parasha Mishpatim* (the portion of Exodus the rabbis called "Laws"). A comparison of Exodus 22 and 23 and Matthew 5 will demonstrate that Jesus' followers live under very strenuous requirements far above those commanded through Moses. In his sermon, Jesus raises the standard of behavior from "do not strike" to "don't even be angry enough to strike"; from "execute kidnappers" to "go an extra mile with them"; from "take life for life" to "turn the other cheek"; from "do not seduce" to "do not even lust"; from "charge no interest" to "give away your money"; from "return your neighbor's property" to "give him your property"; from "be kind to an enemy's livestock" to "love your enemy."[11]

Earlier in this book I explained that Christianity views the Torah in part as an object lesson in my inability to save myself from the corrupting influence of evil through my own actions. The logic goes like this: since the Torah says over fifty times that I must obey *all*—*kol*—of its commands, and since that is something no one can do, and since God surely knew such a thing was humanly impossible long before the Torah was written, then at least one of the reasons for the Torah's existance must be to teach me about my helplessness before temptation. But now comes Jesus with even greater demands. It is as if he wants to put an end once and for all to the fantasy that I can somehow become holy enough to approach God through my own efforts.

The rabbinic idea of building a fence around the Torah strikes me as a hopelessly complicated strategy, and I can always blame my failure to obey on that. After all, I cannot even remember all the laws of the written Torah in the heat of the moment. How can I possibly remember all the others in the oral Torah? Then Jesus

11. Compare Exodus 21:12 to Matthew 5:21–22; Exodus 21:23–25 to Matthew 5:41; Exodus 22:16 to Matthew 5:28; Exodus 22:25 to Matthew 5:42; Exodus 22:26–27 to Matthew 5:40; and Exodus 23:4–5 to Matthew 5:44.

removed my excuse by narrowing down the law to one simple command: love unconditionally.

But I cannot even do that.

I have tried to answer my Jewish friend's question about why Christians do not observe all of the Torah's commandments by comparing the teachings of Jesus and the rabbis. As so often happens, in thinking through my answer I learned that there are as many similarities between Judaism and Christianity as there are differences between us. But one difference cannot be avoided, because it stands at the foundation of Christianity itself. And in order to fully answer my friend's question, that difference must be explained.

On this unusually cold winter morning at Chever Torah, Rabbi Stern is leading a fascinating discussion of the role of faith and action in a believer's life. I am struggling to follow his reasoning on a particularly difficult point, when he quotes the following famous Hasidic commentator:

> In fact everything comes from Torah, and she is the one who blesses both that which comes before her and that which follows her, since all the world was created for Torah.
>
> —Rebbe Yehudah Aryeh Leib Alter[12]

In the earlier chapter on God's self-limitations, I discovered the belief, common to Judaism and Christianity, that the universe was created and continues to exist through the power of God's word, which is seen as identical with the Torah. Rabbinic Judaism teaches that the Torah and the wisdom mentioned in Proverbs as the "craftsman at [God's] side" are identical.[13] In the quote above, Rebbe Alter underscores this idea with the words "everything comes from Torah," but he also links that concept with something new by stating "all the world was created for To-

---

12. Quoted by Arthur Green, *The Language of Truth*, trans. Shai Gluskin (Philadelphia: Jewish Publication Society, 1998), p. 111. Note: Hasidic Jews use the yiddish word "rebbe" instead of the word "rabbi".

13. Proverbs 8:30.

rah." After Chever Torah, I ask Rabbi Stern to explain. He says, "This means the world was created to enable obedience to the Torah."

At my Sunday school class the following day I mention this concept, and Bob, a devout Christian and impressive New Testament scholar, promptly reminds me of the following verses:

> For by him all things were created: things in heaven and on earth, visible and invisible, whether thrones or powers or rulers or authorities; all things were created by him and for him. He is before all things, and in him all things hold together.
>
> —Colossians 1:16–17

Here is a surprising connection between Jewish and Christian theology. The Colossians quote refers to Jesus of course, and Rebbe Alter's quote refers to Torah, but the parallel is impossible to ignore. What can it mean?

In Christianity, there is a mystical link between Jesus and the creative aspect of the Word of God:

> In the beginning was the Word, and the Word was with God, and the Word was God. He was with God in the beginning. Through him all things were made; without him nothing was made that has been made.
>
> —John 1:1–3

I quoted the above verses earlier in this book in a different context. Now they take on an additional meaning when connected with the following:

> The Word became flesh and made his dwelling among us. We have seen his glory, the glory of the One and Only, who came from the Father, full of grace and truth.
>
> —John 1:14

For Christians, this "Word" by which God created the universe is the preincarnate Jesus. And just as Rebbe Alter visualizes a world in which "everything comes from Torah" and says, "all the world was created for Torah," the apostle Paul sees a world created "by him and for him."

I have known these verses from the Gospel of John for most of my life, but it never occurred to me to take them literally. Now, thanks to Chever Torah and the odd parallel between Paul's words in Colossians and those of Rebbe Alter, I begin to wonder—Is it possible that Jesus and Torah are somehow one and the same?

A local community college has invited Rabbi Stern and Dr. George Mason, the minister who spoke at my very first Chever Torah, to discuss Judaism and Christianity in an informal way in their auditorium. The event is open to the public, so I have come to hear what these two men of God have to say.

They sit on stage in comfortable chairs. On the low table between them are a pitcher of water and two glasses. After the introduction by the dean of the college, they begin talking to each other as if the audience of several hundred people is not here, and we are treated to a rare glimpse into the parallel universes of Judaism and Christianity. Everything these two brilliant men have to say interests me, but at one point their conversation flows into comparisons between the Jewish view of Torah and the Christian view of Jesus. I lean forward, fascinated. After the discussion is over, Rabbi Stern and Dr. Mason field questions from the audience. I raise my hand.

"Could you speak some more about the similar ideas of the world being created by and for Torah, and by and for Jesus?" I ask.

Dr. Mason's answer explores the Christian view of Jesus as Creator, but Rabbi Stern responds by saying, "I'm a little worried there might be a sense of Christianity trying to co-opt Judaism here."

This surprises me. After all, Paul's quote about Jesus precedes Rebbe Alter's teaching on the Torah by many centuries (although I doubt the Rebbe had Paul's idea in mind). And it seems to me that Christianity and Rabbinic Judaism are theological branches from a common tree, which is the religion of Moses. We have different Scriptures, but they were written at almost the same time and are to some extent both commentaries on the books of Moses. So if there is any "co-opting" going on, surely it is Christianity and Rabbinic Judaism both absorbing a common ancestor.

Suddenly it occurs to me that this very fact might explain the similarity between the comments of Paul and Rebbe Leib.

While these thoughts rumble around in my mind, Dr. Mason is speaking on a different level. "We have to remember that Jesus said, 'While heaven and earth remain, no part of the Torah will disappear until all is accomplished.' And," says Dr. Mason with a smile, "we also must remember he is not a 'Jesus come lately.'" Everyone laughs, but I wonder if most of the Jews in the audience understand what he means. Dr. Mason continues. "Christians believe Jesus was present at the creation of the universe, just as we agree with Judaism that the Torah has existed since the dawn of time. There's no sense of competition. In fact, on a certain level, there's no sense of difference."

Never one to back away from an idea no matter how controversial or difficult, Rabbi Stern responds, "But if the Word and Jesus were the same, why would we need them both?"

It is a very good question. A Chever Torah kind of question.

We delve deeper into this mystical area a few weeks later at Chever Torah, while discussing God's self-revelations on Mt. Sinai.

When the Israelites stood at the foot of the mountain, the Lord revealed himself in thunder and lightning at the top of the mountain, shaking the earth itself until all the people trembled with fear. That is one aspect of God. But later, when Elijah encountered the same God on the same mountain, the Lord revealed himself with a "still, small voice."[14] According to Maimonides, Moses ascended Mt. Sinai to receive the Torah, heard human words, and wrote them down like a secretary taking dictation. But Israel at the bottom of the same mountain saw nothing but a cloud of fire and heard nothing but a thunderous roar.

The unapproachable thunder and the more accessible Torah were two manifestations of the same God. Christians believe this

14. Compare Exodus 19:16 to 1 Kings 19:12.

is also true of the Torah and of Jesus. If the Torah is a thunderous roar, Jesus is a still, small voice. But both have the same message. So in a way, one could say we Christians do not observe all 613 *mitzvot* of the Torah, because we *do* observe them. We believe that Jesus is God, which means obeying Jesus is obeying God's Torah.

And the Word was with God, and the Word was God.

Like a loving father who expresses his affection to his children with both firm discipline and the gentle example of his own life, the Lord tries to communicate with me on every possible level. For my mind he gives me Torah, but Jesus came for my heart. Why do I need them both? Perhaps for the same reason Israel needed both thunder and a still, small voice. The Master of the universe wants to be very, very sure I understand.

# nine

# Up from the Well

God decided to leave man's conduct to his own free choice, and if
he had not sinned he would have been immortal.

—Bereshit Rabbah, 8, 11

We have been studying forgiveness at Chever Torah today. After
the rabbi leaves, I remain seated at my table with five Jews, discussing what we learned. One of them is Alan, the man who
helped me learn about God's grace over a cup of coffee a few
months ago. He tells an interesting story. It seems Alan's son
lives with Alan's ex-wife, who is raising the boy as an Orthodox
Jew. A couple of weeks ago the boy rose early, donned his
yarmulke and tallis, said his morning prayers, and padded bare-
foot to the kitchen to get a glass of milk. The sun was barely up
and it was a cloudy day, so the room was dark and gloomy. On
his way to the refrigerator, Alan's son absent-mindedly flipped
the light switch. Only then, in the cheery incandescent light, did
he notice his mother already seated at the kitchen table.

"Did you forget it's Shabbat?" she asked.

The boy went pale. Forgetting the glass of milk, he fell into a nearby chair and dropped his head into his hands, moaning, "What did I do?"

His mother looked at him, proud that he took this so seriously, yet concerned that he not reproach himself too harshly. "It will be okay," she said.

Looking up, he said, "How can I make it right?"

"You're already doing the first part. You've admitted it, and you're obviously very sorry."

"Oh yes!" cried the boy.

"Okay. So now you must make amends," she said, nodding. "Then Hashem[1] will forgive."

"But how? I'll do anything!"

The boy's mother thought for a moment, then said, "Think of a new mitzvah to add to those you're already observing."

Puzzled, the boy stared at her for a moment. Then, understanding, he sprang up saying, "I know just the thing!" he ran back to his bedroom, sat on the bed, and opened his Torah, determined to read it for ten minutes every morning before breakfast from then on.

All the Jews listening to this story seem to understand at once, but I am confused. Alan patiently explains that his son switched the lights on during the Sabbath. For Orthodox Jews, this is the sin of working ("lighting a fire") on Shabbat.[2]

"Okay," I say, "But what was his mother talking about?"

"She told him he had already taken the first two steps toward forgiveness," said Alan. "That's to confess the sin to God and then to resolve to never commit that sin again."

"But what about the mitzvah thing?"

"That was her suggestion of how my son could make up for what he did. By adding another commandment to those he's already trying to observe."

With this story and explanation, I am introduced to the classic Jewish threefold response to sin. First, I must admit that what I did was wrong. This is called confession. Then I must resolve never to do it again. This is called repentance. And finally, I must

1. The Orthodox substitute for using God's name or speaking the word "god." It means, "the name."
2. Exodus 35:3.

try to make things right again. This is called reparation. Some Jews would add other steps such as "recognize the sin," and "refrain from repeating the sin," but others see these as contained in the concepts of confession and repentence.

Once again I am surprised to find that Judaism and Christianity are closer than I thought. Both religions agree completely with the first two steps in the process, and while we disagree on important details regarding the third, we all acknowledge the need for reparation.

But now a Chever Torah kind of question comes to mind: Why is *any* process necessary, when God could simply shrug off human disobedience?

Suppose I have jumped into a deep well. If I refuse to admit that I am down in the well, how can I be convinced to grab a rope? Similarly, if I refuse to admit I am disobedient to the Lord, how can I hope for reconciliation? But I am embarrassed to find myself down here and frustrated that I cannot climb out on my own. So although God has dropped a rope and stands at the top ready to pull me up, I go to unusual lengths to ignore him. I pretend there is no rope. I pretend there is no well. I pretend I can climb out anytime I like without his blasted rope. I pretend I am supposed to be exactly where I am. Sometimes I even pretend that God is not really up there or not really willing and able to pull me out. Anything seems preferable to the humiliating admission that I am in a situation beyond my control. But until I admit that, how can I grab the rope? So this is why forgiveness first requires confession: to grab the rope, I must first realize that I need the rope. Confession is admitting that I have foolishly fallen into a bad situation. I am in trouble. I am helpless. I am wrong. Only then can I accept the help God offers.

Now, having confessed, I have the rope in my hands. But a question comes echoing down from the top of the well. God wants to know, "If I start to pull, will you hold on tight?"

The words translated as "repent" in both the Hebrew and the Greek Scriptures carry the connotation of "turning," that is, facing away from my past sinful behavior and back toward

God. I cannot hold the rope yet continue to simultaneously splash around in the muck and mire. Experience has shown that people who try to do both lose their grip and fall right back down. So repentance is agreeing to stop messing about. It is abandoning my sinful ways in order to give God and his rope my full attention. Fortunately, there is a benefit to all those ridiculous excuses I offered prior to grabbing the rope. It is this: now that I have admitted where I am, my pride is well and truly shattered, so when I look up at the small patch of sky and promise, "I won't do this any more," the promise rings true.

The rope tightens and, repentant, I ascend.

I used to believe the sole purpose of confession and repentance was to instill humility, as if God only cares about being in charge, like a bully demanding I "say uncle" before he lets me up. But at Chever Torah I have come to understand that confession motivates me to grab the rope and repentence inspires me to hold on tight. They are for my benefit, not God's. Remembering what I learned before in my study of why bad things happen to good people—remembering that even the Lord cannot make sense of nonsense in a logical universe—I suddenly see that even God cannot lift a person who does not grasp and hold the rope.

But of course, it is not really that simple.

The truth is, I have muddied the water with my floundering about below. I am covered with the muck and mire I stirred up. I have even swallowed some of the filthy stuff in my desperate attempts to escape on my own. So as I am drawn closer to God, a second question comes echoing down the shaft. "Can you leave this well the way you found it?"

It is a fair question. If someone pollutes a well, the only just and proper remedy is to restore the water to its former state of purity. It is not good enough to dig another well someplace else, and certainly not good enough to provide a new bucket and rope while leaving the water muddy down below. This is why the Hebrew Scriptures define justice as "life for life, eye for eye, tooth for tooth." The only real justice is perfect justice—returning things to exactly the way they were before.

All the judgments of the Holy One, blessed be he, are on the basis of measure for measure.

—Sanhedrin 90a[3]

So I dangle here, midway between disaster below and delivery above, wondering how in the world I am going to leave the well the way I found it. One thing is for sure: I must find a way. Since "the soul who sins is the one who will die," apparently my life depends upon it.[4]

Judaism and Christianity agree that four of the Ten Commandments apply specifically to sins directed against God, while six apply to sins against humanity. There is a clear distinction in the Torah between wrongs done against people and those done against the Lord. For example, idolatry—a direct offense against God—is punishable by immediate death, while theft of my neighbor's possessions merely results in a double repayment and a sacrifice.[5] Of course, many sermons and *midrashim* have arisen from the idea that a sin against a person is really a sin against God, because people are his possessions and are made in his image. But for some reason very few sermons and midrashim underscore the fact that there is no solution offered in the Torah for a deliberate sin against the Lord.

The Torah's regulations concerning animal sacrifice for "guilt" and "sin" offerings repeatedly state that these offerings are for *unintentional* sin.[6] When it comes to intentional disobedience to God, the Torah teaches this:

But anyone who sins defiantly, whether native-born or alien, blasphemes the Lord, and that person must be cut off from his people. Because he has despised the Lord's word and broken his com-

3. *Everyman's Talmud*, p. 111.
4. Ezekiel 18:4.
5. Example of death for idolatry: Exodus 32:27; punishment for theft: Exodus 22:7.
6. See, for example, Leviticus 4:2, 13, 22, 27; Leviticus 5:15, 18; Numbers 15:22, 24, 27–29. For differing responses to unintentional and intentional sins against man, see Deuteronomy 19:4–13.

mands, that person must surely be cut off; his guilt remains on him.

—Numbers 15:30–31

I note with dread the words "his guilt remains on him." Apparently, there is no chance of forgiveness for this person. But what does it mean for him to be "cut off from his people"? Perhaps to ensure that I understand the intention of those words, immediately following them the Torah offers this story by way of example:

> While the Israelites were in the desert, a man was found gathering wood on the Sabbath day. Those who found him gathering wood brought him to Moses and Aaron and the whole assembly, and they kept him in custody, because it was not clear what should be done to him. Then the Lord said to Moses, "The man must die. The whole assembly must stone him outside the camp." So the assembly took him outside the camp and stoned him to death, as the Lord commanded Moses.
>
> —Numbers 15:32–36

This man committed essentially the same sin as Alan's son—working on the Sabbath—yet he was killed, while my friend's son was simply advised to add another mitzvah to those he specifically sought to observe. Why such a wide variation of response?

Christianity teaches that God cares most about our intentions. While the boy switched on the light absent-mindedly, it is hardly possible that this man collected firewood during the Sabbath by mistake. Even if he stooped to pick up the first bit of wood without thinking about the fact that it was *Shabbat*, the man could not have continued that activity for long without noticing that he was the only one working in the entire camp. From an Orthodox Jewish perspective the boy sinned, but he did it unintentionally. The man committed a deliberate act of rebellion against God, and the Torah teaches that there is only one possible result of deliberate, intentional sin against God.

"The soul who sins is the one who will die."[7]

7. Ezekiel 18:4.

This reminds me of the puzzling Scripture I discovered in my earlier search for the significance of the *yetzer ha-ra* and original sin, the Scripture that deals with the man who merely thinks of sinning and thereby brings disaster on his entire people. Returning to that passage, I find these words:

> *The Lord will never be willing to forgive him;* his wrath and zeal will burn against that man. All the curses written in this book will fall upon him, and the Lord will blot out his name from under heaven.
>
> —Deuteronomy 29:20 (emphasis mine)[8]

Can it be possible that there are sins God will not forgive no matter what I do in atonement? The question lingers, and months later when I come across the following words, I believe I have found the answer:

> Have nothing to do with a false charge and do not put an innocent or honest person to death, for *I will not acquit the guilty.*
>
> —Exodus 23:7 (emphasis mine)

"His guilt remains on him."
"The Lord will never be willing to forgive him."
"I will not acquit the guilty."
It seems the Torah contains no way out for a person who, knowing what is right and what is wrong, deliberately chooses to disobey the Lord. But it is sour grapes to complain that God is unfair to be so stern, because in his Torah, the Lord offers fair warning many times, beginning in the earliest moments of humanity:

> You must not eat from the tree of the knowledge of good and evil, for when you eat of it you will surely die.
>
> —Genesis 2:17

Warnings like these were surely the inspiration for the apostle Paul's terse statement that "the wages of sin is death."[9] By using the term "wages," Paul implies that death is something I earned

---

8. Deuteronomy 29:19 in Jewish translations.
9. Romans 6:23.

deliberately, much as I would demand a paycheck for services rendered. His phrasing also implies that I might have earned a different lot had I lived a perfect life. The rabbis may have had this idea in mind when they said:

> Had man been perfect in everything he did, he might never have died, but would merely have been summoned to Heaven alive, as was Elijah.
>
> —Zohar, iii, 159.

All Christians and many Jews throughout the centuries have recognized that "the person who sins is the one who will die." Billions of bodies testify mutely from the grave that the curse Adam earned with his disobedience remains in place today, whether one believes in original sin or not. So as I dangle halfway up the well it seems there is no way I can leave things below the way I found them. And since I can do nothing about the muck and mire I stirred up, God demands I repay him in another way, with my very life.

At this point, the Jews of Chever Torah would probably respond that there is an exception to this bleak picture. It is the Day of Atonement, or Yom Kippur.[10] According to Rabbinic Judaism, this is the one ceremony that atones specifically for defiant sins against God. And indeed, the kind of sin forgiven on Yom Kippur is called *pesha*, which means "rebellion," or willful deviation from godly living. So although many verses in the Torah specifically say defiant sins will not be forgiven, it seems possible that Yom Kippur might make up for the mess I've made at the bottom of the well—possible, that is, except for one thorny theological problem.

In at least a dozen places, the Torah prohibits the performance of sacrificial rituals anywhere other than at the tabernacle altar (later, the altar at the temple in Jerusalem):

10. See Leviticus 16 for a description of the rituals, especially verses 16 and 21.

Be careful not to sacrifice your burnt offerings anywhere you please. Offer them only at the place the Lord will choose in one of your tribes, and there observe everything I command you.

—Deuteronomy 12:13–14[11]

But the altar at Jerusalem has been destroyed for almost two thousand years, just as Jesus foretold.[12] If the animal sacrifices of Yom Kippur are the only means in Torah to make reparation for defiant sins, and if the only place where Yom Kippur can be observed has been destroyed, what can I do to compensate God for my deliberate disobedience?

At Chever Torah, I learn that the rabbis of the Talmud were of course well aware of this dilemma. Ironically, their response led them to join the early church in rejecting the notion that the sacrificial death of animals at Yom Kippur was essential to the reconciliation process with God. To support this idea, the rabbis pointed to prophetic Scriptures like one I quoted earlier in this book:

I have no need of a bull from your stall or of goats from your pens, for every animal of the forest is mine, and the cattle on a thousand hills. I know every bird in the mountains, and the creatures of the field are mine. If I were hungry I would not tell you, for the world is mine, and all that is in it.

—Psalms 50:9–12[13]

Statements of this kind—and there are many similar ones in the Hebrew Scriptures—explain what should be obvious: God alone provides everything I possess, therefore offering a sacrifice as compensation for sins against him is like borrowing money from a victim in order to reimburse him for a crime. As the Talmud says:

God asks, "Has anyone ever given anything to me before I gave it to him?"

—Wayyikra Rabbah, 27, 2

11. For other examples of warnings not to offer sacrifices anywhere but at the tabernacle altar (later, the temple altar) see also Leviticus 1:3; 4:14, 18; 6:25–26; 17:3–4, 8–9; Deuteronomy 12:4–11; 16:11; 17:8; 26:2; 31:11; 2 Chronicles 7:5–6, 12.

12. Matthew 24:2.

13. See Isaiah 1:11 for another Scripture making the same point.

So when God wants to know, "Can you leave this well as you found it?" the answer must be that I cannot, because the simple truth is that everything I have to offer as compensation for the mess that I have made already belongs to God.

A second intention of the kind of prophetic verses quoted above is to condemn the type of superficial quid pro quo thinking about holiness and sacrifice that Jesus so consistently opposed. The tabernacle sacrifices were not payments to a divine Judge who could be bribed. This is very clearly stated in the Torah:

> For the Lord your God is God of gods and Lord of lords, the great God, mighty and awesome, who shows no partiality and accepts no bribes.
>
> —Deuteronomy 10:17

But if the animal sacrifices of Torah times were insufficient compensation for sins, why did Torah say God would forgive "rebellion" at Yom Kippur?

The prophets Micah and Hosea both explained the true path of reconciliation in the same way, and it is significant that both of them *contrasted* the path to atonement with the animal sacrificial system. First, Micah asked the question:

> With what shall I come before the Lord and bow down before the exalted God? Shall I come before him with burnt offerings, with calves a year old? Will the Lord be pleased with thousands of rams, with ten thousand rivers of oil? Shall I offer my firstborn for my transgression, the fruit of my body for the sin of my soul?
>
> —Micah 6:6–7

Then Micah provided the answer:

> He has showed you, O man, what is good. And what does the Lord require of you? To act justly and to love mercy and to walk humbly with your God.
>
> —Micah 6:8

When Hosea placed the solution in tension with animal sacrifice, the temple sacrifices came up short again:

For I desire mercy, not sacrifice, and acknowledgment of God
rather than burnt offerings.

—Hosea 6:6

Given Tanakh passages such as these, the early Christians and
many Talmudic rabbis believed the sacrifices of animals—even
the sacrifices of Yom Kippur—were never intended to atone for
deliberate sins against God. Rather, those sacrifices provided a
way for the people to show their humble and sincere desire to
repay God for the damage their sin had done, a desire that they
could not translate into fact. After that point of agreement, the
accord between the rabbis of the Talmud and the early Christians went no further. The tree growing up from Mosaic Judaism—the common root of both religions—forked into two distinct branches. For their part, the Talmudic rabbis took these
prophetic teachings to mean that atonement for human sin can
be achieved without the cost of death. Rabbinic Judaism most
often refers to the following verses to make this point:

Return, O Israel, to the Lord your God. Your sins have been your
downfall! Take words with you and return to the Lord. Say to him:
"Forgive all our sins and receive us graciously, that we may offer
the fruit of our lips."

—Hosea 14:1–2[14]

This, said the rabbis, is proof that the path to atonement for
sin does not require sacrificial death. Instead, I have heard it said
at Chever Torah that God will accept four things as compensation for human disobedience of his law: prayer, Torah study,
obedience to *mitzvot* (especially charity), and repentance combined with fasting. According to the rabbis, these are "the fruit
of our lips." This is exactly what the mother tried to teach the little boy who accidentally switched a light on during the Sabbath.

But it seems to me that the sequence of events in Hosea's passage does not support this thinking. First Israel is told to "return"
(that is, confess and repent), then to request forgiveness, then to
receive it by the grace of God, and only then is Israel told to "offer
the fruit of our lips." In other words, Hosea's "fruit of our lips"—

14. Verses 2–3 in Jewish translations.

Torah study, prayer, obedience to *mitzvot* and repentant fasting—comes only *after* forgiveness has already been received.

Now I recall my earlier exploration of the idea of holiness and purity, and the debate between Jesus and certain Pharisees over the question of external observance versus internal purity. Jesus said impurity does not come from disobedience to the Law, but rather from "out of the heart."[15] He taught that sinfulness is a condition, not a choice, and my disobedience is a symptom of what caused me to disobey, not the disease itself. Similarly, obedience is only a symptom of spiritual health; obedience is not righteousness itself. Real obedience—heartfelt obedience—can only come *after* the scales of justice have been balanced and genuine righteousness restored. Jesus taught that obedience to the commands of Torah is correctly viewed as a result of reconciliation, never as a requirement for reconciliation.

So when God asks, "Can you leave this well the way you found it?" according to Christianity the question contains a double entendre. Of course the Lord is concerned with external behavior—with cleaning up the well—but my behavior is inextricably bound up with the condition of my soul. If Judaism is correct, the requirements of the Torah's *lex talionis* kind of justice can be fully met by offering up obedience to balance disobedience. But Christianity observes that the effects of disobedience are not limited to external actions, therefore actions alone are not enough compensation. Although the mother taught her son to renew his efforts to obey the Torah as a compensation for his sin, Jesus teaches that the Lord does not care nearly as much about obedience to the law as he cares about my loss of innocence. In short, what God is after in return for pulling me up from the well is not just clean water, it is also a clean soul.

Yet I cannot emerge from the well as if the experience has had no effect at all. Sin has had a transforming effect upon me. Each law I choose to disobey makes the next sinful choice that much easier, and therefore that much more likely. I am black and blue from my fall to the bottom, but in a twisted kind of way I find myself longing to repeat the experience. And all around me, everyone else I see is similarly damaged and deranged. When the Psalmist wrote, "Surely I was sinful from my

15. Matthew 15:19.

birth," he meant even the souls of little children are bruised from their first tentative experiments in disobedience. And this was part of Micah's meaning when he said, "Shall I offer my firstborn for my transgression, the fruit of my body for the sin of my soul?" With this rhetorical question, the prophet made it clear that even his firstborn child, the fruit of his body, is inadequate compensation. How then can the mere fruit of my lips be sufficient?

If neither the sacrifice of animals nor the fruit of my lips—that is, a renewed commitment to obey God—are enough to balance the scales, what then will the Lord accept as compensation for my sins?

Jesus taught that the sacrificial death of animals is insufficient compensation for human sin, but sacrificial death is nonetheless part of the redemptive equation. After all, if the prophets intended us to abandon sacrificial death altogether, what are we to make of the following words?

> For the life of a creature is in the blood, and I have given it to you to make atonement for yourselves on the altar; it is the blood that makes atonement for one's life.
>
> —Leviticus 17:11

As I have already pointed out, many prophets spoke against viewing sacrificial offerings as a payment for divine forgiveness, because God cannot be bribed. Furthermore, everything we have to offer is God's already, even our firstborn children. But that is not the same as saying there need not be a sacrifice. When Hosea wrote, "Forgive all our sins and receive us graciously, that we may offer the fruit of our lips," nothing in the prophets' words retracts the requirement, so unanimously established in the Torah, for death in response to sin. Sacrificial death is taught from cover to cover throughout the Hebrew Scriptures, even in the words of the very prophets who spoke against relying on it as a quid pro quo. Perhaps the clearest example of this is found in these verses:

You do not delight in sacrifice, or I would bring it; you do not take pleasure in burnt offerings. The sacrifices of God are a broken spirit; a broken and contrite heart, O God, you will not despise.

—Psalms 51:16–17

Here, once again, the Hebrew Scriptures insist that God does not want me to approach with bribes in my hands and pride in my heart. Instead, he demands the humble acknowledgment that I have absolutely nothing to offer in return for his forgiveness. Through confession and repentance I must throw myself upon his mercy alone. So far, this is nothing new. It is this kind of thing that inspired the rabbis to teach that the sacrifices of animals are totally unnecessary. But consider the very next words of this Psalm:

In your good pleasure make Zion prosper; build up the walls of Jerusalem. Then there will be righteous sacrifices, whole burnt offerings to delight you; then bulls will be offered on your altar.

—Psalms 51:18–19

Although the psalmist began by saying, "You do not delight in sacrifice," he ends by saying, "there will be whole burnt offerings to delight you," and "bulls will be offered on your altar." The psalmist does not intend me to understand that sacrificial death is unnecessary. Rather, he warns against the mistake of relying on the death of a *mere animal,* as if God would be satisfied with such cheap justice.

The rabbis taught that everything at the tabernacle symbolized a miraculous but very real emanation of the divine, from the menorah made in the pattern of the burning bush, to the "shewbread" or "bread of display" that symbolized the manna from heaven. In the same way, Christianity teaches that the animal sacrifices were merely a symbol of a better thing that would later be given by God. According to the New Testament, the message of the animal sacrifices is one of hope. The death of the animals at the tabernacle altar symbolized a perfect justice that would one day be revealed as something miraculous but real, like the burning bush and the manna from heaven, something Israel could see and hear and touch. As the psalmist wrote:

He who sacrifices thank offerings honors me, and he prepares the way so that I may show him the salvation of God.

—Psalms 50:23

The sacrifices of the Lord's tabernacle were an object lesson. They prepared the way for the salvation of God yet to come. Not the cheap, disproportionate justice of a goat's life for the spiritual death of a man, but a restoration of justice that is perfectly balanced. The mere fact that the goats of Yom Kippur had to be offered year after year spoke volumes to the Israelite people about their insufficiency. The death of animals was not enough to balance the scales.

If it could, would they not have stopped being offered? For the worshipers would have been cleansed once for all, and would no longer have felt guilty for their sins.

—Hebrews 10:2

The perfect balance necessary to restore justice is most clearly seen in the Torah's unwavering insistence that the sacrificial animals must be *tamim*, or "without blemish."[16] Logic demands that before the very first sin, there was someone—I might as well call him Adam—who was absolutely righteous, completely without blemish, totally *tamim*. In that case, God lost something more than a spiritual life. He lost a *perfect* spiritual life—a soul that had never been tainted by any disobedience. So even if a flawed human being would agree to offer himself as a sacrifice in return for God's loss, justice would not be served. Yet something somewhere must be sufficient, because the Hebrew prophets promise that the corruption of this world will disappear one day:

The wolf will live with the lamb, the leopard will lie down with the goat, the calf and the lion and the yearling together; and a little child will lead them. The cow will feed with the bear, their young will lie down together, and the lion will eat straw like the ox. The infant will play near the hole of the cobra, and the young child put his hand into the viper's nest. They will neither harm nor destroy

16. See Leviticus 22:21, for example. This is repeated over forty times in connection with sacrificial animals.

on all my holy mountain, for the earth will be full of the knowledge of the Lord as the waters cover the sea.

—Isaiah 11:6–9

According to the Bible, someday peace will rule the earth
again as it was in the beginning. There will be no more violence,
not even to satisfy the carnivorous appetites of lions and bears.
But the Torah's perfectly counterweighted "eye for eye, ear for
ear, life for life" definition of justice means the corruption of the
universe—the spreading imperfection that constantly reminds
me I am no longer in the Garden—can only be reversed by a perfect counterbalance to whatever caused that corruption in the
first place, something equal but opposite in every way.[17]

Before the first sin, before Adam "knew he was naked," and
"hid from the Lord," Christianity teaches that he was physically
and spiritually whole, able to walk with the Lord "in the cool of
the day" without hiding in shame. Then Adam chose to disobey
God, and drove a wedge between himself and his Maker. Being
only human, I usually focus on what Adam lost as a result of this
tragedy: his innocence, his citizenship in the Garden, his immortality. But consider what happened to God: he lost the crowning
glory of his created universe, a flawless companion who shared
his mornings, the one and only creature made in his perfect
image who could approach him without fear or shame. In short,
God lost his most treasured possession.

He has been hoping to get it back ever since:

Now if you obey me fully and keep my covenant, then out of all
nations you will be my treasured possession.

—Exodus 19:5

How does God plan to regain what he values most? If "life for
life" is the definition of justice, and if Adam was spiritually per-

---

17. Exodus 21:26 allows for the exchange of a slave's freedom in lieu of an eye for an
eye, but in my opinion, this is because a slave would consider freedom a more valuable
compensation.

fect before his first sin sent him down to death, it seems that only a second flawless Adam rising up from death could properly compensate the Lord for what he lost. Nothing less could balance the cosmic scales of justice and restore the harmony that allows wolves and lambs to lie down together in peace. Yet no one is blameless as Adam was before the expulsion from the Garden, and no one is capable of reaching that state of perfection.

Which brings me to another reason why I believe in Jesus.

> But God demonstrates his own love for us in this: While we were still sinners, Christ died for us.
>
> —Romans 5:8

Given the absence of a perfect human being to balance the scales, I believe God accomplished the impossible on my behalf, reentering human history as Jesus and accepting all the mortal limitations of Adam except for one: Jesus never sinned. Because I cannot be blameless before the Lord, Jesus became my surrogate, my substitute perfection on the universal scales of justice, providing the perfect life for perfect life that perfect justice requires. Adam went down to death a flawed, divided man. Jesus rose up from death a perfectly whole man. The cosmic scales of justice were balanced. The divided physical and spiritual selves were reunited, and nakedness once again forgotten. And somehow—only God knows how—just as Adam bequeathed his imperfect spiritual condition to Seth and through him down to me, Jesus bequeaths his spiritual perfection to all who accept the gift of his sacrifice in our place.

I believe the annual sacrificial deaths at Yom Kippur prepared the way so that Jesus might show me the salvation of God, the perfect balancing of the scales of justice that was yet to come. I believe in Jesus because I can see no other possibility. Like a Jewish shepherd searching through his flock for an unblemished animal to take to the tabernacle altar, I realize I have nothing to offer God in return for the wrongs I have done. Everything I have is flawed. Moreover, everything is already his. Like any Jew sincerely longing for *teshuvah,* I confess my sin and I repent—I grab the rope and hold on tight—but cleaning up the mess I have made of this well is beyond me. Just as that Israelite shepherd

must surely have known he had no hope of finding a truly unblemished lamb, I also know that everything I can offer has been
damaged while in my possession. Even the promise "I'll be good"
is doomed to be broken from the instant it leaves my mouth to
echo up the shaft.

Some may protest that a God who demands perfect justice
would not accept someone else's death as a penalty for my sins.
But as I learned in my study of paradox, justice without mercy is
not justice at all. And as a Christian, I believe the most merciful
act of all time was accomplished on the cross on behalf of we
who could never meet the standard of pure justice.

If the animal sacrifices of Torah teach anything, it is first that
death is required for death, and second that a substitute death is
acceptable to God. Still, I suspect the shepherd of Moses' day approached the altar with fear and trembling, knowing the flawed
animal in his arms was not enough, but bringing it anyway because God had so commanded, bringing it anyway because he
believed his Lord was a loving God who would somehow find a
way to mend their broken relationship in spite of his pitifully insignificant offering. I believe the sincerity of that shepherd's humility and the depth of his faith was adequate because it was well
placed. The Lord is indeed merciful. He did indeed find a way to
mend their relationship in spite of the fact that the shepherd
could never pay the price for his sins. That way was not Micah's
firstborn child, and certainly not the shepherd's pathetic little
lamb; it was the Lord's only begotten Son, Jesus, the man who is
God, sliding down the rope to take my place because he knows I
cannot leave this well the way I found it.

I believe Jesus' death and resurrection is the very thing the
shepherd trusted God to do, although of course the shepherd
never knew the details. I believe Jesus' death and resurrection
has always been the only basis for anyone's reconciliation with
God, from Abraham to me, although we also do not know the details. I believe Jesus' death and resurrection prepared the way for
the wolf to live with the lamb one day, as they did before in the
Garden. I do not understand how this will happen, but like the shepherd in the days of Moses, like Abraham ascending with the
knife, like Israel gazing at the serpent, I trust the Lord to find a
way.

I believe all of this, but it is not easy to believe. The idea that God can be human is impossible to comprehend. And even that staggering paradox pales in comparison to the notion that the immortal Master of the universe can somehow die to balance the scales of justice. But difficult as the paradox of Jesus is to understand, no other idea in my experience makes sense of what I know about the state of the universe and the love of the God who is One. No other hope I have can reconcile both the justice themes of the Hebrew Scriptures and the spiritual survival of the weak and wounded man I see in the mirror. In short, unless balance is restored by someone else's "perfect life for perfect life," I can see no reason at all why a perfect God should bother with the bruised and blemished sinner that I am, dangling here at the end of his rope.

Still, if I were a Jew, it would be very difficult to believe these things, even if I found them logical and even if they seemed to speak the truth to my heart. For Jews in particular, there is one monumental roadblock to belief in Jesus, as I will shortly see.

ten

# Skeletons in My Closet

To smite an Israelite is as if one smote the Shekinah.

—Sanhedrin, 58

Today I came to temple unaware of the danger lurking here. We are discussing the best way for Jews to defend themselves against future holocausts. I voice the opinion (which I still hold) that Judaism's best chance is to embrace non-Jews as aggressively as possible on an individual level. This strategy is based on the idea that it is extremely difficult to hate decent people whom we truly know as individuals. Prejudice is always based on ignorance.

Suddenly, a man interrupts, disagreeing loudly, accusing all Christians of harboring a deep-seated malevolence toward the Jewish people. Christian anti-Semitism, he says, is ready to rear its ugly head the moment America experiences any national disaster.

Shocked at his words, I vigorously object that the next holocaust will not come from Christians, and will probably afflict Jews and Christians alike.[1]

1. These words were spoken several years before the World Trade Center and Pentagon attacks of September 11, 2001.

183

He tells me I have no idea what I'm talking about. Christians are just waiting for a chance to pounce on Jews again.

"That's a lie!" I shout (yes, I'm afraid I shouted it).

The room is suddenly very still. My face is hot with shame. What kind of a person shouts in anger in a temple? What have I done? Then, hard on the heels of my shame comes a tidal wave of fear. My heart pounds with the terror of standing alone among so many, and with the dread that my time at Chever Torah may have come to an end in this most ignoble way.

The roots of my angry response to this man lie in my first six months at Chever Torah, when very few people at the temple knew I was a Christian. Since Reform Jews are not required to wear yarmulkes, earlocks, or phylacteries, there were no external differences between us. My friend Philip knew I was a Christian, of course, and he told Rabbi Zimmerman and perhaps one or two others, but in a group the size of Chever Torah, it was possible for me to blend in as long as I kept my mouth shut. Since the idea of publicly acknowledging my faith in that particular group was disconcerting to say the least, I decided to simply sit and listen. What I heard was not always easy or comfortable.

The Jews of Chever Torah seemed to think Christians had horribly wronged the Jewish people through centuries of hate and persecution. Deeply insulted, I longed to rise and condemn such an obvious lie, but with so many Jews and only me to oppose them, I was afraid. Also, I realized that entering their place of worship incognito and then confronting them would appear to verify their accusations. Of course, now I have done just that. I am a Chrisitan calling a Jew a liar in his own temple.

But the most shameful thing is this: I know deep down that this man is *not* a liar; I merely wish he were.

Earlier, after hearing all those charges of Christian anti-Semitism while I was still incognito, I decided to go to the history books to prove the innocence of the church. And there, to my deep, deep sorrow, I learned the terrible truth. Christians have persecuted Jews in almost every generation since the third century.

For example, the Crusades were marked by widespread murders of Jews by mobs of Christians, both in Europe and in the Holy Land. The Benedictine monk, Dom Lobineau, wrote the following eyewitness account during the twelfth century:

> The greatest and first expedition of these crusaders was to massacre the Jews, who were not the cause of the evils which the Saracens [Muslims] were inflicting upon the Christians in the East.
>
> —Dom Lobineau[2]

This quote is based on the historical fact that when the knights of the Crusades finally breached the walls of Jerusalem, they did not merely slaughter the Muslim defenders, but every Jewish man, woman, and child living there as well. Then they held a praise and worship service.

The first Passover dinner in ancient Egypt was clouded by an atmosphere of terror, as Hebrew families huddled around their meal listening to distant cries of grief while Egyptian firstborn children were being killed. During the Middle Ages, that horror again dominated the Passover ceremony, but this time it was the distant wails of Jewish families filling the night as a new kind of terror moved from house to house, gaining entrance through an opening provided by the Passover tradition itself. At a late point in the ceremony, "Elijah's cup" of wine is poured and the door opened to allow Elijah's entry so that he can join the family's *Pesach seder,* or Passover ceremony, and hasten the Messianic Age in fulfillment of Malachi 4:5–6. Many medieval Christians believed that Jews murdered children at Passover to use their blood in the preparation of the *matza,* or unleavened bread in the Passover meal. With this outrageous lie as their excuse, Gentiles often waited for the doors of Jewish homes to be opened for Elijah. They would storm inside, overturn the Passover table, and inflict horrible violence upon the worshiping family. Since tradition calls for the youngest son to be the one who opens the door, a child was often the first to be harmed. This tragedy became so widespread that curses on Gentiles were incorporated into the

---

2. Quoted by Dan Cohn-Sherbok in *The Crucified Jew* (London: Fount, 1993), p. 41.

medieval Passover order of service to replace the opening of the door.[3]

Church-sanctioned persecutions of Jews lasted long after the time of the Crusades. During the Spanish Inquisition, over thirty thousand Jews were tortured to death because they would not submit to baptism. Jews today consider them martyrs for the faith, precisely as Christians assign martyr status to the Roman-era Christians who died at Nero's hands. The parallel between Spanish Christians and pagan Romans is disconcerting, to say the least.

Christian atrocities against Jews reach beyond the Inquisition, right into the twentieth century. Catholic authorities in various European countries at various times have required Jews to distinguish themselves through their clothing, often with a distinctive cloth badge. This public branding of Jews was first enforced at the order of the church during the Middle Ages in France, Poland, Italy, and England, as well as Germany—a bleak fact that is codified in a famous thirteenth-century Christian document:

> It is decreed that henceforth Jews of both sexes will be distinguished from other peoples by their garment. . . . Trespassers will be duly punished by the secular powers, in order that they no longer dare flout Christ in the presence of Christians.
>
> —The Fourth Lateran Council of the Holy Roman Church

Of course, one of Nazi Germany's first steps in the "Final Solution" was to force Jews to identify themselves in public by wearing a yellow Star of David on their clothing. It seems the Nazis learned this technique from Christians.

Not that the Catholic Church bears sole responsibility for the horrors endured by Jews over the centuries. When my research leads me to the following quote, I feel the earth shift beneath my feet:

> The Jews, being foreigners, should possess nothing, and what they do possess should be ours . . . their synagogues should be set on fire . . . their homes should likewise be broken down and destroyed . . . they should be deprived of their prayer books and Talmuds . . . their Rabbis must be forbidden under threat of death to

---

3. Lecture by Dr. Ronald B. Allen, Professor, Bible Exposition, Dallas Theological Seminary, November 1996.

teach any more . . . passport and traveling privileges should be absolutely forbidden to the Jews . . . let the young Jew and Jewesses be given the ax, the hoe, the spade, the distaff and spindle, and let them earn their bread by the sweat of their noses . . .

—Martin Luther[4]

Martin Luther, of course, is considered a father of Protestant Christianity.

Why does the church so seldom speak of the horrors committed by our Christian ancestors in the name of Jesus? Perhaps we feel the Crusades and Inquisition have no real connection with our faith. We insulate ourselves by saying that no true Christian could do such things to her fellow man. It is tempting to defend the church by saying that the men and women who did this were not "real" Christians. But although Martin Luther's tract, *Against the Jews and Their Lies,* might just as well have been written by Adolf Hitler, who would deny his Christianity? It seems clear that many sincere Christians in the past have succumbed to the allure of this terrible evil. No doubt some have been wolves in sheep's clothing, but others have been bloodthirsty sheep. How or why I cannot say, but it is undeniable.

I can no longer pretend such history does not matter. I cannot even take comfort in the passage of time, because our century has seen perhaps the greatest moral failure in the history of Christianity, more despicable than everything that went before.

Protestants and Catholics alike love to focus on the courageous acts of great believers like Dietrich Bonhoeffer and Corrie ten Boom, both of whom resisted the Nazis on behalf of Jews; one at the cost of his life, the other at the cost of her freedom and family.[5] But we ignore the dirty fact that most German Protes-

4. *Against the Jews and Their Lies,* quoted in Cohn-Sherbok, *Crucified Jew*, p. 73.
5. Mr. Bonhoffer, a minister, was hanged for his role in smuggling Jews out of Europe, and Ms. ten Boom, a layperson, was placed in an extermination camp alongside the Jews she tried to save. She lost her father and sister to the Holocaust because they too hid Jewish neighbors from the Nazis.

tants and Catholics refused to oppose Adolf Hitler. Some Lutheran pastors actually supported Hitler's government, and Pope Pious XII, when presented with evidence of the death camps, declined to issue a statement condemning the ongoing extermination of the Jews, reputedly saying, ". . . do not forget that millions of Catholics serve in the German armies. Shall I bring them into conflicts of conscience?"[6] Horrible as that is, a papal expression of outrage at that time would probably have been too little, too late. But that does not relieve the church of ethical responsibility. Many Jews might have been safe in a Jewish homeland when the Nazis rose to power had the church supported the Zionist movement of the late 1800s and early 1900s. Unfortunately, in the face of rising European anti-Semitism in 1904, Pope Pious X responded to Theodor Herzl's desperate request for support of a Jewish homeland with these shameful words:

> We are unable to favor this movement. We cannot prevent the Jews from going to Jerusalem, but we would never sanction it. As the head of the church, I cannot answer you otherwise. The Jews have not recognized our Lord, therefore we cannot recognize the Jewish people.
>
> —Pope Pious X[7]

Who knows how many of the six million Jewish dead would have survived safely in the Holy Land had Christians stood together against the rising tide of anti-Semitism in Europe? It is impossible to say. But other questions must be answered.

Why did we fail so miserably to do our duty?

Would I fail again?

The Nazis came for the Communists, and I didn't speak up because I wasn't a Communist. Then they came for the Jews, and I didn't speak up because I wasn't a Jew. Then they came for the trade unionists, and I didn't speak up because I wasn't a trade unionist. Then they came for the Catholics, and I didn't speak up

6. Cohn-Sherbok, *Crucified Jew*, p. 209.

7. Quoted by Pastor Jack Hayford in *Israel, Bewildering Timepiece of History*, taped lecture.

because I was a Protestant. Finally they came for me, and by that time there was no one left to speak up.

—Martin Niemoeller, clergyman
and concentration camp survivor[8]

Of course, Christianity is not the only religion with a bloody history. Christians and Jews today observe the terrorist atrocities of modern Muslim extremists with a sense of outrage, as do the vast majority of Muslims themselves. We wonder how anyone could do such things in God's name. But because of what I have learned about church history, I see those things and think: There but for the grace of God go I.

Drowning in the shame of my own history, I immediately begin casting about for a life preserver. First it occurs to me that these dry old facts may not matter much to Jews today, except in a detached, historical kind of way. Obviously the Crusades and the horrors of the Inquisition were wrong, but that was then and this is now. I hope my new Jewish friends will have a similar common-sense attitude.

Then one day at Chever Torah, my friend Philip leans close to whisper that the woman speaking across the room was saved from the camps by Christians who sheltered her at great danger to themselves. I watch her closely for the rest of the morning. That old woman—that one, right there—stared at Nazi machine guns and heard the pounding of their boots. Those very eyes watched friends and family being dragged away to their deaths. On the one hand, I am gratified that she owes her life to the courage of Christians. On the other hand, a predominantly Christian nation's horrible shirking of responsibility that allowed a man like Hitler to rise to power no longer seems like ancient history.

Some of the Jewish men and women living among us still bear Nazi tattoos on their forearms, still suffer nightmares inspired by real experiences far worse than any fantasy, and still personally feel the sorrow of lost loved ones. Their children, grandchil-

8. Quoted in *From Horror to Hope, Germany, the Jews and Israel,* (New York: German Information Center), p. 43.

dren, and great-grandchildren share in their living pain and will never forget that the church played a role in their suffering. Each new Jewish generation of children is taught the bloody history of the church for their own good, much as African American children are taught about slavery and racism as protection against the painfully confusing realities in our culture. In short, Jews today have not forgotten the crimes committed against their ancestors by the Christian crusaders a thousand years ago, or the church's Inquisition five hundred years ago, or the Holocaust we stood by and allowed to happen fifty years ago.

Jews will never forget.

Nor should we.

Some Christians today actually believe that the Holocaust was ordained by God to punish Jews for their rejection of Jesus. I myself have heard them say it. In fact, for a fleeting moment in my search for an excuse, I even considered this possibility. But then I realized that by this logic, any Christian who tried to help her Jewish neighbors in Nazi Europe was working against the will of God. We might as well say we should not assist the poor or give comfort to the ill. After all, why stop at genocide? Poverty and disease might also be divinely ordained punishment.

Of course, such rationalizing ignores the Torah's admonishment to love our neighbor as ourselves, a command Jesus quoted as second only to loving God with all our hearts.[9] It also demeans the sacrifice and courage of the few "righteous Gentiles" like Dietrich Bonhoeffer and Corrie ten Boom who risked everything to protect their Jewish friends and neighbors. Is it really possible that we would add this sin to all the rest?

God forgive us.

Who am I to say that any disaster is a punishment from God? Even if it were true that the Holocaust was such a judgment (and I do not say it was), that would be a matter strictly between God and those whom he has judged. Jesus was very clear about this.

9. Matthew 22:36–39.

When I assume God's judgment has specifically fallen on anyone, I expose my own actions to judgment as well:

> For in the same way you judge others, you will be judged, and with the measure you use, it will be measured to you.
>
> —Matthew 7:2

Obviously, these words cannot mean that I should make no judgments whatsoever. Every day in order to survive I must make judgments about the company I keep and the things I will and will not do. But although it is the inescapable conclusion of the stories of Adam and Eve, the flood, and the tower of Babel that God will indeed sometimes punish both individuals and entire communities, I must also remember the stories of Job and Joseph. Bad things sometimes happen to people and communities simply because evil exists and they were unfortunate enough to be in the way, or because of the disobedient acts of evil men.

In saying, "Do not judge," Jesus is saying I have no right to decide which neighbor is the subject of divine punishment and which a mere unfortunate bystander in a fallen world. I am not a prophet, that I should know the mind of God. How dare I self-righteously select one neighbor as "worthy" of my love, while smugly abandoning another "sinner" to God's alleged wrath?

Consider Jesus' teaching again:

> Now there were some present at that time who told Jesus about the Galileans whose blood Pilate had mixed with their sacrifices. Jesus answered, "Do you think that these Galileans were worse sinners than all the other Galileans because they suffered this way? I tell you, no! But unless you repent, you too will all perish. Or those eighteen who died when the tower in Siloam fell on them—do you think they were more guilty than all the others living in Jerusalem? I tell you, no! But unless you repent, you too will all perish."
>
> —Luke 13:1–5

Here Jesus says that the possibility that disasters—either man-made or natural—might be caused by God's judgment is no excuse for me to concern myself with anyone else's spiritual guilt. The mere fact that I am thinking that way means I should repent instead. Christians who excuse our past behavior toward Jews by attributing the Nazi extermination camps to divine retribution have forgotten one of the New Testament's foremost truths: ". . . *all* have sinned and fall short of the glory of God."[10]

Many Christians believe Jews bear a unique responsibility for Jesus' crucifixion. It is a very old lie. For example, in his *Expository Treatise against the Jews*, the third-century church father Hippolytus[11] wrote:

> Why was the Temple made desolate? Was it on account of the ancient fabrication of the calf? Or was it on account of the idolatry of the people? Was it for the blood of the prophets? Was it for the idolatry and fornication of Israel? By no means, for in all these transgressions, they always found pardon open to them. But it was *because they killed the son of the Benefactor*, for he is coeternal with the Father.[12]

Oh, what wonderfully convenient propaganda! It allows me to shift my own guilt onto someone else's shoulders. I did not stand against the crusaders or the inquisitors or Hitler because the Jews were being punished for something that they—not I—once did to Jesus.

But Hippolytus should have read the Scriptures more closely.

In the Gospel of Luke, Jesus prophesies that Jerusalem and the temple will be destroyed because most Jews of that time will not accept him as their Lord and Messiah, not because Jews bear a special guilt for his death.[13] In fact, Jesus specifically says the *Gentiles*, not the Jews, will sentence him to death, torture him, and carry out the death sentence.[14] And of course, under the Roman procurator Pontius Pilate, that is exactly what we did.

10. Romans 3:28 (emphasis mine).
11. A presbyter of the Roman church, a bishop, and possibly a martyr during the reign of Maximinus Thracian.
12. Quoted by Cohn-Sherbok, *Crucified Jew*, p. 27.
13. Luke 19:41–44.
14. Luke 18:31–33.

But wait. My New Testament also describes some people called "the Jews" who demanded Jesus' crucifixion and plotted against his followers.[15] Since Jesus prophesied differently, and since the Gospels specify that Roman hands drove those spikes home, who exactly is the Bible describing?

A careful reading reveals that the term "the Jews" is literary shorthand for a group of religious leaders who perceive Jesus as a potential threat to the delicate balance that they have established with their Herodian and Roman overlords. Ironically, at first these religious leaders were afraid to act against Jesus because they feared the crowd—the *Jewish* crowd—would become outraged if harm came to Jesus.[16]

We cannot even say that "the Jews" includes all of the religious leaders of Jesus' time. For example, a Pharisee famous in Rabbinic Judaism named Gamaliel intercedes for the apostles when some in the Sanhedrin wish to have them put to death.[17] Another Pharisee and member of the Sanhedrin, Nicodemus, attends at least one of Jesus' lectures where he asks honest, searching questions. Nicodemus later attempts to dissuade his Sanhedrin colleagues from taking action against Jesus and dares to defy them by joining Joseph of Arimathea in giving Jesus' body a proper Jewish burial.[18] Nicodemus and Gamaliel are not alone. Other Pharisees try to protect Jesus from the powers that be, advising him to "Leave this place and go somewhere else. Herod wants to kill you." Still others genuinely seem to want to understand Jesus' message, otherwise why would they invite him to their homes for that highlight of the Jewish week, the Sabbath dinner?[19] And some of the very first Jews to accept Jesus as a divine messiah are temple priests.[20]

If "the Jews" means the Jewish people in general, how do I account for the fact that all of the Apostles except Luke were Jewish? And of course, although this truth has lost its force through repetition, the fact remains that Jesus was a Jew in every sense

15. John 19:7; Acts 23:12.
16. Matthew 21:46 is one of several examples.
17. Gamaliel was the grandson of the famous rabbi Hillel, and is widely known among Jews today as one of the rabbis of the Talmud's *Mishnah*—see Acts 5:34–39.
18. John 3:1–9, 7:50–51; 19:39.
19. Luke 13:31; 14:1.
20. Acts 6:7.

of the word. If Jesus the Jew from Palestine were to visit the United States today, he would recognize the rituals, prayers, language, and symbols in any synagogue or temple in the nation, but most of the traditions of our churches would be foreign to him. In fact, the only trappings of the Christian faith Jesus might recognize are themselves based on Judaism: the incense in our censors, the skull caps and shawls upon our priests, the full immersion baptismal pools in many Protestant churches, our public readings from the Scriptures, our responsive prayers, and of course that ritual most central to our faith, the wine and bread of the Lord's Table, which was taken wholly from Judaism's Passover feast. So much that is good in our faith—our Bibles, our doctrine of the grace of God, our belief in sanctification by good works and the Holy Spirit, even our moral code—all of this we owe to Jews or Judaism. Yet many of us, including me, have been foolish enough to assume our love for God was somehow superior. Some of us have even dared to attribute unspeakable evils perpetrated against the Jewish people to the justified wrath of God.

I ponder these things for many days, still searching desperately for a loophole, a way to explain away the facts. Finally, a new thought occurs to me. In the Torah, God says:

> Fathers shall not be put to death for their children, nor children put to death for their fathers; each is to die for his own sin.
>
> —Deuteronomy 24:16

This provides a final glimmer of hope. Since I have never personally harmed a Jew (so far as I know), why should I share in the guilt of past Christians? The church of fifty years ago did not include me, much less the church of the Middle Ages. And as I have already seen, Judaism and Christianity both teach that God holds me responsible for my sins alone. Why should I concern myself with the actions of other Christians long ago?

The answer lies within these words:

My prayer is not for them [the apostles] alone. I pray also *for those who will believe in me* through their message, *that all of them may be one,* Father, just as you are in me and I am in you. May they also be in us so that the world may believe that you have sent me.

—John 17:20–21 (emphasis mine)

Here, Jesus prayed for his first-century apostles to be "one" with those of us who would believe in him as a result of their efforts. That means Jesus wants them to be one with me. Jesus also spoke of future believers when he said, "They too will listen to my voice, and there shall be one flock and one shepherd."[21] So Jesus saw all believers throughout time as one great congregation, and for Christians that should be reason enough to accept responsibility for the sins of the church in years past.

But there is another, equally compelling reason.

Jesus said the church is "one" throughout the generations "so that the world may believe." And the world does indeed base its response to Jesus upon the behavior of his followers. For many Jews, the crimes of my spiritual ancestors are the backdrop for everything I do today in Jesus' name, because those crimes were also done in the name of Jesus. Small wonder so few Jews throughout the centuries have believed in him. And how can the damage that was done—the roadblocks to belief in Jesus—ever be removed if I will not even accept responsibility for the evil my brothers and sisters have done in his name?

What response should I offer to the bleak history of anti-Semitism in the church? Is it possible to bind these wounds?

Like anyone else interested in reconciliation, I must begin by viewing the situation from my neighbor's perspective. When I shouted "Liar!" at the angry Jew in Chever Torah, I spoke directly from my own heart without pausing to consider the source of his feelings. This is my greatest area of failure when it comes to interaction with Jewish neighbors. It is an almost universal Christian failure, which is ironic in this era of unparalleled outreach and evangelism by the church. We speak *at* our neighbors,

21. John 10:16.

but we do not communicate. We live in our own insular world, never making the effort to move beyond the confines of "Fort God," never daring to experience life among those who do not believe in Jesus. We do not listen. We do not empathize. Instead, we preach from afar.

There are so many examples I could use, but in order to best demonstrate the vast gulf between the sensitivity we Christians *think* we project and the way we are really seen by many Jews, consider one of Protestant Christianity's best-loved institutions, Campus Crusade for Christ. Millions have taken the first faltering steps on their path to the Lord because of this excellent organization. I have given money and time to their ministries and plan to do so again. The men and women I know who work there are filled with love and compassion, people any religious Jew could respect, and I do not wish to criticize the ministry or its members in any way. But for the sake of making my point, look at the name.

Were I a Jew, I would think, "God forbid they should have another *crusade.*"

Were I a Jew, I would wonder: In nine hundred years, after the facts have been worn down by the church's failure to face them squarely, might some well-meaning Christian organization call itself the "Holy Holocaust for Heaven"?

Obviously, I am not suggesting that the Campus Crusade for Christ change its name at this late date any more than I would suggest that the Talmud be purged of uncomplimentary references to Christians (it includes several, as I will soon discuss). I am suggesting instead that individual Christians ought to face the church's past, confess, and ask for forgiveness rather than remaining so out of touch with our bloody history that we name benevolent Christian organizations after movements intent on genocide.

As an individual Christian I can do nothing about the names of time-honored Christian institutions. But there are other names I can avoid in order to personally show I have learned from the mistakes of the church. For example, when in the company of Jews I can refrain from the Christian habit of referring to Jesus by the word "christ," a word that means "annointed one," and is derived from the Hebrew word for "messiah." Of course, most Jews do not believe Jesus is the messiah, so from their point of view referring to him as "Christ" is tantamount to a theological slap in the face. Some books in the New Testament refer to Jesus simply as "Christ," but nowhere in the Bible am I commanded to do the same. On the other hand, "Jesus" is the name Mary *was* commanded to give to her baby boy by the angel Gabriel, so "Jesus" is what I too will call him.[22] Unless Gabriel was misinformed, I have a feeling God does not mind.

In the Talmud, the rabbis gave Jesus a few titles of their own. Some called him the "Galilean Sectary."[23] Others referred to Christians as "Ishmaelites," that is, members of the other, non-chosen line of Abraham's family. In another place, they called us "falsifiers."[24] To understand how the word "christ" sounds to Jewish ears, I try to imagine how I would feel if my Jewish friends at Chever Torah insisted on calling Jesus "the Sectary," or frequently referred to Christians as "falsifiers," simply because those terms are used in their Talmud. Obviously, I am offended at the mere thought.

Unlike those who refer to Jesus as "Christ" in conversations with Jews, my Jewish neighbors do not insist upon underscoring their ideas about Jesus each time they utter his name. In the spirit of the Golden Rule, I should do the same, especially since here, as in so many other areas, my Jewish friends have already come more than halfway to meet me. After all, each time they refer to "*Christ*ians," and "*Christ*ianity," they use a term with roots in an idea they strongly contest.

The term "Old Testament" also implies something many Jews find objectionable, specifically, the idea that the Hebrew Scriptures are outdated. The term is so widespread I sometimes find it difficult to avoid. But in addition to using the name "Jesus" instead of "Christ" at Chever Torah, I try to respect the feelings and beliefs of my Jewish friends by referring to the Old Testament as "the Hebrew Scriptures," or "the Tanakh." There is no harm in this. In fact, for just this reason, Dallas Theological Seminary, that august bastion of conservative Protestant theology, revised the name of their "Old Testament" studies department some

22. Luke 1:31.
23. *M. Yadaim*, ch. 4, quoted in *Talmudic Anthology*, p. 73.
24. Aggadat Bereshit, 31, quoted in *Talmudic Anthology*, p. 72.

time ago, deciding to use the words "Hebrew Scriptures" instead.[25] Jesus himself used the term "Tanakh" or something very like it when referring to the Hebrew Scriptures.[26] Why not follow his example?

Another way to make amends for the wrongs the church has done to Jews is to celebrate the things we hold in common. For example, compare the following quotes on repentence and the Sabbath from the New Testament and the Talmud:

**On Repentence:**

| | |
|---|---|
| "I tell you that in the same way there will be more rejoicing in heaven over one sinner who repents than over ninety-nine righteous persons who do not need to repent."<br><br>—Jesus, quoted in Luke 15:7 | There is more joy in heaven over one sinner who repenteth than over ninety and nine righteous persons, who need no repentance.<br><br>—Sanhedrin 99a |

**On the Sabbath:**

| | |
|---|---|
| Then he said to them, "The Sabbath was made for man, not man for the Sabbath."<br><br>—Jesus, quoted in Mark 2:27 | The Sabbath is given to you, but you are not servants of the Sabbath.<br><br>—Mekilta Shabbata 1[27] |

I have found many other remarkable similarities between the Talmud and the New Testament. This may be partially explained by the fact that Jesus could have been familiar with the thinking among Talmudic scholars of his day. Hillel, for example, lived and taught in Jerusalem up to the time that Jesus was about thirteen or fourteen years old. Given the Gospel account of the young Jesus engaged in Torah study with the teachers in the temple court, it is quite possible that Hillel and the young Jesus actually

25. Private lecture by Dr. Ronald B. Allen, Professor, Bible Exposition, Dallas Theological Seminary, November 1996.

26. See Luke 24:27; Matthew 11:13; 22:40, and bear in mind that the word "Tanakh" is derived from three Hebrew words meaning "law, writings, and prophets."

27. As quoted by Rabbi W. Gunther Plaut, *The Torah, A Modern Commentary* (New York: Union of American Hebrew Congregations, 1981), p. 551.

exchanged ideas.[28] And of course, the Talmudic rabbis who lived after Jesus would have heard something of his teachings. Since neither the Talmud nor the New Testament cites the other as a source, I do not know who influenced whom in the quotations above, but it is clear that the teachings of Jesus and those of the rabbis have much in common.

Sin and obedience, good deeds and grace, justice and mercy, holiness and evil, judgment and redemption, trials and sanctification, faith and doubt, mystery and revelation, forgiveness and eternal loss—we are so much closer than most of us know on all of these important things. They can bind Christian and Jew together because of our mutual love of God, or, because of our differing responses to Jesus, they can separate us if that is what we choose. But Christian and Jew alike must understand that a choice between suspicion and reconciliation is not a choice about Jesus; it is a choice about our neighbors and ourselves. No Jew should ever expect me to be silent about Jesus —that would be like asking a Jew not to mention the Torah. And of course, I should never equate a Jewish rejection of Jesus with a personal rejection of me.

In short, we continue to love the same God, in spite of two millennia spent growing in different directions from our mutual roots. Why not love each other as well?

Now I am back at Chever Torah on that terrifying day, the day when I defended the church without another Christian in sight, calling one Jew a liar in front of a hundred others. The room is absolutely silent. Everyone's eyes were on me a moment before, but now not even the rabbi will look in my direction. If that word, "liar," were a physical thing, I would grab it and stuff it back inside my mouth, no matter how bitter the taste. But there it hangs in midair, resonating in this peaceful place where I am a stranger—my own ugly word, desecrating this dignified temple.

I am living one of the most disgraceful moments of my life.

28. Luke 2:42–47.

Blessedly, a few minutes later Chever Torah is over. I rise, eyes on the floor, and move quickly toward the door. Someone blocks my way. Too ashamed to look up, I step aside. But he moves too. Sighing, knowing I must face him and take my medicine, I lift my eyes to his face.

The stranger before me steps close, wraps his arms around me, and claps me on the back without saying a word.

In my surprise, I look around. Behind this man stands an elderly woman, watching me with a worried expression. To her right and left are others, moving near. They reach toward me, touching me, comforting me. Rabbi Robbins also lingers to see that I am all right, delaying a Bar Mitzvah for a few minutes because of her concern. More and more Chever Torah Jews move my way, surrounding me, hugging me, offering tender words of comfort.

The Jews of Chever Torah have taught me—have *shown* me—how to love my neighbor as myself.

When you believe you've found the secret to a fulfilled life here and now, and the key to an eternal life of bliss in heaven later on, it is difficult—and selfish—to keep it quiet, especially if you truly believe you must love your neighbor as yourself. The New Testament teaches that Jesus' first and last commandments during his earthly ministry were to become "fishers of men" and to go throughout the earth baptizing all peoples into the faith.[29] Just as Jews honor God through obedience to the Torah's *mitzvot,* as a Christian, I must honor and obey Jesus. Not that this is a burden. Like all sincere Christians, I want all my neighbors to experience the joy of a personal relationship with their Creator, and sometimes I feel a strong desire to shout about Jesus from the rooftops.

But when my Chever Torah friends hear certain Christian denominations announcing that they intend to "save the Jews," most of them view it as the first wakeful rumblings of a threat against their very existence. Now I finally understand why. I

29. Matthew 4:19; 28:19.

have seen my religion as a modern Jew might—not as a safe harbor in the storm but as the tempest itself, a potentially malevolent force looming above the battered ark of Judaism. A Jew, reminded by my words of all we Christians have done throughout the centuries to her people, might well be excused for placing the Christian crusaders in the same category as the rampaging pagan hoards of Atilla the Hun. She might well confuse the coldly methodical Catholic Spanish Inquisition for evil ministrations of the Nazi S.S. She might be expected to ask the obvious question:

"What's the use of Jesus, if he makes so little difference in his followers?"

It is a question to shame every Christian. Jesus prayed that we Christians would all be one because he wished us to provide an irresistible example of his love to all the world. Obviously we have failed to honor his wish. But does an unfulfilled desire on Jesus' part mean his teachings are false?

If that were true, I would also have to assume that Judaism is false, because the Master of the universe once expressed a similar desire for his Hebrews, an unfulfilled desire I quoted once before:

Oh, that their hearts would be inclined to fear me and keep all my commands always, so that it might go well with them and their children forever!

—Deuteronomy 5:29

If the crimes of the church throughout the centuries were proof that Jesus' teachings are untrue, then the repeated failure of Israel to keep all of God's commands would also show the Torah for a lie. But of course the Torah should not be judged on the behavior of Jews, just as Jesus should not be judged on the conduct of Christians. Although the world does indeed draw conclusions about Jesus from my behavior, that merely shows how unwise the world can be, because in this universe it is always cause then effect, never the other way around. My behavior does not change God, of course, so whatever the truth about Jesus may be, it remains true whether I obey his teachings or not.

And what is that truth?

The fact that Christian history makes it an act of bravery for a Jew to even listen to the answer to that question is compounded by the fact that mine is a faith so filled with paradox that it defies complete explanation. But in the chapters to come, I will do my best to tell the truth about Jesus as Christians see it.

# eleven

# One and All

I am first; I have no Father. I am last; I have no brother. And beside Me, there is no God; I have no son.

—Shemot Rabbah, 29, 5

I am early to Chever Torah for once, walking toward an empty seat, when my path crosses Margie's. We kiss each other's cheeks and in seconds flat, somehow, we are discussing Jesus.

"Did you have a good Christmas?" she asks.

"It was okay," I respond. "Sometimes I wish there wasn't so much pressure."

"You have pressure at Christmastime?"

She puts the accent on the "you," and I understand her meaning. Christmas is sometimes difficult for Jews in the United States. Everywhere they turn they find reminders that theirs is a tiny community adrift in a sea of Gentiles. But I decide to press my point.

"You'd be surprised. It's a lot of trouble. Buying presents and putting up decorations and going to parties. . . ."

She is smiling now. "Yes, I can see how all those parties would be a burden."

"Well, sometimes I wish I could just focus on Jesus, you know?"

"No. I don't know, actually." Suddenly she is serious. "I could never be a Christian. I think worshiping Jesus is idolatry."

I have known Margie for over four years now, so her bluntness comes as no surprise. She is eighty-six years old and entitled to forgo beating around the bush.

"Oh no," I respond, "If you were a Christian, you would believe that Jesus is Yahweh, the one God."

She gives me a blank look for a moment then says, "But I don't believe that, so for me it's still idolatry, right?"

With her usual acumen, Margie has zeroed in on the main disagreement between Judaism and Christianity. Rabbinic Jews simply do not believe what Christianity teaches about Jesus, so from their perspective worship of him feels like idolatry. As a man told me while we were standing beside the coffee urn at Chever Torah recently, "You don't need that man between you and God." His remark was a perfect example of the widespread failure among Jews to fully appreciate the simplicity of the way the New Testament views Jesus. There is no man standing between God and me, because Jesus *is* God. But he is also a man.

It's so simple.

It's so confusing.

Perhaps I had better explain.

It is important for Jews to know that a knowledgeable Christian would never say that Jesus is a different god from Yahweh. That would indeed be idolatry. But are Christians trying to have it both ways? Am I saying I believe in Jesus as a distinct person, *and* in Jesus as the one and only God?

Absolutely.

Almost every week at Chever Torah we encounter paradox in the Torah in one form or another. To me, Jesus' humanity and divinity belongs to the same class of impenetrable truths as the apparently ridiculous notion that prayer can modify the decisions of an unchanging God. For that matter, the Trinity is no more difficult to accept than the mutually contradictory ideas that God is an all-powerful Entity, yet we can choose to disobey, so our will is independent of the Lord's power. Christians and Jews blithely refer to the paradoxes of immutability versus prayer and omnipotence versus freewill as if everyone understands them, yet both concepts violate the fundamentals of human logic. For a Christian, it is reasonable to place the Trinity in the same category. God is able to be both a man and God, both one and three, just as he is supreme in authority yet allows disobedience, and just as he is unchanging yet influenced by human prayer.

God is three. God is one. I believe both are simultaneously true, but I cannot hold the concept in my mind. Of course, since I am talking about the Creator of the universe, it would be surprising indeed if I *could* completely understand.

Some will protest that I am trying to have my cake and eat it too.

In the earlier discussion of why bad things happen to good people, I learned that God is limited by logic. In a logical universe, even God cannot make sense of nonsense. Now here I am suggesting that a logical person can believe in the trinitarian doctrine because the Lord is beyond logic, and paradoxes such as "God is three, God is one" are exactly what I should expect from a God who stands outside the laws of nature.

But there is no contradiction here.

The former statement, that God is limited by logic, is predicated not on divine limitation, but on the limits of the human race. Logic limits *me*, not him. Because I am only able to understand things on a logical level, whenever God enters human history to act he must work within the confines of my condition, at least insofar as he wishes me to understand or perceive what he is doing. The Lord's options are much the same as mine when dealing with a difficult dog. I do not waste my time trying to reason with the animal. Instead, I communicate in a doggish way, with monosyllabic commands, doggie treats, and occasional yanks on his leash. I communicate in that way because that is how dogs communicate with each other. I lower myself to his level. But that does not mean I can no longer understand

Shakespeare or work an algebraic equation. In the same way, my inability to understand the divine paradoxes of the Bible has no effect whatsoever on God's ability to exist in ways beyond my comprehension.

All efforts to understand the Lord fall short because of the vast gulf between his state of existence and mine. When trying to envision who and what God is, I am struggling to get a peek at God on a level where the constraints of human logic do not apply. To forget this, even for a moment, is to lose all hope of understanding even the tiny bit I can know about the Lord.

Still, while most Jews will readily agree that it is impossible to understand God, they might also wonder where in the world we Christians got our strange notions about him being both a Father and a Son, a human being and a Holy Spirit. What is the basis for these difficult beliefs?

When Jesus quoted the Shema in response to the question, "Which is the most important commandment?" clearly he considered it a vital concept.[1] This is ironic, since the Shema stands at the center of the dispute between Judaism and Christianity about the Trinity. It is the Scripture Maimonides quoted in support of his second fundamental principle of Judaism, which was in part a denial of the idea of a triune God:

> We are told to believe God is one. . . . He is not like a member of a pair, nor a species of a genus, nor a person divided into many discrete elements.
>
> —Maimonides[2]

But it is interesting to look at the words of the Shema on their most fundamental level. The transliterated Hebrew words are these: *Shema, Yisrael, Yahweh, Elohim, Yahweh, echad.* Translated in the same order, these words mean: "Hear, Israel, Lord, God, Lord, one." So both three and one are there: God is named three times, followed by the simple word, "one." Literally, the

1. Mark 12:29.
2. Helek: Sanhedrin, ch. 10 as quoted in *A Maimonides Reader*, pp. 417–418.

verse does not say, "the Lord is one." There is no "is." The only verb is "hear." The literal point it makes is this: "Lord God Lord one."

At Mt. Sinai, I find something similar. When Moses asks to see God's glory, the Lord's response begins with the words: "The Lord, the Lord, God. . . ."[3] As with the Shema, before anything else is revealed about his nature, God names himself three times.

Perhaps this is all just a coincidence, or some kind of literary device common in ancient manuscripts. But what am I to do with the following observation?

> Yet despite the centrality which the Shema has been accorded in Jewish tradition, its exact meaning (therefore, its translation) is not entirely certain, nor is the reason for the particular writing of its Hebrew text (the third letters of the first and last words are enlarged).
>
> —Rabbi W. Gunther Plaut[4]

Rabbi Plaut makes two important points. First, nobody really knows exactly how to interpret the Shema. It might mean simply that God is one, but the Hebrew allows for other interpretations. Second, no one knows why the Torah author of ancient times chose to enlarge the *third* letters of the words "hear," and "one," any more than they know why the Torah persists in repeating God's name *three* times when he is described in crucial verses. But as a Christian, I have a strong suspicion what the hints are all about.

When deriving his second principle of Judaism from the Shema, Maimonides focused on the Hebrew word *echad,* or "one," taking the word to mean singleness in this context. But *echad* is used in the Bible in the same ways we use the English word "one" today; therefore, it can be given at least three different interpretations. Like "one," *echad* can mean a single, individual thing, as Maimonides said. It can also mean the unity of multiple things. For example, the Torah teaches that Adam and Eve were *echad,* or "one flesh."[5] Yet Adam and Eve were also "members of a pair," to

3. Exodus 34:6.
4. Plaut, *The Torah, A Modern Commentary*, p. 1365.
5. Genesis 2:24.

quote Maimonides again. Finally, the word *echad* can also be translated to mean "first." In fact, it is in this sense that the word initially appears in Torah.[6] So, like its English counterpart, *echad* means singular, unison, and first. Rabbinic Judaism has always understood *echad* in the context of the Shema as meaning only singular and first. Christians try to understand it in all three ways simultaneously, including unity. (Again, we "try to understand" because the Trinity concept is impossible for the human mind to fully grasp, as are all ideas about God's nature.)

In my studies at temple, again and again I have found other reasons to believe the Trinity is true. In fact, many of the Hebrew Scriptures seem awkward to me otherwise. Ironically, the Christian explanation for most of these enigmatic verses eluded me before my time at Chever Torah because I had not yet learned to study the Bible in the Jewish way.

Early in this book I explained that Reform Judaism taught me about the value of asking any question no matter how frightening or apparently heretical, as well as the value of facing Biblical paradox head-on. Part of that approach involves looking for hidden meaning. Toward that end, the Kabbalistic Rabbis studied Torah on at least four levels. But the first of these, called the *p'shat*, or plain sense, was anything but hidden. *P'shat* is the basic meaning of the text. The rabbis believed the more direct the interpretation, the more likely it is to be true, and taught that "No scriptural interpretation ever abandons its p'shat—Plain Sense."[7] The early church fathers also held this view. It is an essential truth in Bible study that all Christians should bear in mind, because sometimes the most amazing ideas in the Bible are hiding in plain sight.

Of course, simply because the *p'shat* meaning is "plain" does not necessarily mean it is obvious. I have already seen one example of this in examining the Shema. Another is found in the following verse concerning God's revelation at the burning bush:

> And God said, "I will be with you. And this will be the sign to you that it is I who have sent you: When you have brought the people out of Egypt, you will worship God on this mountain."
>
> —Exodus 3:12

6. Genesis 1:5.
7. *Studying the Torah*, p. 22.

One *p'shat* reading here is the basic message: God intends to remain with Moses, and promises to prove that fact when Moses returns to Mt. Sinai. But given my newfound Chever Torah ability to read the text with a more open mind, I now find something interesting hiding on the surface of these words. The Lord begins by speaking in the first person, saying, "I will be with you" but then he speaks in the third person, saying, "you will worship God." This shift of God's voice from first to third person seems strange. Why not say, "You will worship Me"?

Something about this seems familiar. Returning to the Bible, I find this dimly remembered verse:

> Then King David went in and sat before the Lord, and he said: "Who am I, O Sovereign Lord, and what is my family, that you have brought me this far? What more can David say to you? For you know your servant, O Sovereign Lord."
>
> —2 Samuel 7:18, 20

Here is a very similar point-of-view switch. David begins in first person, speaking directly as "I," but ends in third person, speaking of himself as "David," as if he were outside this conversation, looking on. Now I wonder, is this simply an ancient form of address, a normal way of speaking that should not be given any deeper implications, or is there some special meaning when people communicate this way in the Bible?

To find out, I need to get more examples and see if there are common elements between them. I search the Torah for the words, "your servant" and, sure enough, find many other places where people mix that third person form of address with first person pronouns like "me," "myself," and "I." Abraham did it when speaking to the Lord and two angels in the hills above Sodom. Lot did it when speaking to those same two angels later on. Jacob spoke this way to God when begging to be saved from Esau. Moses switched back and forth from "I" to "your servant" when speaking to the Lord at the burning bush.[8]

So this was a typical form of address in ancient times, as suspected, but I could not help but notice a common denominator in every example I found. The speaker is always subservient to

8. See Genesis 18:3; 19:19; 32:9–10; Exodus 4:10.

the one being addressed. Ordinary men speak to kings and angels and God as if they are talking about someone else. They are usually entreating him for something or confessing their inadequacy: "please allow your servant . . ." or "your servant is not worthy. . . ." The formality of this third-person form of address underscores the speaker's knowledge of his subservient position and serves to honor the superior personage being addressed. But it was not the habit of those in power back in ancient times to return this favor.

Nowhere in the Hebrew Scriptures can I find kings speaking down to common men this way. Pharaoh did not do it. Neither did Saul or David or Solomon or any of the other rulers mentioned in the Hebrew Scriptures. Yet here is God, the ultimate ruler, speaking this way to a mortal man at the burning bush. Why?

Obviously the Lord is not subservient to Moses, so there must be another explanation.

When God says, "I will be with you . . ." and then ". . . you will worship God," it is as if his voice speaks from one perspective and then another. This is not an isolated example taken out of context. Throughout the Hebrew Scriptures, a mid-conversation shift in point of view is a common phenomenon when God speaks to people. Consider another famous passage, one mentioned before, where God repeats his name three times and describes himself in response to Moses' request to see his "glory":

And he [God] passed in front of Moses, proclaiming, "The Lord, the Lord, the compassionate and gracious God, slow to anger, abounding in love and faithfulness, maintaining love to thousands, and forgiving wickedness, rebellion and sin. Yet he does not leave the guilty unpunished; he punishes the children and their children for the sin of the fathers to the third and fourth generation."

—Exodus 34:6–7

There is a "plain sense" meaning to these words: God tells Moses who he is with a list of adjectives, and descriptions of his behavior. But now I see another clue on the surface, perhaps even more fundamental. As with the conversation at the burning bush, God is speaking here in the third-person verb tense, as if his words apply to someone else. Why this odd form of address? Instead of saying, ". . . he does not leave the guilty unpunished," why not say, "I do not leave the guilty unpunished"? The strangeness of this is underscored by its context. In the verses before and after the passage, God speaks with Moses in the first person tense, ("I will write . . ." and "I am making . . ."), but here, specifically when describing himself, the point of view shifts *as if one person were describing another.*

This only makes sense to me in view of the Trinity. And now that my eye is attuned to see it, I find this kind of "godly schizophrenia" rampant throughout the Lord's dialogue with humanity in the Hebrew Scriptures.[9] In the *p'shat* of these verses, God speaks as if he were outside himself looking in. Given the awkward and imprecise limitations of human language, what better way to describe what it must be like to be one and three simultaneously?

There are other kinds of hints about the Trinity within the Hebrew Scriptures. For example, consider this verse:

> The Lord says to my Lord: "Sit at my right hand until I make your enemies a footstool for your feet."
>
> —Psalm 110:1

Because Jews of Jesus' time did not believe the messiah would be divine (most still do not), Jesus quoted this Scripture to show that the messiah is the eternal Son of God rather than the mortal son of David. The first "Lord" is Yahweh in the Hebrew, leaving only the identity of the second "Lord" (*adon*) in question. "Adon" can mean simply "master," as in one who owns a slave, or it can mean "lord" as in one who is politically superior. But as Jesus said, "If then David calls him 'Lord,' how can he be his son?"[10] After all, David was no slave, and as king, he had no political superiors. Following Jesus' line of reasoning, Christians believe

---

9. For example, see Genesis 9:16; Exodus 34:14, 23–24; Leviticus 19:5.
10. Matthew 22:45.

"the Lord" and "my Lord" in this verse refer to the Father and Son of the Trinity, both of whom are Lords of David.

Many Christian and Jewish readers will be familiar with the various places in the Torah and the prophets where God refers to himself with plural pronouns, such as "us," or "we."

> And the Lord God said, "The man has now become like one of us, knowing good and evil. . . ."
>
> —Genesis 3:22

> Come, let us go down and confuse their language so they will not understand each other.
>
> —Genesis 11:7

> Then I heard the voice of the Lord saying, "Whom shall I send? And who will go for us?"
>
> —Isaiah 6:8

> Then God said, "Let us make man in our image, in our likeness. . . ."
>
> —Genesis 1:26

Why does God speak as if he is one of a group in these verses? Perhaps the most common rabbinic explanation holds that God refers to himself as "us" in the sense of plural majesty, much as the Queen of England might say, "We are not amused," when what she really means to say is, "I am not amused." If this is true, then I should be able to find the mode of speech used by kings and queens elsewhere in the Hebrew Scriptures. But a careful investigation of the Hebrew Scriptures reveals that Pharaoh, King Saul, King David, and King Solomon never refer to themselves in this way. Nor is this "plural majesty" device used in Homer's nearly contemporaneous ancient Greek stories about the royal Agamemnon, Achilles, or Odysseus. So it seems the tradition of ruling authorities referring to themselves as "us" and "we" did not exist in the ancient Greek, Egyptian, or Hebrew worlds at the time these plural self-references by God were written. Based on this, I believe the rabbis have things reversed. God does not refer to himself this way because some scribe believed that is how great rulers should speak; rather, rulers of later times copied how the God of the Bible speaks.

Returning to Genesis 1:27, there is another *p'shat* reading that I believe supports the idea of the Trinity. The words of this verse are: ". . . in the image of God he created him; male and female he created them." Always before when I read this text, I gave the "male and female" portion little thought, because it seemed obvious God created both men and women.

But why state the obvious?

At Chever Torah, as we study the scriptural idea that Adam and Eve were "one flesh," the following concept is presented:

> When a soul is sent down from Heaven, it is a combined male and female soul.
>
> —Zohar, iii, 43b

When I learn about this theory, suddenly the notion that man was created in God's image as both male and female takes on a new level of meaning, and I glimpse an important possibility in the verse that says he made us *male and female* in his image. Could it be phrased in that way because the creation of men and women is meant to be a reflection of the divine plurality? What if men, women, and the third thing that we become when joined together—the "one flesh"—are somehow meant to be an earthly image and likeness of the three persons of God?

This has important ramifications not only in my understanding of God's nature, but also in terms of marriage.[11] It explains why sexual sin is dealt with so severely in the Torah. Adultery equals idolatry.

In Exodus, the punishment of the idolatrous people of Israel began when they were required to drink water mixed with the

---

11. See 1 Corinthians 11:3, which draws a similar parallel between the relationship of the Son to the Father, and the wife to the husband.

ashes of the golden calf they had worshipped.[12] Similarly, any woman accused of adultery was required to drink water mixed with the dust of the tabernacle floor.[13] The Hebrew word translated as "dust" in the latter case is first found in the second chapter of Genesis, with the description of Adam's creation in the image and likeness of God. Surely these connections are not coincidental. If one man plus one woman plus the one thing they become when united in marriage is an image of the triune God, then the Lord's reason for prohibiting sex outside of marriage is the same as his reason for prohibiting the worship of other gods. Both adultery and idolatry are crimes against his "image and likeness."

Throughout this book, when speaking about God's characteristics I have done my best to avoid the word "attribute" because I wish to explore the following idea:

> If one believes him to be One and to possess a number of attributes, one in fact says that he is One and thinks that he is many. This is the same as what the Christians say: he is one, but he is three, and the three are one.
>
> —Maimonides[14]

The famous rabbi goes on to explain his position this way:

Since God is the first cause, he must have established everything, including such things as justice, righteousness, holiness, mercy, and love. As creations, then, these things must not be thought of as part of God, or as attributes of him, because the Lord was first and they came after. They cannot be part of God if he created everything, because "everything" includes them. God is the cause; they are the effect. And as I have said before in this book, it is cause first, then effect—never the other way around.

12. Exodus 32:20.
13. Numbers 5:12–21.
14. Maimonides, *Guide of the Perplexed*, p. 65.

This is part of the reason God said Israel would know him as "I Am."[15] That most personal name for God is significant as much for what it does not say as for what it says. For example, it does not say, "I am love," or "I am holy," or "I am righteous," or "I am just." That would be confusing the effect with the cause.

Maimonides says these "attributes" only apply to God in two ways: to define what he is not, or to describe his actions.[16] In the strictest, most literal sense we must not believe that God is any of these things, because such a mind-set leads to the misconception that God is an amalgam of attributes instead of an entity of perfect oneness. When thinking about God's essence, I must not think that he is love, for example, because even that noble idea leads to a limited conception of God.

God simply is.

Now consider this in a different way. In the Bible where God tells Moses to call him "I Am," the Hebrew verb can also mean, "I will be." In other words, God describes himself as pure potential or the raw ability to cause. He is not really love; he is what causes love. There are no precise analogies for God, of course, but bearing the "I will be" name of God in mind, I might think of the Lord as a fire, and love and justice as light and heat. Light and heat are not fire; they are what travel out from fire, just as love and justice are not God; they are attributes emanating out from him.

Christian readers will be wondering, "What about John's assertion that 'God is love'? Doesn't that contradict Maimonides?" But I think the answer is no, because John's statement was not meant to imply that God is composed of love. In fact, he goes on in the next two verses to clearly state exactly what he means by "love" in that context:

> Whoever does not love does not know God, because God is love. This is how God showed his love among us: he sent his one and only Son into the world that we might live through him. This is love: not that we loved God, but that he loved us and sent his Son as an atoning sacrifice for our sins.
>
> —1 John 4:8–10

15. Exodus 3:14.
16. Maimonides, *Guide of the Perplexed*, p. 18.

So according to John, when it comes to God, love is not an attribute, it is an action, just as Maimonides said.

Of course, there is a major point of disagreement between Maimonides's position and Christianity's. I believe God's existence somehow includes both oneness and three distinct "persons," each with a will, an intellect, and emotions. But unlike Maimonides, I find nothing in the concept of the Trinity that implies a created attribute coexisting with God. Jesus' words in the Christian Scriptures plainly indicate that he himself is not an "attribute" in the sense of being a part or portion of God. To the contrary, when Jesus said, "I and the Father are one," and "Before Abraham was born, I am," he referred to the Shema and the tetragrammaton in order to teach that he is the uncreated God himself, not a portion or an attribute of the Lord.

At this point, Maimonides might reassert his statement quoted earlier: "If one believes him to be One and to possess a number of attributes, one in fact *says* that he is One and *thinks* that he is many." But Maimonides·confuses his terms. Christians do not say God is composed of three attributes. We say he is three persons. "Attribute" and "person" are not the same. In the Hebrew Scriptures, an angel and even God himself can sometimes be perceived by human beings as "a man."[17] Similarly, "person" does not necessarily mean only "human being" in Christian theology. It means any entity demonstrating emotions, intellect, and will—all three of which are exactly what we believe God displays as the Father, the Son, and the Holy Spirit.

The Nicene Creed, perhaps the most widely embraced liturgical statement of Christian faith, includes the assertion that Jesus is "of one substance with the Father . . . ." The word "substance" was selected specifically to guard against the possibility that Christians could adopt the error asserted by Maimonides, and was probably chosen with Aristotle's definition of "substance" in mind. According to Aristotle, the idea of substance means "the absolute or essential . . . in its nature prior to the relative . . . ."[18] The phrase "of one substance" is understood by Christian scholars as meaning "sharing one being with the Father, and therefore

17. See Genesis 18 and 32 for examples.
18. Aristotle, *The Nicomachean Ethics*, p. 17.

distinct in existence, though essentially one."[19] There is a genuine difference between the ideas of multiple attributes and multiple existences.

Christianity teaches both monotheism and the idea that there is a sense of community within the Godhead—three distinct persons who are yet somehow one. Like many wise Jews before and after him, Maimonides took great pains to demonstrate that, on a purely logical level, this teaching is doubletalk. But what Maimonides failed to appreciate (and this is surprising for one so intelligent) is the fact already mentioned several times, that I should *expect* mere logic to be unequal to the task of understanding the eternal, all-knowing, all-powerful, and omnipresent Creator of the universe. Christianity does not teach the Trinity because it is logical. (We are not such fools as that.) We teach God in three persons because we believe that is what the Bible seems to say.

Maimonides had his own problems in this area. For example, as I have mentioned before, the Torah makes it clear that God is everywhere, but it also sometimes describes him as being present in one place in a way that is different from his presence in other locations:

> Then have them make a sanctuary for me, and I will dwell among them.
>
> —Exodus 25:8

Because the Hebrew Scriptures include many similar references to God dwelling in space and time, the rabbis faced a dilemma similar to that of Christianity's struggle to understand Jesus. How can references to God's interaction with creation in a limited way be explained without attributing any kind of limitation or division within his nature? How can he be here in a special way yet everywhere else at the same time unless he has the capacity to manifest himself differently here and there?

19. Henry Bettenson, ed. *Documents of the Christian Church* (Oxford: Oxford University Press, 1963), footnote, p. 25, and text, p. 26.

One rabbi arrived at the following wonderful explanation:

Rabbi Levi said, "The tabernacle was like a cave that joins the sea. The sea rushes in and floods the cave. The cave is filled but the sea is in no wise diminished. By the same token, the tabernacle was filled with the radiance of the Divine Presence, but the world thereby lost nothing of that Presence."

—Shir ha-Shirim Rabbah on verse 3, 10

Rabbi Levi might just as well have been a Christian trying to describe Jesus.

With respect, I believe Maimonides and Rabbinic Judaism have made a fundamental mistake. In no way must the Shema be taken as a limitation imposed on God—not even to the extent that we say he has no limitations. Instead, it should be taken as a statement of his essence, which is limited only in ways he has voluntarily chosen on behalf of his creation. God is outside human logic. He controls what we call "common sense"; it does not control him. Therefore, the fact that I cannot understand or conceive of an entity who is fully one yet fully three in no way limits the Lord's ability to exist in that way.

The Shema is not the only Jewish basis for objecting to the divinity of Jesus or the Trinity, as I learn when I make the acquaintance of Betty, a round and rosy red-headed newcomer to Chever Torah.

Betty has just revealed that she was once a Methodist.

"Why did you convert?" I ask.

"I just couldn't believe all that stuff about Jesus being God."

"Why not?"

"Well, for one thing, if you read the New Testament, he never says, 'I am God,' does he?"

Christians may be shocked to realize that Betty's statement is true. Nowhere in the four Gospels are the simple words "I am God" uttered by Jesus. Betty believes this means Jesus is not God, but there is another explanation.

In modern English, "god" is a generic term that encompasses everyone's understanding of the divine. There was no such term in first-century Palestine. Even the most generic name of God, *El*, when spoken by a Jew to other Jews, was intrinsically understood to be the God of the temple. In that time and place, if Jesus were to say, "I am God," everyone would think he meant, "I am Elohim," or "El Shaddai," or "Adonai," each of which carried specific connotations about the one God. But if Jesus had used any of these terms for God to explain himself, his audience would have misunderstood completely, because the New Testament teaches that Jesus is not God in that way. He is God in a way unlike any other humanity had yet experienced.

In short, Jesus did not say, "I am God," because no word yet existed in any language on earth for the God that he is.

How does one explain a concept that is so completely new and foreign to one's audience? Exactly as Jesus did, by searching for areas of mutual understanding and drawing parallels from that, conveying his revolutionary truth through stories and examples from everyday life.

Suppose I am transported back to Jesus' time and faced with the task of describing the Internet to the people I find there. If I begin by saying, "The Internet is a telecommunications network connecting millions of computers around the world," I will be perfectly accurate but utterly fail to communicate my point. And if I insist on pressing this approach, I will probably be dismissed as a babbling idiot. Instead, I must first explain the concepts of telecommunications and computers. But to explain those things I will have to speak of telephones and microprocessors, and to explain them, I will have to mention speakers and transistors and so forth until I get down to the most basic concept underlying the technology, which I suppose must be electricity, and to explain that, I will probably have to begin with lightning. So I will not use the word "Internet" until long after I have begun with lightning and built my way up, but I will still have been talking about the Internet all along.

The Gospels are filled with exactly that kind of communication between Jesus and his audiences. He does not say, "I am Yahweh." Instead, he says, "I am the bread of life." He does not say, "I am Adonai." Instead he says, "I am the light of the world."

He does not say, "I am El Shaddai." Instead he says, "I am the gate."[20] And if I listen closely, I get his meaning.

Consider this:

> "If you are the Christ," they said, "tell us." Jesus answered, "If I tell you, you will not believe me, and if I asked you, you would not answer. But from now on, the Son of Man will be seated at the right hand of the mighty God." They all asked, "Are you then the Son of God?" he replied, "You are right in saying I am."
>
> —Luke 22:67–70

These words are spoken before the Jewish ruling body of the time, the Sanhedrin. Here I find a hint of the dilemma facing Jesus: "If I tell you, you will not believe me." These Jews, like most Jews today, believe the "christ"—the messiah or anointed one—will be a human king who will deliver them from earthly oppression. They do not believe he will be a divine spiritual savior. They had no frame of reference for Jesus' claims. But they understand the meaning of his final words clearly enough. This is seen in the following verses, when they respond by having him put to death for blasphemy.

Jesus never says, "I am Yahweh," but several times he does say, "I am" in contexts clearly intended to communicate his divinity to those who listen closely. Bearing in mind that the word *Yahweh* is based on the Hebrew words "I am," consider these examples:

> I told you that you would die in your sins; if you do not believe that *I am*, you will indeed die in your sins."
>
> —John 8:24 (emphasis mine)

> So Jesus said, "When you have lifted up the Son of Man, then you will know that *I am* and that I do nothing on my own but speak just what the Father has taught me."
>
> —John 8:28 (emphasis mine)

> "Your father Abraham rejoiced at the thought of seeing my day; he saw it and was glad." "You are not yet fifty years old," the Jews

20. John 6:35; 9:5; 10:9.

said to him, "and you have seen Abraham!" "I tell you the truth," Jesus answered, "before Abraham was born, *I am!*" At this, they picked up stones to stone him, but Jesus hid himself, slipping away from the temple grounds.

—John 8:56–59 (emphasis mine)

Jesus' Jewish audience knows that the most personal name of God is derived from the words "I Am." This, added to the fact that the issue under discussion in each of the above Scriptures is Jesus' nature, makes the meaning of his statements difficult to deny.

It is lamentable that some English translations add words or phrases after the words "I am" in these verses, as if Jesus' statements are incomplete thoughts. In some of the quotations above I have removed these extraneous words because they are not in the original Greek text. Perhaps even the Christian translators missed Jesus' subtle meaning, but his Jewish audience understands immediately. The third example listed above is yet another moment when some of those listening to Jesus attempt to execute him on the spot for blasphemy.

Everyone knows there are ways of saying a thing without saying a thing, just as we all know actions speak louder than words. If Jesus does not intend me to believe he is God, why does he go about forgiving people's sins? Again, the significance of this is not lost on the Jews of his time. They ask, "Why does this fellow talk like that? He's blaspheming! *Who can forgive sins but God alone?*"[21] They might also ask, "Who but God has the power to give life?" because Jesus also claims that divine prerogative:

For just as the Father raises the dead and gives them life, even so the Son gives life to whom he is pleased to give it.

—John 5:21

Almost every word Jesus speaks about himself implies his divinity. He says to dishonor him is to dishonor God, to know him is to know God, to believe him is to believe God, to receive him is to receive God, and to hate him is to hate God. Jesus also says he is the fulfillment of the law and claims the ability to send

---

21. Mark 2:7 (emphasis mine).

God's Holy Spirit. He says he knows the Father in a way we do
not. He says he and the Father are one (remember the Shema),
and he is in the Father and the Father is in him. Jesus does not
say, "I know how to have eternal life," he says, "I *am* life. . . ." He
does not say, "I know the truth," he says, "I *am* truth."[22]

Building on an earlier observation by G. K. Chesteron, C. S.
Lewis once pointed out that there are only four possible explanations for such astonishing statements. Perhaps Jesus never said
them. But this is highly doubtful in light of the well-demonstrated
provenience of the Gospels (we have far more copies dating to
within a couple of hundred years of the events they describe than
any other ancient book, including the Torah). Or perhaps Jesus
said them but he was a lunatic or a liar. But anyone examining his
words must agree that they reveal an eminently sound mind and
an unflinching honesty. So that leaves just the fourth possibility:
Jesus is who he said he is.

Perhaps this is why many Jews in Jesus' day believed him.
Some responded by trying to stone him or have him crucified,
but many fell to their knees and worshiped him on the spot. This
response first occurred with the famous "three wise men" at
Jesus' birth. This was the apostles' reaction when he walked on
water. A man blind from birth worshiped Jesus when he gave
him sight. Many disciples worshiped him when he rose from the
dead. And when Thomas fell to the floor and called Jesus "My
Lord *and my God*," Jesus simply accepted his adoration.[23]

In Thomas's case at least, Jesus has finally gotten his point
across.

I have already mentioned the Gospel incidents when the
crowds around Jesus attempted to stone him on the spot pre-

22. Dishonor him = dishonor God—John 5:23; know him = know God—John 8:19–
20; 14:7; believe him = believe God—John 12:44; 14:1: receive him = receive God—John
15:23; hate him = hate God—John 15:23; fulfillment of law—Matthew 5:17; ability to
send Holy Spirit—John 15:26; unique knowledge of the Father—John 17:25; one with
Father—John 10:30; in Father and Father in him—John 14:10; "I am . . . life."—John
11:25; "I am truth"—John 14:6.
23. Three wise men—Matthew 2:11; walking on water—Matthew 14:25–33; blind
man—John 9:38; risen from dead—Matthew 28:9, 17; Lord and God—John 20:28.

cisely because Jesus' hints became too transparent. This happened when he said, "Before Abraham was born, I am," and later when he said, "I and the Father are one."[24] It is no coincidence that the first statement is so similar to the "I Am" of God's revelation to Moses from the burning bush, and the second is so similar to the Shema. Those very similarities are why his Jewish audience became so angry. Their anger was another reason Jesus never said, "I am God." But if Jesus is God incarnate, why should he worry about the anger of a few Jews?

Apparently, Jesus knows that a plainspoken revelation of his true nature would result in his physical death before his intended purpose on earth could be accomplished.

At first I resist this particular explanation because it seems inconsistent with Jesus' claims of divinity. Would God bother to protect himself from mere humans by being careful in his choice of words? Jesus could drive away an angry mob with a mere thought. Why take all these pains to work within the first-century Jewish mindset? Why not just tell it like it is? Then I remember that God has allowed himself to be influenced by human actions before. I remember prayer. I remember free will. I remember Abraham bargaining with the Lord for the lives of ten people in Sodom, and Moses negotiating with him at Mt. Sinai on behalf of a rebellious Israel. I remember that God seems to relish the idea of my involvement in his plans. Jesus' humble approach to self-revelation is consistent with such a God. Rather than an argument against his divinity, it is just what I should expect if the God of the Hebrew Scriptures reentered history as a man to meet me where I am.

Thinking about Jesus' assertions of divinity and about the Trinity after so many discussions with Jews has expanded my views on the subject. For that, I am eternally grateful to Judaism.

If anything, I now wonder why we Christians stop at just three divine persons. I find the Father, Son, and Holy Spirit within the pages of the Bible, but once the door is opened to the idea of a

24. John 8:58–59; 10:30–31.

plurality within the oneness of God (illogical as that sounds), it seems to me quite likely that God is an infinite number of "persons," not just three. After all, when I say "all the people," and when I say "one people," I am describing exactly the same thing. Similarly, when I say, "God is one," I am also saying, "God is infinity." Anything in between "one" and "all" leaves something out, but thinking about the fact that both are the same thing is the best way I know to grasp the idea of a God who can be everywhere all at once, while being right here in a special way, three persons, yet One, a man, yet divine.

With this concept, perhaps I can meet my Jewish friends at a place very close to where they are without violating anything essential in the Christian faith. I believe in the three persons of God: God the Father, God the Son, and God the Holy Spirit. I also believe in the God who cannot be bound by any limitation, including the logic of numbers or persons, unless he himself has decided to accept that limitation. I cannot find any statement in either the Tanakh or the New Testament that limits God to three persons, but there is a New Testament verse that refers to him as "all in all."[25]

God is much, much more than what he revealed in the Bible. In paradise, I suspect I will encounter the Lord in broader ways that I cannot even begin to guess at now. The Father, Son, and Holy Spirit will all be there for sure, but I believe I will also experience God as One and infinity, as a fellow human being, a spiritual presence, and the Master of the universe, who are somehow all the same.

25. 1 Corinthians 15:28.

# twelve

# The Word in the Word

---

Even matters which in Torah seem as fruitless as thorns, are in reality of the highest significance.

—Shir ha-Shirim Rabbah, 1

At Chever Torah we are studying the famous incident in the book of Numbers when Moses is told he will not be allowed to enter the Promised Land along with Israel. At issue is the question, "Why did God punish him this way?" Together, we brainstorm a long list of possible reasons. In the midst of this discussion, Reid, an attorney and a scholar of philosophy and theology, offers this comment:

"It's interesting to compare the Jewish view of Moses to the Christian view of Jesus in this context. We have a leader who is only human. The Torah includes Moses' punishment to underscore that fact. But when Christianity deified Jesus, they found themselves with a leader they could not criticize, and therefore could not identify with on same level as Jews relate to Moses." (It is a measure of Reid's intelligence that he really does speak this way, as if he has written everything down beforehand.)

I raise my hand immediately, eager to offer the Christian perspective on Reid's comment. But the rabbi, perhaps concerned that our conversation will go in an uncomfortable or irrelevant direction, does not call on me. After the session is over, I seek out Reid to explain that I believe his analogy is flawed. Rather than Jesus, the apostles Peter or Paul might be better Christian parallels to Moses. I tell him, "If your comparison were accurate, you would have to pray to Moses."

Reid's eyes get a faraway look. He seems eager to drop the subject, so I tactfully withdraw. But others apparently sense my concern.

Steve, another Chever Torah Jew who works for the fire department, was listening to our conversation. As Reid walks away, Steve and I move toward the door together. Out in the parking lot a few minutes later, we are still talking. Steve is slightly shorter than I am, and the sun is at my back, requiring him to squint up at me when he asks, "So you really believe Jesus was God?"

"I think he *is* God, yes."

Cocking his head to one side with what appears to be genuine curiosity, still squinting up into the sunshine, Steve asks perhaps the most daring Chever Torah question of all:

"Why?"

Steve has paid me a powerful compliment. In a world filled with zealous Christians who seem to view Jews as mere pagans, he is saying, "I don't think you're one of *them*." But although Steve has come to trust me, he takes a serious risk asking this question. Many Jews get nervous when other Jews investigate Jesus. And if Steve seriously contemplated faith in Jesus, he might well jeopardize the trust and affection of family and friends. If he actually came to believe the New Testament's teachings about Jesus, it is even possible that many people who have known him all of his life would disown him completely. Several Jews I know became unwelcome in their parents' home after believing in Jesus, and I have heard and read stories of many more. Anyone who doubts that this is a common reaction need only ask a few Messianic Jews to tell their conversion stories. A similar pattern of ostracism and disinheritance will soon appear.

The horror inflicted on the Jewish people in the name of Jesus over the centuries is one explanation for this response when a Jew converts, but it is only part of the reason. Another stems from the fact that the Christian view of Jesus is completely foreign to the traditional Jewish way of thinking. Indeed, for Rabbinic Jews, the concept of Jesus as God is a form of idolatry, as my friend Margie recently pointed out to me. That is why a brilliant man like Reid can so completely misunderstand the Christian perspective, to the point of making a comparison between Jesus and a merely human leader like Moses. Obviously, the reality that I actually believe Jesus is God Almighty has not settled very deeply into Reid's intellect, otherwise he would no more compare the Jewish view of Moses to the Christian view of Jesus than he would compare Abraham to Adonai. When I point out the flaw in his analogy, it is significant that Reid withdraws immediately—a typical Jewish response, and a very understandable one given the history of my people and his.

So Steve's question, "Why do you believe in Jesus?" is courageous precisely because Steve is willing to seriously consider the ramifications of a divine Jesus in spite of the potential damage it could do to his relationships, and in spite of the possibility that he is flirting with blasphemy.

In this chapter, I will try to explain why I believe in Jesus. It is not my intention to proselytize. These reasons are my own. They need not threaten Jewish readers, any more than the Jewish perspective threatens me each Shabbat at Chever Torah. Like the lessons I have learned there, I hope these thoughts will help the Christian reader to see his or her faith in refreshing new ways, and the Jewish reader to understand that there are reasonable arguments from the Torah for Christian beliefs, even if we disagree on the conclusions.

Throughout this book I have already given many explanations for my faith in Jesus. Before I offer any more, I will list those explanations again here in order to get everything neatly collected in one place. This way, the reader can fully appreciate the deep foundation that underpins Christian belief.

Here is a quick review:

In chapter 1, "God on the Spot," I observed that Jesus seems to be a natural next step in God's pattern of progressive self-revelation. Since the Torah reveals a God who appears to want me to understand him more and more clearly, since he seems to want more and more intimacy with me, it makes sense that the Lord would eventually come down to my level personally to speak to me directly.

In chapter 3, "God in Chains," I discussed why bad things happen to good people, and mentioned that God seems to have limited himself for the sake of human logic and free will. Continuing in that pattern, it makes sense to me that the Lord drew close through the self-limiting God that Jesus is because I cannot survive more unrestrained contact with him. Prayer, sacrifice, and fasting prove that he has always operated in creation through human beings. Why should he not visit us personally in the same way?

In chapter 4, "Yes and Yes," I explored scriptural paradox and found several in the Hebrew Scriptures that seem to me to hint at Jesus rather strongly. These include the Paradox of Fertility, the Paradox of Blessing, the Paradox of Omnipresence, and the Paradox of the Red Heifer. I noted that God seems to thrive on paradox and can only be explained to the human mind through paradox. The Paradox of Jesus—that a man can be God and that the immortal God can die on my behalf—fits this pattern.

In chapter 5, "The Beautiful Terror," I focused on the need for a direct emotional relationship between God and me. I observed that God sometimes describes himself in human terms in the Torah in order to meet me on a level I can understand. I said I believe Jesus is divine because the Lord knows I need a God I can relate to if he and I are to have a deep and loving relationship. I pointed out that such a relationship is impossible with the Master of the universe because the Creator is too huge to fill this empty heart I have. One might as well try to pass the Mississippi River through a garden hose. But because Jesus is both God and man, I can feel completely connected with the Lord, which is something God clearly wants, if the Hebrew Scriptures are true.

In chapter 7, "Pitching Tabernacles," I pointed out that Judaism and Christianity both teach the concept of grace. This is the idea that only the efforts of God are sufficient to bridge the gap between God and me, and the Lord provides that bridge in spite of the fact that I can never be good enough to deserve it. In light of this I mentioned how significant it is to me that Jesus is the only founder of a worldwide religion who claimed to be God. I believe in Jesus because he makes sense of grace. Since it is impossible for me to climb to heaven, heaven came down—in Jesus—and carried me up.

In chapter 9, "Up from the Well," I explained that I believe the Torah's "eye for eye, ear for ear, life for life" definition of justice leads inexorably to the conclusion that evil in the universe can only be reversed by the balancing influence of whatever caused that corruption in the first place—something equal but opposite in every way. Justice is balance. If Adam was spiritually perfect before his first sin condemned him to death, only a second flawless Adam rising up from death can restore the balance of the Garden. But I cannot pay that price because I cannot be blameless before the Lord, so Jesus became my surrogate, my substitute perfection on the scales of justice, providing the perfect life for perfect life that perfect justice requires. Adam went down to death a flawed, divided man. Jesus rose up from death a perfectly whole man. The cosmic scales of justice were balanced. And somehow—only God knows how—just as Adam bequeathed his tragic flaw to Seth and through Seth down to me, Jesus bequeaths his spiritual perfection to those who trust in him.

In chapter 11, "One and All," I discussed the Paradox of the Trinity and said, for me at least, it is reasonable to place the Trinity in the same category as the many other paradoxes of the Bible. God is able to be both one and three, just as he is supreme in authority yet allows disobedience, and just as he is unchanging yet influenced by human prayer. As I wrote at the end of chapter 4's discussion of paradox, ". . . if Jesus' man/God nature or the Trinity were completely understandable, I would abandon Christianity precisely because . . . all true explanations of God's nature must openly include paradoxical concepts my mind cannot grasp." Thus it is with the Paradox of Jesus.

Now that I have reviewed a few of the reasons for my faith in Jesus already discussed in this book, I wish to present some additional reasons that I find in the Hebrew Scriptures. Everyone knows that Christianity teaches the apparently ridiculous notion that Jesus is somehow both God Almighty and a simple Jewish carpenter. And as I have already learned, this was so previously unsuspected that human language in the first century contained no single word Jesus could use to describe himself. But the New Testament says that he did find a way to tell his followers who and what he is.

> Beginning with Moses and all the Prophets, he explained to them what was said in all the Scriptures concerning himself.
>
> —Luke 24:27

The Hebrew Scriptures we have today are exactly the same as the ones Jesus used to teach those who followed him. I used to wonder what Jesus showed the apostles there. Now, thanks to Chever Torah, I think I know.

He showed them himself.

For example, after Adam and Eve ate the forbidden fruit, Genesis says they ". . . heard the sound of the Lord God moving about in the garden at the breezy time of the day; and the man and the woman hid from the Lord God among the trees of the garden."[1] The Bible is full of such anthropomorphic imagery. The authors of the Scriptures knew of no other way to explain God's interaction in the universe, so they sometimes resorted to describing him as having hands and feet and vision and so forth. But this particular bit of anthropomorphic imagery strikes me as excessive. It seems pointless to describe God "moving about . . . at the breezy time of the day." Time and movement are irrelevant to the story, unless of course the text intends for me to think of this God as an entity that exists *within* time and space. The pointlessness disappears if this God in the Garden who makes noise when he walks is the same God who later reentered history as a Jewish carpenter.

Further on in Genesis, the Torah contains this puzzling statement: "The Lord appeared to Abraham near the great trees of

1. Genesis 3:8 (JPS).

Mamre while he was sitting at the entrance to his tent in the heat of the day. Abraham looked up and saw three men standing nearby."[2] Many Chever Torah Jews believe these two statements are unrelated. After all, what possible connection could exist between "the Lord appeared" and "Abraham saw three men"? Yet for some reason the Torah placed them here together, back to back, as if they apply to the same event.

To discover why, I continue reading the story and find these men not only "stand," but they also have dirty feet and healthy appetites. So the Torah intends me to understand that they are physical beings. Recognizing this, their good host Abraham takes care of their corporeal needs, washing their feet and feeding them. He is rewarded with an intriguing conversation as one of the men—at first called simply "he"—begins asking Abraham questions about his wife, Sarah. But in the middle of this dialogue suddenly it is no longer "he" who speaks to Abraham. The Hebrew text now provides me with the name of this fellow with clean feet and a full belly.

Incredibly, his name is Yahweh.

After their dinner conversation, when their meal is done and these three men rise to leave, the Torah says Abraham "remained standing before Yahweh" as the other two men move on. And just in case I am tempted to believe this story is about three men *plus* Yahweh, the next chapter opens with these words: "The two angels arrived at Sodom. . . ." So now there are only two.

Where is the third "man"?

He is back up on the hill, standing on clean feet before Abraham, discussing the future of the city below. Since the Torah continues to call this person Yahweh, it seems this man with a fully belly is indeed somehow also the God of Abraham, Isaac, and Jacob.

Speaking of Abraham's grandson Jacob, I am reminded of his remarkable experience beside the river Jabbok. There, as I discovered in my earlier examination of biblical paradox, the Torah says ". . . a man wrestled with him till daybreak." But this is no ordinary man. He is capable of wrenching Jacob's hip from its socket with a mere touch. In fact, that is exactly what he does, rather than allow Jacob to cling to him after the sun has risen.

2. Genesis 18:1–2.

When I studied this before, I could not imagine why this fellow cares about the sunlight. But now I finish the story and find that "Jacob called the place Peniel, saying, 'It is because I saw God face to face and yet my life was spared.'"[3]

Jacob saw God?

If that fantastic statement is true, if the "man" who wrestles with Abraham's grandson really is the Lord of the universe, it occurs to me that he might be concerned about the rising sun for Jacob's sake. This "man" may want to hide his face in the darkness for the same reason God will later say to Moses, "no one may see my face and live."[4]

Over my years at Chever Torah, I have heard many Jews refer to Jacob's opponent as an "angel," but the word "angel," or *malak*, is not present in the story.[5] And the text of Genesis clearly says this "God" whom Jacob saw "face to face" is an *enowsh*—the Hebrew word for "man."

The first time I mentioned Jacob's wrestling match at the river Jabbok, I wrote, "It occurs to me that all of these questions may overlay a deeper truth, perhaps the fundamental reason for the story." Now I believe I know what caused that nagging sense of something hidden just beneath the surface. Before, I read the story of Jacob and the "man" wrestling beside the waters of the Jabbok and I marveled that a man could struggle with God. Now I marvel that God could be a man. Now I believe Jacob's opponent, this man who is God, was none other than the preincarnate Jesus.

These stories are so fantastic, I wonder if they might be mistranslations or anomalies. But that possibility becomes more and more remote as I continue studying Torah. For example, the Hebrew Scriptures describe a scene centuries later when Moses, his brother, his nephews, and seventy others climb Mt. Sinai and see God.[6] In case I am tempted to interpret this divine encounter

---

3. Genesis 32:30 Note: "Peniel" is Hebrew for "face of God."
4. Exodus 33:20.
5. Hosea 12:4 says that Jacob struggled with an angel, but the event described by Hosea takes place at Bethel, while Jacob's wrestling match takes place at Peniel. (Jacob does encounter angels in a separate event at Bethel, mentioned in Genesis 28:12, 19). And whether we call Jacob's opponent a man or an angel has no effect upon my thesis, as will soon be seen in this chapter's discussion of the "Angel of the Lord."
6. See Exodus 24:9–11.

as merely metaphorical, the Torah states "they saw God" twice in back-to-back verses. And in case I am tempted to write the experience off as something strictly spiritual, the Torah anchors this God in the physical universe with a floor beneath his "feet." This floor is real enough to be described in great detail, as "something like a pavement made of sapphire, clear as the sky itself." If the floor is real, why not the feet upon it? The Torah also describes Moses and the elders eating and drinking with this God on Mt. Sinai, much as Abraham once did with a mysterious God/man in the hills overlooking Sodom. So it seems that once again the Hebrew Scriptures have gone out of their way to describe a God interacting in creation in a physical way, a God with an image that can be seen, a God who gets his feet dirty and sits down to dinner with believers.

Even after Torah times, people kept encountering a mysterious man cloaked in divinity. For example, just before the famous Battle of Jericho, Moses' protégé Joshua "looked up and saw a man standing in front of him with a drawn sword." This word "man" is not an anthropomorphism on the Scriptures' part. He is a "man" so apparently human that Joshua feels he can challenge just as a soldier might confront any other intruder in the camp. So "Joshua went up to him and asked, 'Are you for us or for our enemies?'" But when the man speaks in reply, suddenly Joshua understands the truth. His next question says it all: "What message does my Lord have for his servant?"

The word "Lord" here is *Adonai,* perhaps the most commonly used name for God among Jews today. But as I learned before, sometimes that word is also used in the Hebrew Scriptures to address a king or other person of superior authority, so this is inconclusive as proof that Joshua perceived the intruder as God Almighty. Inconclusive, that is, until this "man" offers an answer to Joshua's question:

"Take off your sandals," he says, "For the place where you are standing is holy."

The last time I saw these words in the Bible—indeed, the only other time they appear in all the Scriptures—they were spoken to Moses by Elohim himself at the burning bush.[7] How remarkable! Who is this man with the name of God, this man who de-

---

7. Compare Exodus 3:5 and Joshua 5:15.

mands respect equal to the One who spoke from the burning bush? Here he is called the "Commander of the Lord's Army," but centuries later I believe people will begin calling him Jesus. And after his death and resurrection, the apostle John will see him in a vision, still in command of the Lord's army:

> The armies of heaven were following him, riding on white horses and dressed in fine linen, white and clean.
>
> —Revelation 19:14

Speaking of the burning bush, a careful reading of that story back in Genesis reveals another interesting fact. Contrary to most people's recollection, it is not God who first appears there in the flames. It is someone called "the Angel of the Lord." But then two verses later, suddenly it *is* God speaking to Moses from the bush.[8] This odd midmoment transition is a phenomenon I find again and again in the Hebrew Scriptures. When the Angel first appears in many of these stories, he speaks of God in the third person, as if he and the Lord are separate entities. Then, in the midst of his appearance, a peculiar shift in point of view occurs and suddenly the Angel is speaking as if he is God himself.

For example, as Abraham faces the greatest trial of his life on top of Mt. Moriah with his son Isaac bound and ready for sacrifice at God's command, it is the "Angel of the Lord" who stops him from the deed with these words:

"Do not lay a hand on the boy. Do not do anything to him. Now I know that you fear God. . . ."

This is how I expect an angel to speak of God—as a separate entity. But then I read the rest of the sentence:

". . . because you have not withheld from me your son."

Here in midsentence this angel is claiming that *he* is the one to whom the sacrifice is being offered! This pompous angel is praising Abraham because his son was "not withheld from *me.*" But Isaac was to be a sacrifice to God, not to the angel! No self-respecting Hebrew would sacrifice anything to a mere angel, especially not Abraham, the father of all the Hebrews.

Of course this is all based on that one little word—"me." It could be some kind of mistake. But then a few verses further, the

8. See Exodus 3:2–4.

angel calls from heaven a second time, saying, "I swear by myself declares the Lord. . . ."[9] There is no room for misunderstanding this time. This "angel" speaks as if he is God himself.

The Hebrew word *malak*, translated as "angel" in these verses, actually means "messenger," that is, someone who proclaims the news. I believe when he returned to earth as a Jewish carpenter, this messenger's job remained the same:

> At daybreak Jesus went out to a solitary place. The people were looking for him and when they came to where he was, they tried to keep him from leaving them. But he said, "I must preach the good news of the kingdom of God to the other towns also, because that is why I was sent." And he kept on preaching in the synagogues of Judea.
>
> —Luke 4:42–44

Earlier, the angel appeared to Abraham's concubine Hagar and spoke these words: "I will so increase your descendants that they will be too numerous to count." If this angel is not God, he is a very presumptuous fellow to take personal credit for the propagation of the human species. And Hagar certainly thought he was God, because after their conversation, "She gave this name to the Lord who spoke to her: 'You are the God who sees me. . . .'"[10]

Was Hagar wrong to call the angel "God?" Was the Torah wrong to say it was "the Lord who spoke to her"? Apparently not, if the angel himself is to be believed, because later when he meets Abraham's grandson Jacob, the Angel of the Lord says, "I am the God of Bethel. . . ."[11]

The angel says, "I am God."

What could be more clear?

But could this angel/messenger be delusional—a heavenly being with a god complex? If so, it seems he has the Lord fooled too, because later while introducing Moses to this angel, Yahweh himself says, "Pay attention to him and listen to what he says. Do not rebel against him; he will not forgive your rebellion, *since my Name is in him.*"[12] There are two star-

9. Genesis 22:15–16.
10. Genesis 16:10, 13.
11. Genesis 31:13.
12. Exodus 23:21 (emphasis mine).

tling aspects to this statement. First, as far as God is concerned, this angel has the right to forgive sins (or not). As the
Pharisees said to Jesus, isn't that the right of God alone?[13] Second, as any rabbi will agree, God's "Name" is biblical shorthand for his essence, which is that part of him that dwelt
among Israel in the Most Holy Place of the tabernacle.[14] The
Name is the aspect of God that exists inside time and space (as
he did in the Garden). So when Yahweh says his Name is in
this angel, he is designating the angel as a sort of moving tabernacle, a portable manifestation of the divine. When I came
to this realization about the angel and the Name, it reminded
me of the following prayer Jesus offered for the followers he
would leave behind:

> I will remain in the world no longer, but they are still in the world,
> and I am coming to you. Holy Father, protect them by the power
> of your name—*the name you gave me*—so that they may be one as
> we are one.
>
> —John 17:11 (emphasis mine)

The Lord's Name is indeed in him.

These are just a few of the things I believe Jesus showed his
apostles in the Scriptures concerning himself. In the marvelous
words of Dr. George Mason, Jesus wanted them to know "he is
not a Jesus come lately." If what Jesus claimed to be is true, he
did not pop up all of a sudden two thousand years ago as a Jewish carpenter. If there really is an entity who is fully God and
fully man, he must be uncreated and eternal. He must have lived
a timeless existence before the moment of creation. He must
have existed in the Garden in the cool of the day, and continued
to exist all along. That is what the Torah says to me again and
again with enigmatic passages like these.

Each story I have told can be explained individually with a
wide variety of complicated theories, but I am aware of only one
idea that explains them all so simply and so elegantly: Jesus is
the eternal God.

13. In the New Testament Jesus is accused of blasphemy because he claims to be em-
powered to forgive sins. Some in his audience ask, "Who can forgive sins but God
alone?" (Mark 2:7).

14. Deuteronomy 12:5.

Many other clues about Jesus exist within the Hebrew Scriptures. For example, Judaism and Christianity both acknowledge that the instructions for the creation of the tabernacle are so specific and so unique there can be no doubt that it was intended to symbolize something. The only question is, what?

There are many theories. Some Talmudic rabbis assumed it is symbolic of heaven because that is where God dwells. The New Testament draws the same conclusion.[15] Other rabbis believed the tabernacle symbolizes the related concepts of the Sabbath and the creation of the universe. They based this conjecture in part upon the fact that the Torah passages concerning the tabernacle's construction are sandwiched between reminders of the commandment to sanctify the Sabbath. The rabbis also thought the tabernacle might be a monument to commemorate Israel's exodus from Egypt. For example, when God commands Moses to return to Egypt and lead the people, he speaks from within a bush that burns but is not consumed. Inside the tabernacle is a menorah made in a botanical pattern, and its flames are to be tended forever. Also, just as a cloud on Mt. Sinai conceals God's glory, God is hidden behind a cloud of incense in the tabernacle. In fact, the Torah specifically states that the purpose of the incense smoke is to conceal God from view.[16] There is both a "consuming fire" at Sinai, and an altar for a constant flow of burnt offerings at the tabernacle. When the Hebrews are hungry, God gives them manna, and inside the tabernacle is the table bearing bread. God parts the Red Sea as a final sign of his superiority over Pharaoh and the Egyptian gods, and the tabernacle includes a basin in the courtyard for washing the priests' hands and feet. When the tabernacle is replaced by Solomon's temple, the corresponding but much larger basin comes to be called the "sea."[17]

So the rabbis saw at least four levels of symbolism in the tabernacle: heaven, Sabbath, creation, and the exodus. At Chever

---

15. See Hebrews 8:5.
16. See Leviticus 13:2, 16.
17. Cloud of incense—Leviticus 16:11–13; consuming fire—Exodus 24:17; bread of display—Exodus 25:23–30; basin of water—Exodus 30:17–21; lampstand—Exodus 25:31–33; 27:21; "sea" at the temple—1 Kings 7:23–26.

Torah, I have learned that many other truths were communicated with the tabernacle, which brings me back again to the connections I see between the Hebrew Scriptures and Jesus.

For example, in an earlier exploration of Christianity and the Mosaic Law, I mentioned that the New Testament portrays Jesus as the "Word," which "became flesh and made his dwelling among us."[18] The use of the phrase "dwelling among us," focuses my attention on the tabernacle of the Torah because of its connection with this verse:

> I will put my *dwelling place among you,* and I will not abhor you.
>
> —Leviticus 26:11 (emphasis mine)

In my earlier exploration of the tabernacle sacrifices, I noticed that the psalmist says sacrifice, "prepares the way so that I may show them the salvation of God." If that salvation is found in Jesus' sacrifice as Christianity teaches, then surely there must be other connections between Jesus and the enigmatic tent of God. This idea has been the subject of many thousands of pages written over the centuries, so I will not explore it comprehensively here, but I cannot resist the temptation to offer one or two thoughts.

At Chever Torah I have found that the tabernacle was the physical establishment of a means of worship, signifying a shift from Israel's passive role to a more active, personal relationship with God. I believe it is no coincidence that Jesus is my means of encountering God in an even more active, personal way.

Also, the tabernacle provided the focal point for the entire Hebrew community and became a symbol of unification for a people. It was the first thing they accomplished together after God set them free, since materials and skills from everyone were required. Similarly, Christianity teaches that Jesus is the head of a body of believers spanning all centuries, nations, and races. People as diverse as a stockbroker in twenty-first-century New York City and a slave in a first-century Roman household are united across time as brothers and sisters by their faith in Jesus.

The tabernacle used sanctified physical things (holy matter) to create holy space, and as I have already seen, the rabbis were the first to notice it was also connected somehow with the Sabbath,

18. John 1:14.

or holy time. When God's presence or Spirit took up residence in the tabernacle, it incorporated the fourth fundamental building block of the universe: holy energy. Thus, the tabernacle symbolized the arrival of complete holiness within all four components of physical creation: holy space, holy matter, holy time, and holy energy. But God did more than that with the tabernacle. He also sanctified the building blocks of the universe in ways relating to humanity. The Lord did not simply make time holy on the Sabbath; he expects a change in human behavior on that day. He did not simply make space holy in the tabernacle; he expects Israel to approach this holy space in a certain way. The Holy Spirit did not simply enter the tabernacle; he entered into Bezalel, the Spirit-filled man who crafted the ornaments of the tabernacle.[19] Everything science understands about the composition of the universe begins with time, space, energy, and matter. As a Christian, I join the rabbis in believing that God used the tabernacle to sanctify these universal building blocks. But I believe he sanctified them in relationship to humanity so we could later understand the complete holiness of a human being named Jesus.

At Chever Torah I have learned that the tabernacle was a metaphor for God's omnipresence. Its temporary nature (it was, after all, a tent) indicated that God's presence among the people was not tied to a physical location. The carrying poles of the ark were always in place as a reminder of this truth. And lest the symbol be mistaken for what it symbolized, the sacrificial altar was hollow, probably to allow it to be filled with soil or stones to dissipate the heat of burnt offerings. This filler material was collected from wherever the people camped. Cut stones were specifically prohibited for this purpose, so that whenever the people moved on, the altar could be lifted up and carried away, and the natural soil and stones within the altar would simply fall back to the ground rather than leaving behind a structure to be misinterpreted as the source of holiness.[20] Although the tabernacle was the glorious dwelling of eternal God, it was also merely a tent made of wool and skins and filled with portable objects that could be dismantled, moved, and re-erected among the soil and stones of another place to establish new holy space and time. In

19. Exodus 31:2–3.
20. Exodus 20:25.

the same way, Jesus was God in a mortal body, the eternal Creator in a perishable, portable container that could be killed then resurrected to begin the process of renewing universal balance.

Someone at Chever Torah once called the tabernacle "Heaven's Embassy," a tangible reminder of God's presence in the universe.[21] This is a perfect expression of the tabernacle's most amazing function: it was a place where God came down to earth. Only once before has the Bible described the Lord and people dwelling together—at the Garden of Eden before the fall. There, the Lord appeared to humanity as someone whose footsteps were physical enough to be heard. Even then he was an ambassador, just as the tabernacle was an embassy—Almighty God in a physical body, just as the Lord occupied the Most Holy Place in a pillar of fire.

A Chever Torah Jew once called the tabernacle a "portable cleft." She meant that it provided physical protection from God's presence in a way similar to the cleft in the rock where Moses was placed for his protection while God revealed his glory on Mt. Sinai.[22] As I have already learned, virtually all of the priestly rituals were designed to provide human beings with a "God suit," or a way to approach God in his dwelling place without being physically consumed by his presence. And just as the tabernacle protected Israel from the sheer power of the Lord's presence, Jesus was a touchable God, a kissable God, a God whose face could be safely seen, a God who did not sterilize the unclean with holy fire, but healed instead with a holy touch.

The tabernacle taught Israel wonderful lessons about faith. Just as the Hebrew slaves in Egypt had been forced to build structures that meant nothing to them, the tabernacle's meaning was concealed at the time of its construction. But the Israelites willingly provided the materials and labor for it anyway. Only after this communal act of faith did the Lord enter their midst in a cloud of fire.[23] In the same way, before I encountered Jesus personally, I could not understand the true potential of his presence in my heart. To experience him, I had to accept his death and resurrection in faith. Only then did his Spirit fill my

---

21. See Exodus 17:7; 25:8.
22. Exodus 33:22.
23. Exodus 25:2; 40:34–38.

heart in ways as clear and undeniable as any pillar of smoke and fire.

The tabernacle gave structure to the religion of the patriarchs—a formal, rigidly established means to approach God. Any attempt to draw near to the tabernacle apart from the strict rules set forth in the law of Moses would result in the fiery fate of Aaron's sons, Nadab and Abihu. In that sense, the tabernacle symbolized the doctrine known by Christians today as "one way." The tabernacle's religious system was known by all of Israel, in contrast to the secret rituals of a privileged priestly cult, as was the rule among the surrounding cultures. So long as Israel respected the holiness code God had established, anyone was welcome to approach. Jesus continued this oddly contradictory tradition, formally establishing himself as the one and only means to approach God, yet publicly offering himself to anyone, rich or poor, Jew or Gentile.

Each of these connections between the tabernacle of the Torah and the life and teachings of Jesus represents another reason why I believe in Jesus.

There are too many other Jesus "coincidences" in the Hebrew Scriptures to include them all here, but I cannot resist one more. We are all familiar with the story known to Jews as the *akeda,* or "binding" of Isaac. With less precision, Christians call this story the sacrifice of Isaac. The parallels between the *akeda* and the New Testament account of the Passion of Jesus are striking.

For example, consider that both stories begin with an angel's announcement. Both involve a miraculous birth. Both revolve around the idea of a father's only son being sacrificed at God's command. Since Mt. Moriah is where Jerusalem was later established, the location of both events is the same. In both cases, the central character in the drama approached the place of his sacrificial death on a donkey. Both stories include the idea of resurrection on the third day (since it is the third day of the story when Abraham tells the servants to wait at the bottom of the mountain until both he and Isaac return). The son in both tales carries the wooden means of his own destruction. Both involve the idea that one life can be sacrificed for another (a ram for Isaac; Jesus for me). In both cases, the son faces death voluntarily. And the final result of both stories is said to be the same: all nations are blessed, and the son lives on.

Many theories have been offered to explain the meaning of the story of Isaac and Abraham on Mt. Moriah. Both the Talmud and the New Testament point to it as an awesome example of faith, but our Jewish and Christian traditions agree that the Bible never functions on only one level. With that in mind I believe this famous story is both a parable of faith and a remarkable prophecy of Jesus, but I also believe it is something more, something that speaks to the heart of everyone who trusts in Jesus here and now.

> Abraham enjoys honor and glory as the father of faith, whereas he ought to be prosecuted and convicted of murder. . . . Why then did Abraham do it? For God's sake, and (in complete identity with this) for his own sake. He did it for God's sake because God required this proof of his faith; for his own sake he did it in order that he might furnish the proof. . . . It is a trial, a temptation. A temptation—but what does it mean? What ordinarily tempts a man is that which would keep him from doing his duty, but in this case the temptation is itself the ethical—which would keep him from doing God's will.
>
> —Søren Kierkegaard[24]

It seems to me that anyone who is in awe of God and is considering faith in Jesus is in exactly the same position as Abraham standing with his knife lifted over Isaac's breast. To drive the knife home is to commit murder if Abraham's vision is untrue, just as belief in Jesus is idolatry if Christianity is a lie. Since we are made in the image and likeness of God, murder and idolatry are inextricably intertwined.

An ancient tradition in Rabbinic Judaism holds that Sarah never spoke to Abraham again after learning what he almost did to their son at the top of Mt. Moriah. In every way, it would have been much easier for Abraham to write off God's command as a figment of an overactive imagination. But Abraham believed in spite of the spiritual risk of murdering his son and earthly risk of

---

24. From *Fear and Trembling,* as quoted by Robert Bretall, ed., in *A Kierkegaard Anthology* (Princeton: Princeton University Press, 1946), pp. 118, 130, 133.

estrangement from his wife, just as some have been willing to risk persecution—even risk idolatry—in response to Jesus. To obey is to disobey. It is the Paradox of Obedience, an impossible dilemma, which Abraham and I have both survived by keeping our eyes firmly fixed on the Truth between the truths.

I am reminded of another example of the paradox, one I discussed earlier in this book.

> Just as Moses lifted up the snake in the desert, so the Son of Man must be lifted up, that everyone who believes in him may have eternal life.
>
> —Jesus, quoted in John 3:14–15

Idols are evil, but look at the man-made serpent and be healed. Jesus is a man, but look to him and be reconciled with God. The message of the snake and pole is the message of the man and cross. It is is the message of faith I learned from Rashi and his *koshim*, or difficulties. Do not fear questioning God. Do not fear idolatry. Fear the Lord instead.

Why would God require such a bizarre test of me?

He wants me to have a full-circle faith. Faith enough to fear the Lord, and faith enough to forget my fear and rush into his arms. So after all of my carefully constructed explanations for belief in Jesus, the reader may be surprised to learn that I also believe in him because my belief makes no sense at all.

There is a divinely erected barricade at the end of the path to God that cannot be circumvented with pure reason. The uselessness of logic at this vanishing point is a finely calculated test akin to the *akeda*. If the idea that a man can be God was a more reasonable proposition, I might rationalize my way to acceptance on my own terms, thinking, "Yes, this makes sense. I can accept this." But where in the Torah has God ever been prepared to meet me on *my* terms? In this universe, he makes the rules, not me, and as the Creator, God stands outside the rules he made, beckoning Abraham and me to step beyond them too.

So my final and strongest reason for believing in Jesus is also the most subjective. It is indescribable, akin perhaps to the way it feels to be a parent. Something fundamental seems to change in people's hearts when their baby enters the world, something so basic it lies beyond their ability to explain. They are no longer "Jill" or "Jack." Suddenly they are "Suzie's mom" or "Timmy's dad," redefined by a tiny other who has seized their minds, imaginations, and hearts. The change is total. It is irreversible. But ask a brand new parent *why* this is true and somehow no words—not even the word "love"—can begin to explain.

Something similar happened when I believed in Jesus. The transformation was not instantaneous but it was irreversible, and it caused changes I can see and hear and feel. My mind, imagination, and heart have been seized by an Other at a level I never thought possible.

Ironically, once I have thrown logic to the wind and passed to the far side of this barrier, I find myself on solid ground again. Mine is not a blind faith; it is the conviction of experience. After placing God above even the law (a remarkable leap of faith), the Abraham who descended Mt. Moriah had a certainty about the Lord that the man who climbed that mountain could not know. My choice to believe in Jesus—even at the risk of idolatry—has given me the same assurance, because when I accepted the gift of Jesus' sacrifice for me, the sin-addicted man I used to be died with him, and together we rose again.

# thirteen

# One Way

Rabbi Simeon ben Nathaniel said: Do not make your prayer a
fixed task, but a plea to God for grace and mercy.

—Abot 2, 18

It has been more than four years since I first set foot in temple to
attend Chever Torah. As I walk along the hallway now, the sur-
roundings feel familiar, as if I belong. People greet me cheerfully
by name. There is much good-natured kidding back and forth. I
no longer think of myself as a Christian out of place; rather, this
has become one of the more comfortable parts of my life.

Rabbi Stern strides up to join me. He is in a hurry to begin a
Bar Mitzvah, so I pick up my pace to match his and together we
head toward the sanctuary with his robes flying behind. I am
proud of the fact that the senior rabbi of this, one of the largest
Reform congregations on earth, seems to enjoy my company.
There is a moment or two of small talk, and then he surprises me.

"You know," says the rabbi, "Sometime I'd like to talk to you
about this 'one way' business."

All of my warm sense of belonging vanishes in an instant with this, the single question I fear the most from a Jew, the one I would do almost anything to avoid. So rather than setting a time to discuss the topic as Rabbi Stern suggests, I take the coward's way out. I wait a few days, then send him a long letter. I pride myself on the honesty of the letter, but it is really just a way to avoid the issue. I prefer avoidance to a face-to-face discussion, because I know if there is one thing that angers Jews almost as much as the church's horrific persecution in years past, it is this: Christianity teaches that faith in Jesus is the only path to God.

Now it is a year later. On this lovely spring morning, the sun shines brightly and a fresh breeze stirs the tender new leaves outside temple. I stand near the main doors talking to Henry, a newcomer to Chever Torah who struck up a friendship with me before he knew I was a Christian. But now that he knows, the dreaded question has come up again.

"You people believe there's no other way to God, right? I mean, except for Jesus."

"Yes. That's true." I desperately try to keep smiling.

"So anyone who doesn't believe in Jesus is going to hell?"

"Uh . . ."

"Do you realize what that means? That means my grandmother is in hell! And my favorite aunt and my uncle!"

"Well . . ."

"They loved God! How can you believe he would send them to hell?"

This time I must stand and face the issue. Henry expects an answer here and now and there is no imminent Bar Mitzvah to save me. But this time I am ready (I think) to explain the Christian point of view. Henry and I will disagree of course, for I must tell the truth about what Jesus taught. It is a teaching Judaism rejects in general, and proudly pluralistic Reform Jews find particularly offensive, but I may still be able to explain Christianity's position in ways that do not anger my new friend. At least that is my sincere hope.

This chapter contains the answers I gave Henry just the other day.

Of all people on earth, Christians should know better than to tell Henry his deceased relatives have gone to hell. The founder of our faith warned against just that kind of thing when he said:

"Do not judge," said Jesus, "or you too will be judged."

—Matthew 7:1

Unfortunately, in our age of increasing tolerance at the expense of scriptural values, some have used this command to avoid passing judgment on the behavior of humanity. Adultery, divorce, drunkenness, gluttony, anger, unforgiveness, and many other practices prohibited in the Bible are being ignored within the church because we fear that condemnation of such behavior could violate Jesus' commandment not to judge. But this is a mistaken interpretation. Jesus' words do not prohibit judgment of human activities. Jesus is a realist, never demanding the impossible, and he knows that civilized life and holiness itself would be impossible without ongoing judgments of behavior by us all.

Parents must judge children's actions if their little ones are to become responsible adults. Employers must judge employees' performance if fair increases in pay are to be given to those who earn them. Men and women engaged in courtship must judge each other's character if marriages are to succeed. I could go on for pages demonstrating that judgments are required to maintain virtually every kind of healthy human relationship, but hopefully this point is beyond dispute: civilized people must be allowed to judge each other's behavior or civilization will dissolve into anarchy.

In the same way, holiness depends upon the judgment of what is holy. Put differently, holiness by definition depends upon the separation of what is holy from what is not, and that is only possible if we can judge one from another. Should newspaper hawkers shout the headlines among those praying at the Western

Wall? Should Bibles serve as doorstops? Should one eat ham at Bar Mitzvahs or drink vodka at communion? Again, I could fill pages with these kinds of questions, but I hope it is quite clear that holiness can only be maintained if we judge between the holy and profane.

The Christian Scriptures command us to judge each other.[1] Another word for this concept is "discernment," something that the Hebrew Scriptures say is both a virtue and a gift from God.[2] So when Jesus warns us not to judge, is he opposing a biblical virtue that stands in the breach between civilization and anarchy, holiness and profanity?

Of course not.

Some Christians believe Jesus' command not to judge means we must not impugn the motives of others. While I think this is getting closer to the truth, it is still not quite on point. Discernment applies not only to judging past or current actions, but also to predictions of the future based on my best guess about another person's motivation. If a drunken stranger asks for a handout, should I give him cash, or buy him a meal instead? If a man stares openly at my wife's décolletage while offering her a ride, should she get into his car, or should she take a cab? Does Jesus' commandment "do not judge" prohibit consideration of the possibility that these people might have something wrong in mind? Again, of course not.

There is no sin in using common sense to judge probability, motivation, or intent. And once this judgment has been made, I would be foolish not to act accordingly. After all, this same Jesus who warned me not to judge also said, "Be on your guard against men," and taught his apostles to be "as shrewd as snakes."[3]

So, since Jesus encouraged the use of common sense to judge both the external behavior and the internal motivation of others—the physical and the psychological aspects of my neighbor—it seems to me just one interpretation remains. In saying, "Do not judge or you too will be judged," I believe Jesus has commanded me not to presume to know my neighbor's spiritual sta-

---

1. 1 Corinthians 6:1–5.

2. See for example, Deuteronomy 32:29; 2 Chronicles 2:12; Psalm 119:125; and Proverbs 3:21.

3. Matthew 10:16–17.

tus before God. A few of the Pharisees of Jesus' day made it their business to point at those who did not observe their brand of Judaism and say, "God has excluded you." But in commanding "Do not judge," Jesus warns that the treatment of souls is God's business and none of mine. Faith in Jesus does not entitle me to pronounce spiritual judgment on any specific person any more than the Pharisees gained that right through obedience to the Torah. According to Jesus, when I condemn any individual as unworthy of heaven, I put my own immortal soul at risk.

> For in the same way you judge others, you will be judged, and with the measure you use, it will be measured to you.
>
> —Matthew 7:2

This warning holds particular weight in terms of the Jewish people, because more than a thousand years before the Son spoke these words, the Sprit of God caused these to be spoken to Israel:

> . . . may those who bless you be blessed and those who curse you be cursed!
>
> —Numbers 24:9

Far be it from me to pretend to know God's plans for anyone's soul, especially a Jew's. So my first response to Henry's question is to assure him that I do not know what God has done with his grandmother or favorite aunt and uncle, and I would not dare to guess.

Within these pages I have gone to some trouble to explain why I believe a good relationship with God is only possible as a result of accepting the gift of Jesus' death and resurrection in my place. I believe these are historical events that somehow balanced the cosmic scales of justice. But again and again I have also admitted there is much about Jesus that I do not understand. I do not understand how a man can also be God. I do not understand how the one God can also be three persons. And I do not understand how the cross and empty tomb threw open the Garden gate. I do not understand because the New Testament leaves plenty of room for debate on all these things. For example, consider Jesus' words:

> But he who disowns me before men will be disowned before the angels of God.
>
> —Luke 12:9

This is a familiar statement to many Christians, one we file away in memory alongside the more widely known, "No one comes to the Father except through me."[4] Many Christians believe these verses mean I must publicly announce my faith in Jesus, or at least consciously believe the gospel, in order to reach harmony with God. But look at Jesus' very next words:

> And everyone who speaks a word against the Son of Man will be forgiven, but anyone who blasphemes against the Holy Spirit will not be forgiven.
>
> —Luke 12:10

This is a whopper of a paradox. First Jesus says God will disown anyone who disowns him. That seems to imply I must do the reverse to achieve the reverse effect; that is, if I wish to be adopted by the Lord, I must adopt Jesus. But Jesus' very next words say I can actually *speak out against him* and still receive God's forgiveness, so long as I do not revile the Holy Spirit.

Christians who are certain I must publicly announce faith in Jesus in order to be forgiven for my sins tend to ignore the second verse and focus on the first. But if I have learned anything about biblical paradox at Chever Torah, it is that I must never deny one Scripture in favor of another. The truth is always inclusive of them both. So I have reached a final Chever Torah kind of question: If Jesus is the "one way," can my soul be drawn to God even though I speak against him?

As the title of this book implies, it is my intention here to explain the gospel. I believe everyone must confess their sin, repent, and place their trust solely in the reparation made possible

4. John 14:6.

through Jesus' atoning death and resurrection in order to find peace with God. But while these are conscious steps on my part, I am not at all certain that the divine redemptive process depends upon my consciousness of these steps.

Consider this quote from a giant in the Christian world:

A partisan of the most rigid orthodoxy . . . knows it all, he bows before the holy, truth is for him an ensemble of ceremonies, he talks about presenting himself before the throne of God, of how many times one must bow, he knows everything the same way as does the pupil who is able to demonstrate a mathematical proposition with the letters ABC, but not when they are changed to DEF. He is therefore in dread whenever he hears something not arranged in the same order.

—Søren Kierkegaard[5]

Kierkegaard is saying the truth is true whether I think of it in terms of ABC or DEF. In other words, the gospel's so-called spiritual laws are not *the* truth; they are merely our meager way of communicating the *idea* of the truth as best we can. Who knows how many ways there are of understanding this one truth, this one way?

So long as I make a heart connection with the one God, is it necessary that I also call him by the name "Jesus"? Most evangelical Christians say yes. They say I must trust Jesus specifically and consciously, must understand the gospel as it is explained in Christian tracts and make a "public profession of faith in Jesus" in order to be at peace with God. But the New Testament book of Hebrews is clear that God embraced many men and women long before the pre-incarnate Word entered history as Jesus, long before anyone ever made a public profession of faith in the second person of the Trinity as we now understand him. For example, Abel did not know the name of Jesus, but Hebrews teaches that Abel awaits me in heaven. So do Enoch, Noah, Abraham, Sarah, Isaac, Jacob, Joseph, Moses, Gideon, Barak, Samson, Jephthah, David, and Samuel. They are all mentioned in the book of Hebrews as examples of those who were "commended

5. *The Concept of Dread* (Princeton: Princeton University Press, 1957), trans. Walter Lowrie, p. 124.

for their faith," yet none of them "received what had been promised." That is, none of them knew the name of Jesus or made a
public profession of faith in him, yet they are now at peace with
the Lord.[6] If a conscious acceptance of Jesus on the cross is the
only path to a relationship with God, how is this possible?

Peter Kreeft, a widely published Catholic scholar, explained it
this way:

> On the one hand, no one can be saved except through Christ. On
> the other hand, Christ is not only the incarnate Jewish man, but
> also the eternal, preexistent word of God. . . . So Socrates was
> able to know Christ as word of God, as eternal Truth; and if the
> fundamental option of his deepest heart was to reach out to him
> in Truth, in faith and hope and love, however imperfectly known
> this Christ was to Socrates, Socrates could have been saved by
> Christ too.[7]

Many Christians will respond that the people listed in Hebrews were redeemed without specifically trusting in Jesus the
Jewish carpenter because they lived before his death and resurrection. According to them, when Jesus rose from death God
changed his requirements for redemption.

There is a strong argument against this position, which I
will make in a moment, but first I have some questions: What
about the mentally disabled, who cannot understand who Jesus
is? What about the fabled lost tribes of the Amazon, who never
heard his name? What about a baby who dies within hours of her
birth? If making a "public profession of faith in Jesus" is a necessary step in the redemptive process, are such people forever
damned?

Of course not.

Acknowledging that this would be inconsistent with a God of
love, most Christians say the Lord makes exceptions for people
who are incapable of freely choosing faith in Jesus. This idea is
called the doctrine of accountability. But again, I have some
questions: Who is accountable and who is not? Does the Lord
base this decision on one's age? Intelligence? Culture? It is be-

---

6. See Hebrews 11.
7. *Fundamentals of the Faith* (San Francisco: Ignatius, 1988), p. 80.

yond my capacity to know, which is precisely why Jesus forbade such speculation, such judgments.

The doctrine of accountability argues against the idea that God has changed the rules. One cannot accept this doctrine without acknowledging that people are brought to God through Jesus without ever knowing his name, even now. It is still possible for someone who has never heard of Jesus to somehow be touched by him in a redemptive way. This means God has no external formulaic requirement, not even a "public profession of faith" or a conscious belief in Jesus the Jewish carpenter who died for my sins, which must be followed in order to reach harmony with him. If he did, then everyone who ever died without making such a profession—everyone from Abel to a stillborn baby—would be in hell today, for they did not know the gospel as we now write it in our tracts.

Where does the doctrine of accountability begin and end? Is it possible for people of this age who were taught since birth to "speak against the Son of Man" to be forgiven for doing exactly as they have been trained to do? I dare not say, for who am I to judge? But I do know that understanding with the mind is not like knowing with the heart. When parents, teachers, friends, spouses, aunts, uncles, brothers, sisters, cousins, and rabbis spend a lifetime shaping a Jew's understanding of Jesus, when a Jew's family history is filled with torture and death at the hands of Christians, is there always a chance to really *listen* to the gospel with the heart, or do some Jews live and die without that opportunity? Will a gracious God consider their situation, look into their hearts to see if they truly love him, and forgive their "words spoken against the Son of Man?" It does seem that the doctrine of accountability includes at least the possibility of forgiveness for such people.

Some Christians will call the mere suggestion of this possibility a heresy, but I am in good, orthodox company. For example, C. S. Lewis said the following:

> . . . although all salvation is through Jesus, we need not conclude that he cannot save those who have not explicitly accepted him in this life.[8]

8. "Christian Apologetics," *God in the Dock*, (Grand Rapids: Eerdmans, 1970), p. 102.

So this is my second response to Henry. Although I dare not take a firm stand either way for fear of judging and being judged in turn, so long as ". . . the fundamental option of his deepest heart was to reach out to him in Truth, in faith and hope and love, however imperfectly known . . ." so long as a person has a "a broken and contrite heart" that desires nothing more than to "act justly, love mercy and walk humbly with the Lord," so long as that person loves Jesus in spirit, even if not in name, it seems to me that Jesus' teaching allows for the possibility of redemption.[9]

As I mentioned a moment ago, many Christians believe the rules were changed with Jesus' life, death, and resurrection. Their belief is based in part on something Jesus said at the Last Supper (a Pesach seder, by the way):

> This cup is the new covenant in my blood, which is poured out for you.
>
> —Luke 22:20

The words "new covenant" imply a turning point on the path to redemption. All Christians think it is a seminal moment in history, and some believe it established a new standard that must be met if I am to reach accord with God. Jeremiah is often quoted in support of this position:

> "The time is coming," declares the Lord, "when I will make a new covenant with the house of Israel and with the house of Judah. It will not be like the covenant I made with their forefathers when I took them by the hand to lead them out of Egypt, because they broke my covenant, though I was a husband to them," declares the Lord.
>
> —Jeremiah 31:31–32

Obviously, the prophet's revelation means there will indeed be a change in God's covenant with Israel. The change seems to be

9. See Psalm 51:17 and Micah 6:8.

brought on by Israel's failure to honor the previous covenant. Like all Christians, I believe that change is the redemption of humanity through Jesus' life, death, and resurrection. But does this change include a stricter requirement to publicly profess faith in Jesus? Is it the end of the possibility that Jews can enter God's good graces as Abraham and Moses did, without knowing Jesus by name? Consider the rest of the passage:

> "This is the covenant I will make with the house of Israel after that time," declares the Lord. "I will put my law in their minds and write it on their hearts. I will be their God, and they will be my people. No longer will a man teach his neighbor, or a man his brother, saying, 'Know the Lord,' because they will all know me, from the least of them to the greatest," declares the Lord. "For I will forgive their wickedness and will remember their sins no more."
>
> —Jeremiah 31:33–34

Nothing in these words implies this change in the covenant will exclude more Jews. On the contrary, "they will all know me, from the least of them to the greatest." Jeremiah is saying the Lord intends to draw his chosen people closer, to embrace them, to "forgive their wickedness and remember their sins no more." That hardly sounds like he is closing a loophole or making the redemption process more restrictive.

If there is one way to God, then there has always been one way to God, and it has always been exactly the same way. The Bible says, "I the Lord do not change. So you, O descendants of Jacob, are not destroyed."[10] This is why, in the eleventh chapter of his book to the Romans concerning the covenant made with the patriarchs, Paul says, "God's gifts and his call are irrevocable."[11] In other words, the Lord does not change, and neither does his arrangement with Israel. On the same subject, Paul also said:

> And so *all Israel will be saved,* as it is written: "The deliverer will come from Zion; he will turn godlessness away from Jacob."
>
> —Romans 11:26 (emphasis mine)

10. Malachi 3:6.
11. Romans 11:29.

This is the same man who wrote, "If we disown him, he will also disown us."[12] But now Paul says all Israel will be saved. Why? Because he knew his Hebrew Scriptures. Consider:

> Then he said to me: "Son of man, these bones are the whole house of Israel. They say, 'Our bones are dried up and our hope is gone; we are cut off.' Therefore prophesy and say to them: 'This is what the Sovereign Lord says: O my people, I am going to open your graves and bring you up from them; I will bring you back to the land of Israel. Then you, my people, will know that I am the Lord, when I open your graves and bring you up from them. I will put my Spirit in you and you will live, and I will settle you in your own land. Then you will know that I the Lord have spoken, and I have done it, declares the Lord.'"
>
> —Ezekiel 37:11–14

I see at least four important points here. First of all, Ezekiel must be talking about every Jew, since he refers to "the whole house of Israel." Second, it is likely this vision applies even to Jews who have already died, because it says God will "open your graves and bring you up." Third, it appears to apply even to Jews who lived apart from the Lord, to those whose "hope is gone," and who "have been cut off." Fourth, it seems these Jews who were formerly "cut off" will be given a second chance, and there will be a spiritual and physical redemption, since the Lord says he will "put his Spirit in you and you will live, and I will settle you in your own land." Like all interpretations of prophecy, this must come with the caveat that there are other feasible understandings. But if one follows the plain sense of Ezekiel's words, there can be little doubt that the future redemption of all Jews who love the Lord is at least possible.

Perhaps this is because the new covenant that began with Jesus' crucifixion and resurrection is still a work in progress. Christianity teaches that Jesus ascended to the presence of the Lord, where he continues to minister on our behalf because his work is not yet done.

> In my Father's house are many rooms; if it were not so, I would have told you. I am going there to prepare a place for you. And if

12. 2 Timothy 2:12.

I go and prepare a place for you, *I will come back and take you to be with me* that you also may be where I am."

—John 14:2–3 (emphasis mine)

The italicized words refer to something Christians call the "second coming," a future revisitation of earth by Jesus, who will then complete the new covenant by banishing evil from creation. Rabbinic Jews, finding many prophecies of this coming time in the Hebrew Scriptures, call it the "World-to-Come." It will be a time when all living creatures are once again in perfect harmony with the Lord as we were in the Garden, and as Jeremiah foresaw when he wrote, "I will put my law in their minds and write it on their hearts . . . they will all know me, from the least of them to the greatest." This may be what Ezekiel saw and tried to explain with the words, "I will put my Spirit in you and you will live, and I will settle you in your own land." It may be what Paul meant when he wrote, "All Israel will be saved."

So here is the third thing I want Henry to know: although some Christians are unaware of it, the Bible seems to foretell a coming time of redemption for Jews—even those who are already dead. It appears to be promised in the Hebrew Scriptures. It appears to be promised in the New Testament. And this promise appears to apply to all Jews who accept God's Holy Spirit.

I am certain this promise will be fulfilled through Jesus somehow, but I am far from certain how it will happen, and I must take care not to pretend to know too much. That was the stereotypical Pharisee's mistake. Some of them were convinced the Anointed One would usher in the World-to-Come with military force, that he would be a king in the earthly sense, a mortal man like David, only greater, bringing paradise on earth. Because they were so certain of their prophetic interpretation, they could not see the big picture when he stood as flesh and blood before their very eyes. In the same way, I must avoid carved-in-stone ideas about how God draws others near, who I can expect to meet in heaven, precisely how they will get there, and exactly what will happen when Jesus comes again. All redemption has been and will be accomplished through Jesus, but I know very little about how Jesus accomplishes redemption. I know he died for me and physically rose again to repair

the damage sin has done, but exactly how did his death and resurrection acomplish my spiritual restoration? What are the
nitty-gritty details of how that worked? No one knows. Similarly, I know the Lord loves me, forgives me, and has a place
prepared for me within his presence, but beyond that his future
plans are a mystery. Although the Bible contains many hints
about God and his plans for all creation, in truth, the knowledge in the Scriptures barely scratches the surface. For all of its
vastness and wonder, the Bible is merely a footnote in the Lord's
autobiography. There are many answers not written there and
many yet to come.

If I know so little about what God has done and still intends to
do for me, I know absolutely *nothing* about the Lord's intentions
for anyone else. Paul was well aware of this and summed it up
with these words:

> Oh, the depth of the riches of the wisdom and knowledge of God!
> How unsearchable his judgments, and his paths beyond tracing
> out!
>
> —Romans 11:33

Jesus said, "no one comes to the Father except through me,"
and that obviously means Jesus is the one and only way to the Father. But Jesus also said even if I "speak against" him I may still
be forgiven, and the Bible leaves no room for doubt that God has
a future plan for his chosen people, even those who have been
cut off, because "God's gifts and his call are irrevocable." Is a
conscious acceptance of Jesus the one way to God, or can I be
forgiven of my sins even though I speak against Jesus? The answer lies in discarding the "or" between these statements and accepting the fact that according to the New Testament, somehow
both are true. If that seems too difficult, or too easy, perhaps it
will help to think about Jesus' role in our reconciliation with God
this way: Jesus is the one and only path to God, but there are
many paths to Jesus.

For all I know, some people may even be on that path without
realizing where they are. So my friend Henry from Chever Torah
shouldn't worry so much about what we Christians think of his
grandmother and his favorite aunt and uncle's status in the

World-to-Come. If his family loved the Lord, the Bible seems to prophesy a future hope for them, just as it does for me.

"For I know the plans I have for you," declares the Lord, "plans to prosper you and not to harm you, plans to give you hope and a future."

—Jeremiah 29:11

The Bible says God loves us, every one. According to both the Christian and the Jewish Scriptures, that means he "is not willing that any . . . should be lost," he "wants all men to be saved," and he "takes no pleasure in the death of anyone."[13] Although some will always presume to know whom God has excluded, the Bible is blessedly clear on this: The Lord loves Henry and his family, and he can be trusted to do the right thing.

Does all this mean I should refrain from telling the world about the gospel?

Heaven forbid!

There are at least two excellent reasons to proclaim the gospel far and wide. First and most important is the simple fact that Jesus commanded me to spread the word. After all, I believe Jesus is God, and who am I to refuse the Lord?

As for the second reason, consider C. S. Lewis once again:

Is it not frightfully unfair that this new life should be confined to people who have heard of Christ and been able to believe in him? But the truth is God has not told us what his arrangements about the other people are. We do know that no man can be saved except through Christ; we do not know that only those who know him can be saved through him. But in the meantime, if you are worried about the people outside, the most unreasonable thing you can do is to remain outside yourself. . . . If you want to help those outside, you must add your own little cell to the body of Christ who alone can help them.[14]

13. Matthew 18:14; 1 Timothy 2:3–4; Ezekiel 18:32.
14. *Mere Christianity*, Book II, chapter 5.

Since I cannot say what God's "arrangements about the other people are," to use Mr. Lewis's tactful expression, concealing this wonderful way that I have discovered would be like failing to announce a newfound cure for cancer on the off chance someone else has already mentioned it. Because Jesus said so, I believe he is the one and only path to God. I cannot know for certain who else has found this path, but I do know what Jesus has done in *my* life, and it really is the very best of all possible news, so I will tell it at a moment's notice to anyone who cares to listen.

Now that I have explained what "one way" does *not* mean, it is time to broach the topic from an affirmative point of view. Why do I believe Jesus is the only path to God?

Over the years at Chever Torah, I have found many reasons.

For example, if I say there are many paths to God, I must assume one of two things: either the differences between the teachings of Jesus, the Hindus, Buddha, Mohammad, and the Talmudic Rabbis are irrelevant to the Lord, or else there really is no important difference between these religions.

The first possibility is the simplest to refute. If one believes that God's nature is unchanging because he is One as traditional Christianity and Judaism teach, then the truth as it relates to God must also be unchanging. And if divine truth is constant, then wherever I find a fundamental contradiction about God between the teachings of two religions, at least one of them must be mistaken.

Remembering what I wrote earlier about paradox, some may protest that I am being inconsistent. If two contradictory teachings about God within one belief system can both be true, why not contradictory statements in different religions? But here I am not talking about affirmative paradox within a single belief system—two statements that appear to be incompatible yet do not specifically deny each other. Instead, I am dealing with direct contradictions between different religions in areas that address our most basic ideas about humanity and God—ideas that overtly reject each other. A response of "yes" does not harmonize these kinds of contraditions, because the contradictions lie at the very root of belief.

For example, Rabbinic Judaism insists that Jesus was at best a human prophet or teacher. But Christianity teaches that he was the incarnate Creator of the universe. To accept the position of Rabbinic Judaism is to disavow the heart and soul of Christianity. There is no truth between these truths, because each side of the question specifically calls the other false. Only one can really be true, hence, one path to God.

To avoid this difficulty, I usually hear the second possibility that I suggested earlier: the world's great religions teach essentially the same truth under different guises. According to this theory there is no real difference between them, just different ways of communicating the same ideas. Compassionate people feel a strong desire to believe in this fundamental agreement of religions, because they long to think of everyone in blissful fellowship with God and with each other. The notion that the world's religions are essentially the same also stems from confusion about the meaning of "ethics" versus "religion." Ethics deals with the relationship of man and man. On the other hand, religion deals with the relationship of man and God. Therefore, the "man and man" and "man and God" concepts must be rigorously separated when comparing religious belief systems. Try to tell an atheist there is no difference between ethics and religion and you will quickly see what I mean.

Confusion enters in when we note that there are indeed remarkable similarities between the world's great religions in terms of the ethics they teach. In a previous chapter, I listed some parallel ideas found in both the New Testament and the Talmud. Another example involves a famous Talmud story about Rabbi Hillel, a near contemporary of Jesus. It seems the Rabbi was approached by a Gentile who said he would convert to Judaism on condition that Hillel teach him the entire Torah while standing on one foot. Rabbi Hillel's answer was wonderful in its simplicity:

What is hateful to yourself, do not do to your fellow man. That is the whole of the Torah. . . .

—Shabbat 31a

Of course, this is the famous Golden Rule stated in the negative. The Christian version is "Do to others as you would want them to do to you." It is universal wisdom, also taught by Buddha and Confucius. (Buddha's version, "Consider others as yourself,"[15] sounds like the Torah's "love your neighbor as yourself," while Confucius actually taught it in the negative, like Hillel.)[16] The similarities go even further when Jesus joins Rabbi Hillel in teaching that the Golden Rule "sums up the law and the prophets."[17]

But while there are areas of agreement, even the ethical teachings of the primary religions contain significant differences. For example, only Jesus specifically commanded his followers to love their enemies. Although the Talmud exhorts Jews to forgive enemies and not to hate them or bear resentment toward them, it stops short of suggesting they must be actively loved. While Buddha taught nonresistance to violent enemies (as did Jesus), he also taught that love is essentially irrelevant. And the Muslim Scriptures contain the following exhortation:

> Believers, take neither the Jews nor the Christians for your friends.
>
> —Koran, "The Table," 5:51[18]

So important ethical differences do exist between the world's great religions. When we leave ethics behind and examine ideas about the nature of God and the various paths humanity may take to reach him, the differences between our religions become positively vast. For example, as I mentioned earlier, Christianity is radically different from all other religions in one important way: it teaches that its human founder is God. No other worldwide religion makes this claim. If it is true, the God/man idea gives a level of authority to everything Jesus taught that no other religion can match, and this includes his famous "I am the way" assertion. Understanding the Christian's commitment to the one-

15. Marcus Borg and Ray Riegert, "East Meets West, The Uncanny Parallels in the Lives of Buddah and Jesus," *Bible Review* 15, no. 5 (1999):22.

16. Tsesze, *Chungyung* (*The Mean, or Central Harmony*), ch. 12, as quoted by Lin Yang in *The Wisdom of Confucius* (New York: Random House, 1966), p. 110.

17. Matthew 7:12.

18. N. J. Dawood translation (London: Penguin, 1993), p. 85.

way doctrine must begin by recognizing that we believe this teaching comes directly from the lips of God Almighty. Either Jesus is God, or he is not. If he is, I had better believe everything he has to say, including "no one comes to the Father except through me." If Jesus is not God, Christianity is a farce at best and an abomination at worst.

Also, except for Judaism, most of the world's great religions essentially ignore another Christian idea, the one called "grace." As I mentioned previously, Jesus said we can do nothing to earn reconciliation with God, while Buddhists, Hindus, and Muslims teach the exact opposite: that peace or salvation is available through the four noble truths of Buddhism, or the dharma of Hinduism, or the five pillars of Islam. Each of these paths involves human effort leading to a harmonious existence or to acceptance by God. But Jesus taught that acceptance by God leads to good works, not the other way around. The importance of this difference cannot be overstated. If Jesus is right, the Buddhists, Muslims, and Hindus are simply wrong about the path, and vice versa. There is no middle ground.

There are many other fundamental differences. Hinduism itself contains adherents to virtually every opinion on the nature of God; a Hindu may be monotheistic, henotheistic, polytheistic, or pantheistic, depending upon his village or temple of origin.[19] On the other hand, the three Western religions are strictly monotheistic. Both Buddhism and Hinduism teach reincarnation, a concept completely foreign to Christianity, Judaism (except among some fringe medieval mystics), and Islam. Many Buddhists and some liberal Jews actually deny the existence of God. And since Judaism and Islam bluntly deny Jesus' divinity claim, either they are right and he is wrong, or vice versa. We cannot have it both ways.

These are not trifling variations or slippery paradoxes; they are fundamental differences, which prove it is no more possible for all of the world's major religions to be equally correct paths to one God than it is possible to play baseball, football, and soccer simultaneously on one field. The "many paths" of the world's religions head for all points on the compass. Most of them say we

---

19. David Crystal, ed., "Hinduism," *The Cambridge Encyclopedia* (Cambridge: Cambridge University Press, 1990), p. 569

can find our own way up to God. By contrast, Christianity and (to some extent) Judaism say we must ask God to come down to us. Of course, Christianity and Judaism disagree on how and why God will honor that request. Either he will accept repentance, *mitzvot*, Torah study, prayer, and fasting as reparation for my sins, or he will accept Jesus' death and resurrection. Again, it cannot be both. The words of Jesus do not allow that luxury.

In short, if I choose to believe there are many paths, at least one of those ways—the way of Jesus—is closed to me.

That last statement may remind some of a "members only" mentality, which has nothing to do with God's will and everything to do with the rampant ego of someone who wants to feel superior. When charged with such elitism, many Christians point to the fact that our one-way doctrine did not begin with us; we simply comply with the teachings of Jesus. But in truth, the idea of a single path to God did not even originate with Jesus. It is firmly entrenched within the Torah, appearing as early as the fourth chapter of Genesis.

Able's offering pleases the Lord, but Cain's does not. One way.[20] Nadab and Abihu, Aaron's unfortunate sons, are killed by "fire from the Presence of the Lord" because they try to approach God on their own terms. One way. Aaron is cautioned to draw near to God in the Most Holy Place only through the prescribed ritual and at the prescribed time upon pain of death. One way.[21] All of Israel is warned not to allow a person to remain among them who "practices divination or sorcery, interprets omens, engages in witchcraft, or casts spells, or who is a medium or spiritist or who consults the dead." That pretty much rules out the New Age religious concepts of today. And the reason for this prohibition? "Anyone who does these things is detestable to the Lord." One way.[22]

20. Genesis 4:4–5.
21. Leviticus 16:2.
22. Deuteronomy 18:10–12.

Of course, sorcery, witchcraft, spiritualism, and the like are not what most of us would consider organized religions. What does the Torah have to say about them?

Consider God's response to the Egyptian belief system. Each of the ten plagues of the Exodus was intended to prove his superiority to a specific god in the Egyptian pantheon, from Hapi, the spirit of the Nile, who was conquered when the Lord turned the Nile to blood; to Seth, protector of crops who was defeated when the locusts devoured Egypt's grain; to Ra, the sun god, who was vanquished when the Lord caused darkness to cover Egypt at midday; to Pharaoh himself, the ultimate god of Egyptian polytheism, who could not even defend his first born child from Yahweh. It seems that one of the motives behind God's flamboyant approach to freeing his chosen people was to teach the children of Abraham that the Egyptian religion's "path" was a dead end.

The other popular religious systems of that era fared no better. Consider the following divine instructions concerning the Canaanite religions:

> Destroy completely all the places on the high mountains and on the hills and under every spreading tree where the nations you are dispossessing worship their gods. Break down their altars, smash their sacred stones and burn their Asherah poles in the fire; cut down the idols of their gods and wipe out their names from those places. *You must not worship the Lord your God in their way. . . . You are not to do as we do here today, everyone as he sees fit. . . .* Be careful not to sacrifice your burnt offerings anywhere you please. Offer them only at the place the Lord will choose in one of your tribes, and there observe everything I command you.
>
> —Deuteronomy 12:2–4, 8, 13–14 (emphasis mine)

The God of Abraham, Isaac, and Jacob did not wait at the end of many paths in the time of Moses, and God does not change. Why should I believe he waits at the end of many paths today?

I make no claims of benign selflessness, but in addition to the fact that the one-way doctrine is as old as the Torah, the accusation that it is an arrogant creation of Christians—a sort of "members only" mentality—strikes me as ironic for two reasons.

First, the "many paths" theory can be disrespectful of the billions of believers who view their particular religion as unequaled. Given the critical differences between our religions, I may respectfully tell a Muslim I disagree with his views, but I ought not be so patronizing as to downplay our disagreements in the interest of harmony, no matter how deeply felt my compassion or how uncomfortable my sense of cognitive dissonance. Where we agree, it is good to acknowledge agreement. But the statement that our differences do not matter carries the implication that beliefs are unimportant, and that, quite frankly, is insulting to anyone with strong convictions.

Second (and this is where the irony is most striking), rather than inspiring arrogance, the one-way doctrine is intended to create exactly the opposite effect. Again, it is not we Christians who demand the one-way doctrine; it is Jesus, whom we believe is God. And if Christians really do believe he is God, then one way means we must approach the Lord on his terms, not our own. Thus, the very heart and soul of the teaching is humility.

The *American Heritage Dictionary* defines arrogance as "making or disposed to make claims to unwarranted importance or consideration out of overbearing pride." Given that definition, if I genuinely believe Jesus is God Almighty, then ignoring Jesus' teaching would be the height of foolish arrogance. "One way" is not prideful; on the contrary, it is based on the *humble* acknowledgment that Jesus is God, and I am not.

Those who believe in "many paths" invariably mention the tremendous diversity among his creation. Why would God create so many kinds of people, they argue, yet require us all to approach him in just one way?

It seems to me this argument rests on a flawed basic assumption. I might as well say that there are many people at a firing range, so it is acceptable for everyone to shoot in any direction they please. Doesn't it make more sense to say there is one target, and one way to hit the target, just as there is one God, and one path to God?

Thinking further along these lines, imagine the chaos at a firing range where targets are set up all over the place. How would I know where to aim? Far better to place the targets in a single area with just one direction in which to aim. In the same way, when Jesus said, "no one comes to the Father except through me," he provided a simple, clear path to God, a way that cannot be missed among the clutter of life. Jesus said the gate is narrow and hard to enter.[23] But it is not a maze. If there were multiple paths to God, I would have a role to play in plotting my own course, exercising my free will to choose this path or that one. Inevitably, I would fail in plotting that course because I lack the necessary moral discipline to stick to the path.

Again and again the Torah tells me to obey *all* of God's commandments. But I cannot obey all 613 *mitzvot*. I cannot even obey the first ten. In fact, I have not yet managed to unfailingly obey the two most basic commands to love God wholeheartedly and to love my neighbor as myself. And in this moment of embarrassing honesty, I must also admit I cannot even obey the simplest command of all, the one Hillel and Buddha and Confucius and Jesus all agreed upon: "Do to others what you would have them do to you." Just one simple command, but I cannot obey.

Can you?

If living a moral life is a path to God, it is choked with weeds from lack of use. So God must reach down for me, not only because that is the one way he seems to want on his end but also because of the dismal condition of things here on mine. That divine reaching down is the "one way" that the Torah and Jesus taught. It is what I believe Jesus did for me on the cross and in the empty tomb. All God asks in return is that I believe in him enough to accept his help, as Abraham did when the covenant began.

Christianity is not a system of man's search for God, but a story of God's search for man.

—Peter Kreeft[24]

23. Matthew 7:13–14.
24. *Fundamentals of the Faith,* pp. 76–77

Miraculously, my relationship with Henry survived our discussion about "one way." Perhaps because he could see I had no intention of setting myself up as the judge of his immortal soul, Henry continues to speak to me today in friendly terms. But Henry tells me he is not at peace with God, so I do pray for him from time to time. I hope he does not mind a Christian's prayers. If he heard the words I speak to God on his behalf, I think he would approve. My prayer is not that he will "make a public profession of faith in Jesus as his personal Lord and Savior," as the Christian tracts all say. I can tell Henry has been too deeply wounded by Christians over the years to express faith in those terms. The name of Jesus has been corrupted for Henry by some among those who claim to love it best. So my prayer instead is that he will come to know the God who loves him, the One who was there in the beginning, who was with God, and was God, and through whom all things were made, who is the way, the truth, and the life, and the light of men. Henry tells me he has no peace with God, but who knows? Maybe some day he will come to believe that God became flesh and dwelled among us, first in the Garden, then at Mamre and Peniel and Sinai and Bethlehem, and Henry might take his hand, and let the God who has felt the pain of living here on earth gently lift him up.

That is my prayer for Henry and for all the world.

Made in the USA
Middletown, DE
02 September 2022